6½″

Each clear area gives the outline for one frame of a single-frame filmstrip made with a standard 35mm camera. The toned area surrounding the clear areas indicates the position and spacing of the two frames

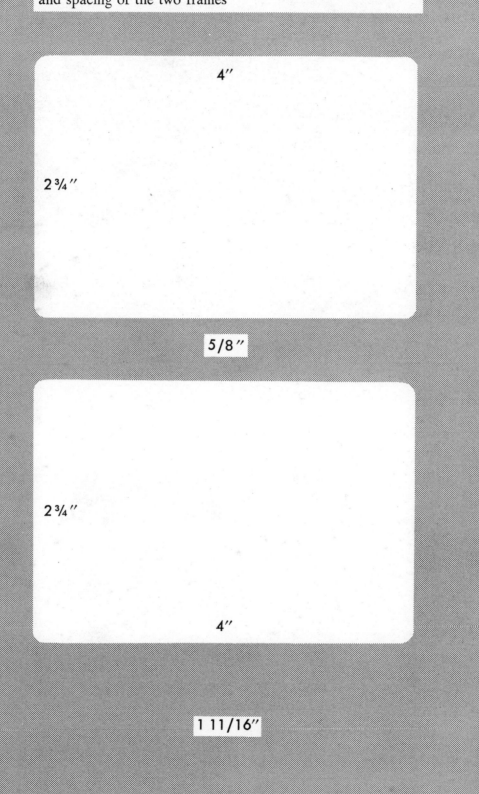

4″

2¾″

9½″

5/8″

2¾″

4″

1 11/16″

6½″

Planning and Producing
Audiovisual Materials

Chandler Publications in

AUDIOVISUAL COMMUNICATIONS

Operating Audio-Visual Equipment

Sidney C. Eboch

Planning and Producing Audiovisual Materials

Jerrold E. Kemp

Preparation of Inexpensive Teaching Materials

John E. Morlan

Planning and Producing Audiovisual Materials

Second Edition

By JERROLD E. KEMP

Professor of Education and Coordinator, Audiovisual Production Services
San Jose State College

With the assistance of

RON CARRAHER (Art)

University of Washington

WILLARD R. CARD (Photography, First Edition)

Brigham Young University

RICHARD SZUMSKI (Photography, Second Edition)

San Jose State College

CHANDLER PUBLISHING COMPANY
An Intext Publisher • Scranton, Pennsylvania 18515

Contents

Preface

A reader often skips the Preface in a book, so this one is purposely printed in a large type in the hope that it will catch your attention. I want to persuade you to read it before you turn to any particular section of the book. There are things about the content, organization, and correlated materials you should know.

First, if you are familiar with the first edition of this book, you will find here the addition of a new Part comprising the first three chapters. For those interested in the careful planning of audiovisual materials, these chapters provide a necessary background. They treat these areas—the newer roles of audiovisual materials as changes and improvements take place in education and training programs; a pattern for instructional design and the selection of media to serve specific objectives; principles of perception, communication, and learning theory that are basic to all teaching and need consideration during your planning phase; and a review of research findings concerning factors that can affect the design of your audiovisual materials.

In order to do things like mount pictures, plan a slide series, write a script, copy pictures, record narration, shoot an 8mm film, or make transparencies, people need specific, detailed, step-by-step instructions, not generalized suggestions. First, carefully integrated words and pictures give you the background for fundamental skills in photography, graphics, and sound recording. Then detailed procedures for producing each of seven kinds of audiovisual materials are presented. Cross-references through the book help you to make use of the fundamental skills in your specific area of interest.

A number of 8mm *single-concept* films and other materials have been prepared that correlate with specific topics to provide further visualization for effective learning. You will find reference to these films at appropriate places in the text. A list of the films and their source for distribution are included in the Appendix.

Review questions and suggested activities that help you apply the skills and procedures being learned round out the plan of instruction in this book. The questions and activities are found at the end of chapters and of sections within chapters. Feedback to check your answers is provided in the Appendix.

Try to make use of all the instructional elements described here. Each one provides reinforcement for the others.

Now read on . . .

Acknowledgements

I was pleased to acknowledge the assistance I received from many colleagues and friends while preparing the first edition of this book. Their contributions were noted in that edition and much of their help is still evident in this, the second edition. My thanks to them again.

Now I wish to express my gratitude to those who have assisted in the preparation of the second edition. First, to those who offered comments on the new, first part of the book—David Curl, Western Michigan University; Malcolm Fleming, Indiana University; Vernon Gerlach, Arizona State University, and Harold Hailer and Richard Lewis, San Jose State College.

Second, I greatly appreciate the suggestions, effort, and time spent by my colleagues, who with me, formed the production team for this edition—Ron Carraher for art and Richard Szumski for photography. Much of the work of Willard Card, prepared for the first edition, is carried to this edition.

Finally, I again thank my wife, Dorothy, and Tinker Belle and Wendie for their understanding and patience during the preparation of this second edition.

Jerrold E. Kemp

San Jose, California
January, 1968

Part One

BACKGROUND IN AUDIOVISUAL COMMUNICATIONS

1. Audiovisual Materials in Instruction

The purpose of this opening chapter is to review developments in the field and to put media in perspective in terms of changes and emerging developments in education. This is necessary background information for the producer of audiovisual materials.

The first edition of this book, in 1963, contained this introductory paragraph in its preface:

As increasing recognition is given to the audiovisual media and as more suitable facilities are provided for their use, we will see increased dependence on various media to serve many instructional purposes—and not as enrichment devices to be used if time permits, but rather as carefully planned and integrated parts of the teaching-learning environment.

Since 1963 the concept of audiovisual materials (more broadly referred to today as part of the *educational media* field) has been extended further and their roles in instructional programs, on all levels, have received greater attention.

AUDIOVISUAL "AIDS"

Audiovisual materials have been among the resources for teaching and learning in educational programs for many years. Most often they have been secondary to verbal presentations by teachers, to textbooks, to the chalkboard, to library materials, and to other traditional and convenient methods of communication. Often they were introduced into a class lesson at the whim of the teacher, perhaps just to occupy spare time. For these reasons audiovisual materials generally have been considered as "aids" to instruction.

Audiovisual *aids* came into prominence with the development of 16mm motion-picture films, at first silent and then with sound, in the 1920 and 1930's. For many people in education, *audiovisual aids* have been (and still may be!) synonymous with the use of films. Many research studies soon showed an increase in learning when a motion picture was added to a lecture, as compared with the lecture by itself. Films proved their value in serving military training needs during World War II. On the basis of these and other contributions to improve teaching, a number of educational film companies have produced quantities of films for classroom uses. Many films are excellent

in content and creatively designed, and they do play important roles in providing visual experiences for students of all ages.

But in large measure 16mm films—along with filmstrips, slides, recordings, and other typical audiovisual materials generally—have remained just *aids* to instruction. They have not reached a level of widespread acceptance and careful integration into present-day teaching and learning experiences. As Heinich expresses it:[1]

Materials of instruction were more often afterthoughts of curriculum planning than results of the curriculum development process. Audiovisual materials usually entered the instructional process at the classroom application level, either when the teacher was casting about for materials that might "aid" instruction, or when the audiovisual director instituted a search of catalogs for appropriate materials.

This peripheral status of audiovisual materials in educational programs is the result of such factors as these:

- Most teachers have not understood or do not accept the instructional value of audiovisual resources. Many feel that unless they were in front of the class talking, doing, or showing, no learning is taking place. Others react to the use of pictures in one form or another as being a "low level" of teaching; academic respectability as they see it can be maintained only through verbal communication and reading. This attitude was easily understood since "we teach as we were taught" and most teachers experienced little but verbal classroom instruction during their own education.
- The use of *visual aids* was difficult in the past. Equipment and materials had to be scheduled long in advance, machines were cumbersome and difficult to operate, rooms needed darkening, and so on. For these reasons it often was not worth trying to use a film or a filmstrip.
- The content of commercial materials often left much to be desired with respect to a teacher's immediate instructional needs. A typical classroom film included many concepts. Generally students cannot grasp and retain this much material, even if all of it is important to the immediate lesson. Possibly only a small section of a film had the content that fit the topic

[1] Robert Heinich, *The Systems Engineering of Education II: Applications of Systems Thinking to Instruction,* page 7.

under study, but it was too difficult to advance to that part for use. Or again, the treatment of the subject was not handled in the way the teacher wanted to present it.

• Finally, overzealous and premature promotion of audiovisual materials, by salesmen and some educators, without adequate follow-through, has had understandably adverse effects on teachers in their acceptance and future use of these resources.

So, for many teachers, the traditional audiovisual materials unfortunately, have been *aids*—enrichments to be used "if we have the time," after the lecture and textbook are studied.

RECENT MEDIA DEVELOPMENTS

The mid 1950's have been established as the beginning of modern developments in *instructional technology*[2]—that area of endeavor that has brought machines, materials, and techniques together for educational purposes. Many of these developments have bearing upon presently emerging new instructional patterns and the roles of media to serve them.

One of the most influential media of communication is television, including both instructional (for direct classroom learning) and educational (for cultural and community enrichment). The medium has extended the influence of the 16mm film so as to reach students with up-to-date topics and with newly organized approaches to subjects. The detailed planning incident to television instruction, plus its potential for efficiently incorporating most other audiovisual materials within its format, have made many educators aware, for the first time, of a way to approach instruction systematically with audiovisual materials.

One important result of television has been the availability of complete courses presented by one or more subject experts in a series of 100 to 160 30-minute programs (films). The film courses, with their up-dating of subject content, have contributed to a reexamination of most subject fields. The results have been the development of new course structures, primarily in the sciences, social studies, and mathematics, and the availability of new texts, manuals, and correlated visual materials (mainly films).

In recent years, of all types of audiovisual equipment, more overhead projectors have been purchased than anything else. With these the teacher, at the front of the room, when wanting to explain or show, could turn from the blackboard and face the class—an important psychological component in the relation of teacher with students. Simple but effective techniques are available for using the overhead projector to present information at the best pace for the class.

Language laboratories have applied the potentials of magnetic tape for instruction to groups and individuals. Today extensions of the language laboratory are found in remote-control electronic equipment like dial-access systems. Some marvels of equipment development now permit pushbutton random-accessing of information in many forms. These "hardware" items have developed spectacularly. But the "software" (the instructional materials for use with the equipment) have not always developed along with the "hardware."

A particularly impressive instance was the teaching-machine movement, which introduced various devices, but very few programs to be used with them. Recently, the term *teaching machine* has given way to the expression *programed* instruction (as process *with* materials). The emphasis is now on carefully designed and tested materials to serve specific objectives.

Reasonably priced equipment for slide projection is now available. Remote-controlled slide projectors are commonplace. Slides are held in trays or drums and proper sequencing is guaranteed. Also, simple-to-operate slide-making cameras are here and tape recorders, for synchronization with slide projection, can be had. Teachers have gained the confidence to use these types of equipment in developing materials of their own for specific teaching purposes.

In addition, there have been developments in the motion-picture field. Self-threading 16mm projectors make film use easier. But, the biggest potential lies in the 8mm field. One outstanding development is the cartridge projector with its simplicity of operation. This opens many possibilities for independent study and demonstrates that the motion picture does *not* have to be at least 10 minutes long or cover a whole chapter of a textbook. Short "single-concept" films serve to illustrate a particular skill or process and thus put learning right at the level and the pace of the student. The development of the Super-8 format has brought 8mm film quality near to the level of 16mm film and optical and magnetic sound for 8mm film will lead to further instructional potentials.

Besides these noteworthy technological developments (and there are many more that cannot be included in this brief survey), there are other important areas to recognize along the trail leading to the emerging future. One is the "cross media" or "multimedia" presentation. These terms refer to the simultaneous or sequential use of a number of visual and audio materials. In projection it is typified by the presentation auditorium in which two or three images (no more, we hope!) are shown simultaneously for large groups. The visuals may be in the form of slides, motion pictures, and/or overhead transparencies. These may be controlled remotely by the presenter or may be run automatically on cue. The planning and "programing" for such presentations are extensive and, to date, have been successful in only a few situations.[3]

2 James D. Finn and others, *Studies in the Growth of Instructional Technology I: Audio-Visual Instrumentation for Instruction in the Public Schools, 1930-1960: A Basis for Take-off.*

3 Gerald F. McVey, "Multimedia Instructional Laboratory," *Audiovisual Instruction,* February 1966, pp. 80–85. Alvin B. Roberts and Don L. Crawford, "Multiscreen Presentations: Promise for Instructional Improvement," *Audiovisual Instruction,* October 1966, pp. 528-530.

Another less ambitious use of the multimedia concept is in the development of "kits" of materials, organized around a single topic. Such a kit contains a variety of materials—filmstrips, recordings, still pictures, concept films, worksheets, printed booklets, and even real objects. Many are now available, such as those on a country (Mexico), a process (bread making), a concept (water pollution), and those providing lessons in foreign languages. They are being developed commercially and also locally, as in the San Diego Community Resources project[4] wherein local industries and scientific institutions cooperate with the schools to produce materials that are too current to be available any other way.

On the horizon are the applications of computers for instruction. Already computers are used for record keeping and scheduling, for counseling, for simulating learning environments for instruction, for information storage and retrieval, and for publication work. Research is being conducted to determine how computers and media can be best adapted for direct instruction to individuals.

In sum, technological advances in the last ten to fifteen years have been extensive in providing improved devices and techniques for bringing the best, the most relevant, and the widest range of experiences to students. It has been shown that the use of various media can improve student learning and at the same time significantly reduce instructional time and some personnel requirements.

It should be evident that audiovisual and related educational media are proving to be far more than *aids*. Media of these kinds are often the vanguards of change in education and, when properly considered, can affect the development of curriculum and influence the learning process itself. They are essential to effective communication in group instruction; they are the only means of communication for direct instruction in many independent-learning programs.

But along with the positive results of instructional technology, some important concerns must be recognized. Admittedly, some setbacks and negative results have been connected with the introduction and trial of new resources. In some situations the proponents of major types of audiovisual materials or other media operate in isolation, separated from each other and ignoring other components of the instructional environment. This aloofness has been in some degree characteristic of educational television, of programed instruction, and of complete film courses. It produces inefficiency, waste, duplication, and in some of the products a sad lack of purpose and quality.

There are strengths and weaknesses in all media. The possible integrated use of media, so that each may serve for its best specific purposes, seems to offer much potential for instruction. We have a technological capability for making great strides in

reaching toward educational goals. Instructional media, if carefully planned, selected, produced, and used within an over-all pattern, can become key elements in such developments.

THE CONCERNS OF EDUCATION

In the last five to ten years the perspectives in United States education have started to undergo upheaval and change. The federal government and private foundations, through many programs, have encouraged innovation and experiment with change. Newly formed business concerns consisting of "hardware" manufacturers (electronic companies) and "software" producers (book publishers) are entering the educational market with equipment and materials for instruction that most certainly will influence education.

There is much concern that education has been missing the mark, that its *product*—the *educated* child—has not been up to anticipated standards. The emphasis on *teaching* has somewhat neglected, in other than generalized and verbal ways, the real intent of education: *learning,* by the *learner.* With growing awareness, the process of education is shifting emphasis from *teaching* and the imparting of knowledge, directly from teacher to student, to having *greater concern for the learner*—for his needs, for his interests, and for ways to structure instruction and motivate him so he will be an active participator in the process of learning.

Another way to express this is to recognize that the fundamental purpose of an educational system is to manage learning so that it will occur most efficiently. The essential *input* in this system is the *student.* The *output* is the *student's changed behavior.* The objectives of this management are to insure that the greatest positive changes in student behavior occur in the shortest period of time (a measure of efficiency).

This new emphasis has made educators alert and active in serving such concerns as these:

• That students differ greatly in their ability to perceive and learn, and in their individual requirements for learning. Some learn easily and rapidly from printed or oral presentations, with a minimum of more "direct" experiences. Others require experiences that are more concrete, including the use of visual media. Most students require a combination of various avenues to learning.

• That many cultural factors affect learning. Students need a whole range of experiences involving real things, visual representations, and abstract symbols.

• That new ways to organize subject content encourage greater participation in the learning activity through discovery and inquiry methods.

• That instructional programs themselves need to be reorganized in terms of efficient and flexible use of space, time, personnel, and resources.

---

4 Ronald L. Hunt, "The Schools, Industry, and New Knowledge," *Audiovisual Instruction,* March 1964, pp. 162-165.

ORGANIZING FOR LEARNING

The implications of these concerns and the attempts to find solutions require new ways of approaching and organizing for learning. It is now more clearly recognized that learning is an activity; *what students do* determines what they learn; and they learn by working with ideas and with things.

The teacher or teaching team, now managers of learning, must determine realistic curricular goals and specific objectives —to make these clear and meaningful to the students, to plan how they can be met through effective use of selected resources, to implement the instruction and learning, and to evaluate progress with the students.

For efficiency, when topics are introduced or when essential information must be transmitted to numbers of students, it is appropriate to do this in regular classes or in large groups, using proper educational media. But a new major theme has been to individualize instruction. In an environment conducive to study, a student can take increasing responsibility for his own learning, proceed on his own level and at his own pace. Many media resources for independent study are available and improved ones are coming.

Thus, various systematic patterns for learning are emerging. For the transmission of information to a number of students at one time, large groups may meet; for individual learning, a student can work by himself at his own rate; and for the necessary personalized interaction, to stimulate the give-and-take between teacher and students, for committee work, for reviewing and for evaluation, small discussion groups can be formed. Audiovisual and other media help to give shape and substance to these patterns in a school program.

Underlying these patterns for improved learning are changes in the roles of teachers and other personnel. No longer need the teacher stand in front of a class, verbally presenting information. The mere presentation of information can be done very effectively with appropriate media, be it for transmission to a group, for an individual to use by himself, or for use by a committee in a discussion group. Now teachers, frequently as teams, are free to guide learning—the creative and truly professional work that has long been neglected. This guidance includes some responsibilities for the planning and preparation of audiovisual materials to fit the needs of groups and individuals.

The use of technology to improve communication forces changes in the methods by which educational objectives can be achieved—changes that frequently are resisted as disturbing and discomfiting to personnel imbedded in the status quo. Resistance to the introduction of instructional media in education also stems from the concerns that media will dehumanize teaching, that teachers will be replaced by machines, and that education will be automated with consequent loss of the personal quality between teacher and student.

In actuality, with the broadening of subject content and in-creasing enrollments, what *is* often overlooked is that the human quality and the genuine personal touch can *only* be had by using the resources of technology, thus freeing the teacher from repetitive work and from the simple presentation of information.

DESIGNING FOR INSTRUCTION

The patterns for learning described above require careful planning and attention to detail usually neglected in traditional procedures. Now, attention must be given not only to subject content and student variables, but also to many other factors that influence the success of the learning process. Taking all these elements together, we may develop an *instructional design*. The design requires this sequence of activities:

1. Set objectives in terms of the individual's needs in a changing society.
2. Select subject content to serve the objectives.
3. Develop learning experiences in terms of the most efficient and effective instructional methods, keeping in mind the requirements and limitations of budget, personnel, facilities, equipment, and schedules.
4. Select and prepare instructional materials that fit the learning experiences and methods.
5. Test the materials with a sampling of learners.
6. Revise materials as necessary to satisfy the objectives.
7. Carry out the instruction.
8. Evaluate the results and revise elements in the design, as necessary, for future uses.

This instructional-design approach can be the starting level from which, eventually, a true *instructional system* may be developed. The concept of the instructional system is much broader than the instructional-design approach and is beyond immediate application in most school situations. References on page 232 provide information on the instructional system.

Media personnel can work with teachers to develop effective instructional designs for daily class lessons, for units of work, or for whole courses. Success in instructional design demands careful planning and realistic facing of the numerous problems that must be answered. This is not a casual activity. It is a rigorous method in which the designer-teacher must face up to decisions and then take action. He may himself apply the design in a limited application, or it may be applied by a number of people, each with a required speciality, but united in their attack on a common instructional problem.

Professional film production, instructional television, and programed instruction have all contributed to the instructional-design approach. Film production, when properly carried out, is a systematic way to plan, to involve personnel, to consider content, and to select visual experiences that will serve a particular objective. Television includes all that film production does and in addition considers the interrelationships of all media and how they can best be brought together to serve a specific purpose. This purposeful combination is a key attribute of the instructional-design approach.

Programed instruction has been the real seed for the *process* of developing instructional design in education. Here, at the outset, the desired behavioral change in the student, in terms of a specific instructional objective, is defined. The content associated with the change is broken into small steps to facilitate student learning. The learning is then reinforced with continuous encouragement through immediate recognition of correct understanding. Finally, the program is tested to determine, quantitatively, whether the sought behavioral changes have occurred. If necessary, the program is redesigned and reapplied until the desired results are obtained.

MEDIA IN THE INSTRUCTIONAL DESIGN

Media to be used within the instructional design are determined by the requirements of objectives, content, and instructional methods. Media are *not* supplementary to or in support of instruction, but *are* the instructional input itself. In this light, the old concept of audiovisual *aids* can no longer be accepted. Determination must be made of which media, in what form, and at what time, will most effectively and efficiently provide the most relevant experiences for learners.

Just as various instructional objectives require different kinds of learning, appropriate instructional resources require matching to required tasks. Each separate concept to be taught should require a separate consideration of resources. Certain media can best serve certain purposes (sound or print; motion or still pictures). In other cases available equipment, convenience, costs, and such factors may be the determiners of choice.

This approach to teaching and learning is developed around specificity—specificity in terms of behavior objectives to serve the needs of particular students. Commercial materials generally will not be suitable, since in the main they are too generalized and too broad in treatment of subjects. On the other hand the dependence on local production for all necessary materials seems unduly costly in time and money. Perhaps forward-looking producers will treat the most commonly taught subject topics and concepts by providing carefully designed and interrelated materials that may be of use in a variety of locally developed instructional systems. But openings will remain for the addition of materials having local applications or particular local emphases. For example, a unit on community health includes the study of water-purification methods. Commercial materials may describe the principles of water treatment with examples taken from various general processes, but the particular method of local water treatment will need to be learned with locally prepared materials.

AN EXAMPLE OF ELEMENTS WITHIN AN INSTRUCTIONAL DESIGN

```
Subject: Community Health

General purposes:
       1. To understand that the health of the people in a
          community is protected through control of pollution
          in water, air, food, and other parts of the environment.
       2. To understand that lack of protection may cause illness
          and disease.

       [Other pertinent purposes]

Topics:
       Water pollution and purification
       Sewage treatment
       Air pollution
       Food processing and preservation

       [Other pertinent topics]

[The following treats only the topic "Water pollution and
purification."]

Objectives:
       1. To identify the major causes of water pollution.
       2. To describe the effects that water pollution can have
          on a community.
       3. To list the steps in general water treatment.
       4. To demonstrate the local methods of water treatment.

       [Other pertinent objectives]
```

Instructional design:	Media resources
A. Presentation: Teacher to student group	
1. General sources of water supply	Overhead transparencies
2. Causes of water pollution	16mm commercial film clips
3. General methods of water treatment	Printed sheets
[Other pertinent presentations]	
B. Independent study	
1. Local method of treating water	Slides--tape recording; programmed review;laboratory exercises
2. New, emerging methods of water purification (desalting, for example)	Library research
[Other pertinent independent study]	
C. Discussion group: Teacher with students	
1. Review of independent-study activities	
2. Student reports on emerging methods	Overhead transparencies; slides; chalkboard
3. Discussion of anticipated problems in water shortage, overuse, and so forth	Tape recording of comments by water conservationist
[Other pertinent discussion activities]	

(Note: The slides and tape recording for B-1 above are planned in detail in the chapters of Part Two.)

IMPLEMENTING THE INSTRUCTIONAL DESIGN

If you are a media specialist, training director, or teacher who contemplates developing a design for instruction as described here—either by yourself or in conjunction with other teachers or instructors—here are some guidelines and recommendations:

• The instructors most receptive to the approach described here, whether for reexamination of a topic or for planning an entire course, are likely to be those who already are users of audiovisual services. An instructor who is entirely verbally oriented has more difficulty accepting audiovisual methods than one who has used them.

• Get to know the instructors with whom you work—their approach to the subject, abilities to select illustrations of content, and understanding of the roles of media in instruction.

• As an initial experience with the instructional-design approach, start small with only a few immediately controllable elements (possibly to serve one or two lesson objectives) and build toward an ultimate design.

• Help instructors to be *specific* with examples and illustrations. The generalized statements used in a lecture will not suffice when planning for *learning* experiences. Observe the instructor while he is teaching the topic under consideration. What you see should offer clues for organization and visualizations.

• Often the logical organization of content, as developed by the instructor or subject expert, must be revised as the instructional design is planned. Often the development of media for instruction will affect the organization of content and plans for specific experiences.

• The matter of developing objectives is a complex, difficult, and often frustrating process. Spell out general purposes, move to content, and then backtrack to the behavioral objectives, planning to refine them even later when materials are being planned.

- Develop general guidelines for evaluation when objectives and content are considered. Then plan and prepare the specific evaluation instruments (tests, performance, and so forth) during the planning and production of media for instruction.
- Carefully consider the selection of media to carry content and to serve objectives. Such questions as these should be asked:

What will be the costs?

How much time is available to locate or prepare each item?

What technical skills or services are required?

Should available materials (commercial or previously prepared) be considered for use?

Will there be problems in utilization—are appropriate facilities, equipment, and supervision available and convenient?

Are the planned materials the most appropriate to objectives and content?

- Recognize that an extensive quantity and a wide variety of instructional materials probably will be needed for this method of group and individual instruction.
- Benefit by what is known about how people learn. Make use of the research findings in the next two chapters as you plan the instructional design and then develop specific materials.
- Refer to the details in Part Two of this book, since many of the same planning principles apply both to an instructional design and to individual audiovisual materials.

LEVELS OF AUDIOVISUAL PRODUCTION

The local production of audiovisual materials can take place on any of three levels.

Mechanical level: preparation

First, there is the *mechanical* level; here the concern is solely with the techniques of preparation. Mounting pictures on cardboard or cloth, copying pictures on film for slides, and running a printed page or clipping through a copy machine to make a transparency are examples of the mechanical preparation of materials. Even though the individual has a purposeful use in mind, little planning is required and the actual preparation follows a routine procedure. Many persons start at this level in audiovisual production and go on to other levels of activity.

Creative level: production

A step above the mechanical level is the *creative* level. Here,

materials being considered for production require decisions; planning accordingly becomes an important forerunner of production. *Production* implies an order of activity beyond *preparation,* with its more routine connotations. The design and production of an instructional bulletin board, of a slide series with a recording, of a filmstrip for self-instruction, of a set of thoughtfully designed transparencies to teach a concept, or of an 8-millimeter film that illustrates a process—all are examples of materials produced on the creative level. The skills developed on the mechanical level become tools for use on this level.

Design level: conception

As will be seen, the production of audiovisual materials that are carefully integrated into learning activities to serve specific instructional objectives may be part of a *design for instruction.* This is a third level to be served by locally planned and produced materials. Now audiovisual materials are conceived within a carefully designed instructional framework for group or individual uses. The skills developed on both the mechanical and creative levels serve important functions here.

While your interest in using this book may start with the mechanical level, it is hoped that you will find potentials for developing materials on either the creative or design levels.

Now, review what you have read about the place of audiovisual materials in emerging instructional programs.

1. Do you view audiovisual materials as "aids" or as integral parts of the instructional process? Justify your answer.
2. What is meant by the expression instructional design? What are its sequential elements? Give an example of a concept you might wish to develop in the instructional design pattern.
3. What are the particular contributions of television, film production, and programed instruction to the concept of instructional design?
4. What three patterns for teaching and learning are emerging in educational programs? What roles might audiovisual media have in each pattern?
5. What might be the relationship or coordination between commercial materials and locally prepared materials in an instructional program?
6. Which of the guidelines listed for implementing the instructional design seem most important to you? Would you add any other ones to this list?
7. By example, differentiate among the three levels of audiovisual production activity.

2. Perception, Communication, and Learning Theory

Slides, filmstrips, motion pictures, and other audiovisual materials have been produced for many years. Some of these materials do excellent jobs of imparting knowledge, of teaching skills, of motivating, or of influencing attitudes. Other materials are less effective, and some are of poor quality or may even be detrimental to accomplishing the purposes for which they were made to serve.

Too often the production of a film or the planning for multimedia instruction is based on intuition, subjective judgment, personal preferences for the way you like to do things, or even on a committee decision. These unfortunately may be relatively ineffective ways for insuring satisfactory results.

How can you be somewhat more sure that the materials you plan and produce will be effective for the purposes you intend? Is there evidence from research and some general principles to guide you?

Three areas should be of particular concern. One is the logical steps of developing objectives, of planning, and getting ready to take or draw pictures and to make recordings. These procedures will insure some degree of success for your audiovisual materials. Part Two of this book presents the planning steps you should consider using.

The second area from which you can obtain help in designing effective audiovisual materials includes reports on experimental studies measuring the effectiveness of such materials. In such studies specific elements that affect production have been controlled, thus providing evidence for handling such elements in audiovisual productions. Summaries of these research findings are reported in the next chapter.

Third, and fundamental to both audiovisual research and careful planning for media production, is the need to know how people perceive things around them, how people communicate with each other, and how people learn. Therefore our immediate concern is to examine evidence from the fields of psychology and communication.

The discussions that follow have one purpose—to make the reader aware of (or to review for him) some generalizations from the areas of perception, communication, and learning theory. Admittedly the treatment of each topic is greatly simplified and only the minimum essentials are presented. But even these can be useful to you as you plan your materials and consider the place of your materials in an instructional sequence.

PERCEPTION

Perception is the process whereby an individual becomes aware of the world around him. In perception we use our senses to apprehend objects and events. The eyes, ears, and nerve endings in the skin are the primary means through which we maintain contact with our environment. These, and other senses, are the tools of perception; they collect data for the nervous system. Within the nervous system the impressions so received are changed into electrical impulses which then trigger a chain of further electrical and chemical events in the brain. The result is an internal awareness of the object or event. Thus, perception precedes communication. Communication hopefully leads to learning.

Two things are of major importance about perception. First, any perceptual event consists of many sensory messages that do not occur in isolation, but are related and combined into complex patterns. These become the basis of a person's knowledge of the world around him. Second, an individual reacts to only a small part of all that is taking place around him at any one instance. He "selects" that part of the world he wants to experience, or that attracts his attention, at any one time. (Hence one needs to design materials that will attract the attention and hold the interest of the learner.) The experience of perception is individual and unique. It is not exactly alike for any two people. A person perceives an event in terms of his past experiences, present motivation, and present circumstances.

Evidence from research on perception indicates the following:[1]

- There is no purposive behavior without perception.
- Behavior is an outcome of past perceptions and a starting point for future perceptions.
- The perceiver and his world do not exist independently.
- Meanings are given to things by the perceiver in terms of all prior experiences he has accumulated.
- Perceptual experiences are personal and individual.
- A percept is a link between the past which gives it its meaning and the future which it helps to interpret.
- Those things that have been tied in most closely and most often with past personal experiences predominate perceptually over the unusual or the unfamiliar.
- Since two people cannot be in the same place at the same time, they must see at least slightly different environments.
- Though no two people can have exactly the same meanings for things observed, common experiences tend to produce shared meanings which make communication possible.

From these statements we can conclude that while any one perceptual experience is uniquely individual, a series of perceptions by different persons can be related to become nearly identical. If you walk around a statue, its shape will constantly change as you change the angles at which you look at it. If someone else then walks around the same statue and looks at it from the same angles, he will have different individual experiences, but the series for him will be much the same as it was for you. Thus a succession of individual experiences enables us to agree upon what we have experienced, even though the individual experiences are somewhat different.

The audiovisual field rests on the assumptions that people learn primarily from what they perceive and that carefully designed visual experiences can be common experiences and thus influence behavior in a positive way.

Therefore, as you design audiovisual materials, keep in mind the importance of providing carefully for desirable perceptual experiences in terms of the learner's experience background and of the present situation. Such production elements as methods of treating the topic (expository, dramatic, inquiry, or other), vocabulary level, kinds and number of examples, pacing of narration and visuals, graphic techniques, and others can each contribute to successful perception. In this way communication will be more effective and learning should be positive.

_____
[1] Selected from Hans Toch and Malcolm S. MacLean, Jr., "Perception, Communication and Educational Research: A Transactional View," *A V Communication Review,* vol. 10, no. 5, September–October 1962, pages 66-68.

COMMUNICATION

Perception leads to communication. In all communication, however simple or complex, a sequence similar to this occurs:

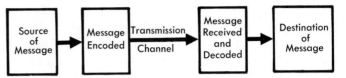

This model illustrates that a *message* (at the mental level), generally in the form of information, originated by a *source* or *sender* (the brain of an individual), is *encoded*—converted into transmittable form (a thought verbalized by being turned into sound waves, words of script). The message then passes through a *transmitter* (print, film, television) via a suitable *channel* (air, wire, paper, light) to the *receiver* (a person's senses—eyes, ears, nerve endings), where the message is *decoded* (within the nervous system, conversion into mental symbols) at the *destination* (brain of the receiver).

Effective communication depends upon the receiver being active. He reacts by answering, questioning, or performing, mentally or physically. There is then a return or response loop of this cycle, from receiver to sender. It is termed *feedback.*

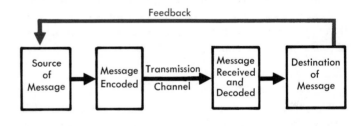

Feedback enables the originator to correct omissions and errors in the transmitted message, or to improve the encoding and transmission process, or even to assist the recipient in decoding the message.

One additional element must be added to this communication model:

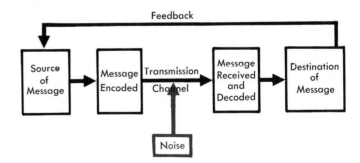

Noise is *any* disturbance that interferes with or distorts

transmission of the message. The factor of *noise* can have serious impact on the success or failure of communication. Static on a radio broadcast is a simple example of noise. A flashing light can be a distracting "noise" when a person is reading a book. Ambiguous or misleading material in a film can be deemed noise. Noise, can be created internally, within the receiver, to upset satisfactory communication—for example, a lack of attention. Even conflicting past experience can be an inhibiting noise source. Recall the importance of an individual's background experience in affecting perception. Noise clouds and masks information transmission to varying degrees and must be recognized as an obstacle to be overcome.

At times noise cannot be avoided and in planning materials the factor of *redundancy* is often used to overcome the effect of evident or anticipated noise. Redundancy refers to the repeated transmission of a message, possibly in different channels, to overcome or bypass distracting noise. Examples of redundancy may be showing and also explaining an activity, projecting a visual and distributing paper copies of the same material for study, or providing multiple applications of a principle in different contexts.

In working with audiovisual materials you should understand where the materials, as channels of communication, fit within the framework and process of message movement between senders and receivers, and how the various elements, along with factors of noise and redundancy, function to affect the success of your efforts to communicate effectively.

LEARNING THEORY

The process of learning is an individual experience for each person. Learning takes place whenever an individual's behavior is modified—when he thinks or acts differently, when he has acquired new knowledge or a new skill, and so forth.

Since a major purpose for preparing audiovisual materials is to effect behaviors that serve objectives, it is appropriate to turn to the psychology of learning for some help in locating principles that would guide the planning of effective audiovisual materials. Unfortunately, learning theory, as a body of knowledge, as yet has contributed little directly to the design of such materials. All we can do is offer some interpretations of generalizations.

Learning theories fall into two major families. One is the so-called *behaviorist* or *connectionist* group which interprets man's behavior as connections between stimuli and responses. This is the *S-R* pattern of learning. Each specific reaction is an exact *response* to a specific sensation or *stimulus*. Spoken and written words, simple pictures, and all audiovisual materials are examples of stimuli. Some are more effective stimuli for certain purposes than are others.

Much instruction is of this stimulus-response type. This concept is implicit in the "programed-instruction" approach introduced by B. F. Skinner. The emphasis here, as in most newer approaches to instruction, is on the learner and his response. In programed instruction, each sequence of learning is broken into small steps, requiring an appropriate response to each item followed by immediate knowledge of results. If the response is correct, the knowledge is a *reinforcement*, a rewarding recognition of each correct response.

The second group of theories is referred to variously as the *organismic, gestalt, field, or cognitive theories*. The common feature of these theories is that they assume that cognitive processes—insight, intelligence, and organizational abilities—are the fundamental characteristics of human behavior. Concern is more for the *how* of learning than for the *what*. Human action is seen as marked by a quality of intelligence and the ability to create relationships. The psychologists supporting these theories believe that in each new perception the object or event is seen differently because the cognitive structure within an individual has been reorganized by each of his prior perceptions (experiences).

Various psychologists have pointed out areas of emphasis and agreement among all learning theories. Two writers in the media field have offered practical interpretations of selected psychological concepts. C. R. Carpenter, a psychologist, and Edgar Dale, an educator, focus on audiovisual materials in terms of learning. Ten of their principles follow, the first seven from Carpenter[2] and the other three from Dale[3]:

• *Importance of motivation to the learner*. The most important and persistently basic task of teaching is to release, instigate, and increase such motivational processes and forces as interest and the need, desire, and wish to learn.

• *The personal relevance concept*. Teaching materials are effective in an ordered manner depending on the degree of their *personal relevance* (meaningfulness) to individual students. The production and use of teaching materials require judgments of their relevance to the individuals to be taught—abilities, levels of achievement, activated and latent interests, and accepted objectives of academic achievement.

• *Selected processes and audiovisual instruction*. What is presented to students and what is accepted and learned by them are very different. Chains of communication, which include teaching, can be conceived as a sequence of events with selective filters operating between each major contiguous link in the chain. The "output" or response can be expected to differ greatly from the "input" or stimulus. The individual interposes his entire *relevant* life history between the stimulus material and his own response.

2 C. R. Carpenter, "Psychological Concepts and Audio-Visual Instruction," *AV Communication Review,* vol. 5, no. 1, winter 1957, pages 361-369.

3 Edgar Dale, "Principles of Learning," *The News Letter,* vol. 29, no. 4, January 1964, Bureau of Educational Research and Service, Ohio State University, Columbus.

• *The need for organization.* More information can be learned more enduringly when materials are meaningfully and systematically organized than when they are unorganized or poorly organized.

• *The need for participation and practice.* Learning is activity. A widespread criticism of audiovisual materials and methods is the lack of participation and overt practice. Seeing and hearing are activities. Perception is an activity. Thinking is action. Using symbols, abstracting, deducing, generalizing, inferring, and concluding are all activities intimately involved in learning.

• *Repetition and variation of stimuli.* Generally it may be said that nothing absolutely new is ever learned effectively with one exposure. Repetition functions to reinforce and extend learning and to make the learned information more enduring. Variations operate to sustain attention, to instigate interest, and to broaden the pattern of learning. Variations of stimuli in all probability aid students to generalize and apply more widely and surely what they have learned. Repetition with variation provides *time* for learning and time for learning is absolutely essential.

• *The rate of presentation of material to be learned.* The rate of presentation of information in relation to the comprehension rates of students is a fundamental consideration in learning. Rate is determined in part by the number, complexity, and subjective difficulty of the materials to be learned.

• *Clarity, relevance, and effectiveness.* The clearer, the nearer, the more realistic, and relevant the statement of desired outcomes, the more effective the learning. If a learner can't see the target clearly, the chances of his hitting it are not good. Be sure he knows what is expected of him from the first.

• *Teaching for transfer.* Old learning doesn't automatically transfer to new learning. You must teach for transfer. Students need guided practice in learning to transform or reconstruct habitual ways of doing things. Teachers and planners can increase transfer by providing for new learning in varied contexts, by generalizing experiences, and by building attitudes favorable to learning.

• *Reporting results promptly.* Learning is increased by knowledge of results. Information about the nature of a good performance, knowledge of mistakes, and knowledge of successful results aid learning.

A useful addition to this list of psychological concepts is a statement from principles by Bugelski.[4] This statement is in keeping with the changing approach to teaching and learning described in Chapter 1.

• *Learning is done by the learner and not by some kind of transmission process from the teacher.* The function of the teacher is to prepare the situation and the chains of events in such fashion that the learner has the maximum possibilities of acquiring the proper "connections."

Kinds of learning

Robert Gagné, another psychologist, classified observations about learning and decided that various educational objectives require different *conditions of learning.* He found that eight kinds of learning, organized sequentially and cutting across all theories, could be described.[5]

1. *Signal learning.* Learning to respond to a signal. This is the involuntary *conditioned* response typified by the Pavlovian experiments with dogs.

2. *Stimulus-Response learning.* Voluntary learning that involves making a specific response to a specified stimulus, such as a child saying "doll" when mother says "doll."

3. *Chaining.* Learning to connect together, in a sequence, two or more previously learned *S-R* situations, as when a child learns to call an object by its name.

4. *Verbal association.* Learning on the verbal level, related to chaining, such as learning to translate an English word into a foreign language.

5. *Multiple discrimination.* Learning an extensive series of simple chains, as when distinguishing the names of a variety of plants and calling each one by its correct name.

6. *Concept learning.* Learning to make a common response to a number of stimuli that may differ from each other in appearance, as recognizing that various objects are all "plants."

7. *Principle learning.* Learning a chain consisting of two or more previously and separately learned concepts, such as geometric propositions based on axioms, or the names of chemical compounds related to the names of individual chemical elements.

8. *Problem solving.* Learning, based on two or more previously acquired principles, that requires internal thinking toward the result of a new, higher level principle; an example is the housewife's making decisions for the selection of items in a market on the basis of price or contents.

Gagné points out that in his pattern each higher-numbered condition (above the first) depends on the former ones as prerequisites. Thus for *chaining,* the individual has previously learned *S-R* connections so they can be chained; and so forth, building to the highest level of problem solving. Gagné also recognizes that his treatment of the conditions of learning is restricted to knowledge (cognitive tasks) and skill types (motor and psychomotor tasks) of educational objectives and does not treat objectives of motivation and the establishment of attitudes and values (the affective domain of learning).

Applications of Gagné's conditions for the design of instruction have been made in a research project and are described as

---

4 B. R. Bugelski, *The Psychology of Learning,* page 457.

5 Robert M. Gagné, *The Conditions of Learning,* pages 33-57.

part of a publication.[6] In this report, after statements of behavioral objectives are made, types of learning involved (from Gagné's list) are identified, then media and experiences are selected to serve the indicated conditions of learning. The report provides further details of how Gagné's learning principles are related to media selection.

In a subsequent paper Gagné summarized what to him are the most important events of instruction:[7]

• Gaining and maintaining attention
• Insuring recall of previously acquired knowledge
• Guiding learning by verbal and pictorial materials that provide "cues" or hints to new principles
• Providing feedback of his accomplishments to the learner in terms of stated objectives
• Establishing conditions for recall and transfer of learning through the use of carefully designed problems and situations to which application of the newly learned principle is made
• Assessing outcomes through test and other evaluations

Some investigators from the engineering sciences explain thought and behavior in terms of models derived from the study of control mechanisms (known as *cybernetics*). Such mechanisms operate by *negative feedback*. This involves adjustments in a system to keep it in a steady state by compensating for any deflections from that state (like a thermostat which, reacting to a drop in temperature, turns on the furnace to make the temperature rise). There are many such mechanisms and cybernetics attempts to apply their principles to problems in psychology and related fields. The feedback model has the advantage of combining stimulus-response analysis with a recognition that behavior is not merely a collection of stimulus-response units but a continuously on-going process. For the most part, to what extent this approach will prove useful in dealing with learning still remains to be seen.[8]

Finally, recognition must be given to one other thought bearing on learning. Where formerly it was generally accepted that only the *content* of the stimulus material (book, film, television, radio, or whatever) was important to the learner, there is now some concern, notably by the Canadian philosopher and communications theorist Marshall McLuhan, that the *medium* itself (film, radio, television) is more than a transmission belt.[9]

---

[6] Leslie J. Briggs and others, *Instructional Media: A Procedure for the Design of Multiple-Media Instruction*, chapter 2.

[7] Robert M. Gagné, "Learning Theory, Educational Media, and Individualized Instruction," a paper presented at the Faculty Seminar on Educational Media, November 16, 1967, Bucknell University, Lewisburg, Pennsylvania.

[8] Karl U. Smith and Margaret F. Smith, *Cybernetic Principles of Learning and Educational Design*.

[9] Marshall McLuhan, *Understanding Media: The Extension of Man*.

Media have certain characteristics of their own which influence the reception of the message. Furthermore, the exposure to each medium is a direct experience itself, according to McLuhan. His expression, "the medium is the message," may hold important implications for the design and effectiveness of audiovisual materials.

It should be clear from the information in this section that there are no concise principles of learning that can be directly transferred to the practical design of audiovisual materials. But the generalizations relating to motivation, careful organization, participation and practice, repetition, rate of presentation, and so forth, summarized by Carpenter and Dale, and the conditions of learning described by Gagné, do have definite bearing both on the selection of media to serve instructional objectives and on the planning of specific materials. Keep these generalizations in mind. In effect, many of the findings related to production elements reported in the next chapter are examples of the applications of these broad principles.

But lacking more direct guidance from psychology, educators must proceed with planning for instruction starting with objectives, then to designing of materials largely on an *empirical* basis, using experience, reactions of others, and "best-guesses." Then they must be tried with the potential student group, refined or changed as necessary, and tested again until ready for operational use. This approach applies to materials for group use or materials for independent student use.

Now, review what you have read about perception, communication, and learning theory.

1. In your own words, what is "human perception"? How does perception relate to the design of audiovisual materials?
2. Relate the seven (7) elements of the communication process in a communications model. Where do audiovisual materials fit into the model?
3. List the ten (10) principles of learning enumerated by Carpenter and Dale. Give a practical application of each one in a subject area. Which of these principles are related to the "important events of instruction" summarized by Gagné.
4. If possible, obtain a copy of the publication by Briggs indicated as a footnote. After studying it, suggest your own subject examples for each of Gagné's conditions of learning.
5. What is your reaction to the importance that McLuhan has placed on the *medium* itself used in communicating subject matter? Read one or more of his recent publications that treat this topic.

3. Research in the Design of Audiovisual Materials

Much research has been conducted about audiovisual materials. A large portion of the studies concerns utilization practices and proof of the instructional value of specific materials as compared with traditional teaching methods. In a smaller number of experiments a particular aspect of an audiovisual presentation was varied in order to determine the effect on learning of that particular variable. Results of the latter group have relevancy for the planning and subsequent production of audiovisual materials.

Summaries of research findings, including production elements, have been prepared by a number of writers. From these summaries the findings relating to production aspects of audiovisual materials are abstracted and presented in this chapter. Readers who have access to the original reports can profitably refer to them for full information.

These findings are fairly numerous and probably cannot be remembered or applied easily. To assist in your understanding and recall of these findings, at the end of the chapter, applications are offered for appraisal in a review exercise. The number of each finding is referred to in the review exercise.

HOBAN AND VAN ORMER (1950)

In 1950, Hoban and Van Ormer (*Instructional Film Research, 1918-1950*) surveyed a large number of experiments and other studies that had been made in the previous thirty years concerning the instructional values of motion pictures. Among their findings were some directly relating to variables in film production. Most of these points are also of value in the production of other materials such as slides and filmstrips. Only the briefest summary statements of the detailed explanations are included here.

1. *Camera angle.* Show a performance on the screen the way the learner would see it if he were doing the job himself (subjective camera position).

2. *Rate of development.* The rate of development or pacing of a film should be slow enough to permit the learners to grasp the material as it is shown.

3. *Succinct treatment.* Presenting only the bare essentials or too rapid coverage of subject matter may be very ineffective.

4. *Errors.* The learning of performance skills from films will be increased if you show common errors and how to avoid them.

5. *Repetition.* Organize a film so that important sequences or concepts are repeated. Repetition of films, or parts within a film, is one of the most effective means for increasing learning.

6. *Organizational outline.* Films which treat discrete factual material appear to be improved by the use of an organizational outline in titles and commentary.

7. *Introduction.* Present the relevant information in an introduction and tell the viewer what he is expected to learn from the film.

8. *Summary.* Summarize the important points in the film in a clear, concise manner. Summaries probably do not significantly improve learning unless they are complete enough to serve as repetition and review.

9. *Visual potentialities.* Take advantage of the ability of the motion-picture medium to show motion, to speed motion up and slow it down, to telescope and otherwise control timing of events and processes, to bridge space, and to organize events and action.

10. *Picture-commentary relationship.* The commentary of a typical informational film appears to teach more than the pictures of that same film when learning is measured by verbal tests. This observation does not necessarily mean that the commentary has greater inherent effectiveness than pictures; it may mean that producers rely more heavily on commentary than on pictures or on the optimum integration of the two. With films designed to teach performance skills, where learning is measured by nonverbal tests, the pictures appear to carry the main teaching burden.

11. *Concentration of ideas.* Ideas or concepts should be pre-

sented at a rate appropriate to the ability of the audience to comprehend them.

12. *Commentary*. The number of words (per minute of film) in the commentary has a definite effect on learning. Care should be taken not to "pack" the sound track. Application of readability formulas to improve a commentary may not do so.

13. *Use of personal pronouns*. Use direct forms of address (imperative or second person) in film commentaries. Avoid the passive voice.

14. *Nomenclature*. Introduction of new names or technical terms in a film imposes an additional burden on learners, and may impede the learning of a performance skill.

15. *Special effects*. Special effects used as attention-getting devices have no positive influence on learning.

16. *Optical effects*. A film in which straight cuts have replaced optical effects (such as fades, wipes, and dissolves) teaches just as effectively as a film which uses these effects.

17. *Color*. Experimentation has not yet demonstrated any general over-all increased learning as a result of using color in instructional films.

18. *Music*. Preliminary experimentation suggests that music does not add to the instructional effectiveness of an informational film.

19. *Pretesting*. Scripts, workprints, demonstrations, and final prints can be evaluated quickly using the learning-profile method of film evaluation, which requires a group of trainees to estimate their own learning.

20. *Film loops*. Short film loops, which can be repeated continuously as many times as desired, appear to be good materials for teaching difficult skills.

21. *Participation*. Learning will increase if the viewer practices a skill while it is presented on the screen, provided the film develops slowly enough, or provided periods of time are allowed which permit the learner to practice without missing new material shown on the screen.

22. *Dramatic sequences*. Incorporation of dramatic sequences such as comedy, singing commercials, or realistic settings in films to teach factual information have not been shown to improve the film.

23. *Filmograph*. Filmographs, which incorporate still shots rather than motion, may be equally effective and less expensive.

24. *Visual recordings*. Films may be produced to make a visual recording of a task that may be difficult to describe with words alone.

25. *Inexpensive films*. Because color, optical effects, and dramatic effects have little to do with increasing learning from films, it is possible to eliminate them. Films prepared in this manner can be made inexpensively and can be produced quickly.

SAUL (1954)

Another review of literature, relating this time to graphic training aids, was done in 1954 under the direction of Ezra V. Saul (*A Review of the Literature Pertinent to the Design and Use of Effective Graphic Training Aids*). The objective of this report was "to prepare annotated reviews of the literature in specific areas pertinent to the problem of developing standards and criteria on the design, preparation, and utilization of effective graphic training aids."

Materials for the report were derived from the literature on psychophysiology of vision, visual perception, experimental aesthetics and art, advertising, visual education, psychology of learning, engineering drawing, and instructor utilization of graphic materials. Many of the reports are valuable for such findings as relate to design principles, uses of color, and graphic depiction of relationships, to mention just a few. Evaluations of findings are provided at the end of each section, but no generalized factual summaries are made from which specific principles can be drawn.

MAY AND LUMSDAINE (1958)

Between 1946 and 1954 a series of experimental studies concerning problems in production and utilization of teaching films were conducted under the Yale Motion Picture Research Project (*Learning from Films*). Some findings correlated closely with the results reported by Hoban and Van Ormer in these categories: *concentration of ideas, color, music, participation,* and *dramatic sequences*. In addition, other findings were:

26. *Pictorial quality*. A crude presentation (pencil sketches of visuals) may be at least equal in effectiveness to a polished color film.

27. *Live dialogue and off-stage narration*. Except where the use of live dialogue can have marked superiority for meeting particular objectives, the narrated film has great advantages.

28. *Printed titles and questions*. Liberal use of titles, questions, and other printed words can improve teaching effectiveness.

MAY (1965–1966)

A different approach to reporting research results was taken in May's series of papers [*Enhancements and Simplifications of Motivational and Stimulus Variables in Audiovisual Instructional Materials* (1965); *The Role of Student Response in Learning from the New Educational Media* (1966); *Word-Picture Relationships in Audio-Visual Presentations* (1965)] for the United States Office of Education. He examined selected areas of instructional variables as related to the production of audiovisual materials. These were treated from the standpoint of the functions they perform for *motivating, reinforcing, cueing,* and *simplifying* the responses that are required for learning.

29. *Motivators* are devices, effects, and procedures to cause the learner to pay close attention, to look or listen for relevant and crucial clues, to have a "set" or put forth effort to learn, and to respond or practice. Positive motivators may include the use of color (to gain and hold attention); dramatic presentations; humor and comic effects; and inserted printed questions.

30. *Reinforcers* are techniques to increase the probability that the learner will remember and can reproduce what was presented. There are no clear indicators of ways to accomplish this increase, but there is evidence that stimuli in materials that are pleasing, interesting, and satisfying are positive reinforcers.

31. *Cue identifiers* are devices and effects that help the learner identify and recognize the relevant cues. These include color, arrows and pointers, animation, "implosion" techniques (having assembled parts fall into place without being handled by the demonstrator), subjective camera angles, and directed narration.

32. *Simplifiers* are procedures for making presentations more effective. They include improving the readability of narration, eliminating irrelevant pictorial materials, repeating illustrations or adding additional illustrations, or using filmstrips or filmographs (still pictures or diagrams on motion-picture film) in place of live film action for some purposes.

In this review May, as did other writers, indicated that some techniques did little or nothing to improve learning in audiovisual materials. These included musical backgrounds, introductory and review sections, and optical effects for transitions (fades, dissolves, and wipes).

TRAVERS (1967)

In 1964 Travers, a psychologist, made available an interim report on his project, sponsored by the United States Office of Education. The preliminary report, with additions, was the basis for Travers's *Research and Theory Related to Audiovisual Information Transmission* (1967). His purpose was to search the literature relating to the transmission of information through the senses and to point out implications for the design of audiovisual teaching materials. This report differs from that of Hoban and Van Ormer in two ways. First, Travers examined reports of psychology-oriented studies and those involving other media as well as motion pictures. Second, the majority of the studies described by Travers were performed after 1950, whereas the Hoban and Van Ormer report included studies from 1918 to 1950.

Here are the major findings reported by Travers. Compare them with the summary list from Hoban and Van Ormer.

• *Embellishments and simplifications*

33. The fact that color adds to the attractiveness of a training device does not necessarily mean that it improves learning. Black-and-white is as effective as color for instructional purposes except when the learning involves an actual color discrim-ination. Learners prefer color versions despite the fact that the addition of color does not generally contribute to learning.

34. A demonstration should include only the basic elements of what is to be demonstrated, but oversimplification can have a deleterious effect.

35. The special effects (fades, dissolves, and the like) that are used to represent lapses of time and other events were not effective in conveying the intended meanings. Print titles seem to be more effective. Special sound effects appear to provide much more challenge to the film producer than aid to the learner. The same can be said of humor and of other special means intended to retain the interest of the learner.

• *Audio readability, density of information, and rate of presentation*

36. Verbal simplification in film commentaries increases teaching effectiveness. Comprehension of audio inputs can be predicted by readability formulas to measure their difficulty.

37. Some verbalization is better than none, but there is no optimum amount. Slow speeds for transmitting verbal information are favored, but they can be too slow.

38. If time is not a factor, listening comprehension is likely to be most effective at speeds of around 160 words per minute. This generalization is probably true only for relatively simple material and the intellectual level of the audience must also be taken into account. When narration is accompanied by video, the optimum rate of the narration appears to be slower.

• *Audience participation and practice*

39. Overt (visible) response, practiced by the learner during the film, results in increased learning.

40. Furnishing knowledge of results as part of the participation process also has positive effects upon learning.

41. Activities related to the presentation of a film indicate that learners experience difficulty in following a continuous demonstration and, at the same time, undertaking the task themselves. But when the film or other continuous flow of information is stopped and the learner then participates, learning is more effective. Participation does not have to be overt. Mental practice is as effective.

In 1966 Travers completed his project, including a series of experiments designed to investigate the validity of certain accepted elements in the design of audiovisual materials. On the basis of the results of his experiments, he builds a useful case for presentations via a single sense with this conclusion:

42. "The simultaneous use of two senses (visual and audio) are likely to be of value only when the rate of input of information is very slow. The silent film with the alternation of picture and print would appear to find much theoretical support as a teaching device."

Hartman (1961)

This matter of single- versus multiple-channel presentation is of particular importance with attention being given to 8mm silent- and sound-film production. Hartman ("Single and Multiple Channel Communication: A Review of Research and a Proposed Model") had reviewed the literature to that date on single- and multiple-channel communication and concluded with these two points:

43. The meaning of a visual message is often ambiguous and subject to personal interpretation. The use of words to direct attention is essential.

44. The audio channel is much more capable of obtaining attention if it is used as an interjection on the pictorial channel rather than being continuously parallel with the pictorial.

Gropper (1966)

Finally, the relation of visuals and words for developing *programed* audiovisual materials had been studied by Gropper ("Learning from Visuals: Some Behavioral Considerations"). He found that:

45. While concepts and principles can be acquired on the basis solely of visual presentations, to rely *only* on visual lessons is inefficient. Gropper concluded that words serve an important cueing role and should be incorporated, for this secondary purpose, into a visual presentation.

A person interested in planning and producing audiovisual materials should review and weigh all the evidence from research findings and theory reported in this and the preceding chapter. Many of these findings, rather than intuition, should be considered as you design your own materials for instruction. Start with these results and recommendations, realizing that some may have been derived from situations far afield of the applications you plan to make. (Yet they are starting points with positive evidence for improved learning at lower costs in terms of time, materials, and services.) Then adapt and change as you gain experience and test the results of your efforts.

Now, review what you have read about research findings for the design of audiovisual materials.

Following are statements concerning audiovisual materials that apply one or more of the findings described in this chapter. Some make recommended applications, while others apply elements in nonrecommended fashion. For each example indicate your *agreement* or *disagreement* with the proposed plan. Then check your answer, using the reference numbers at the right to locate the relevant numbered finding(s) used as a basis for each example.

	Agree or Disagree	*Evidence*
1. When demonstrating the proper method to use in casting with a fishing rod, show errors commonly made and ways to avoid them.	_____	4
2. In demonstrating a skill, like fingering a musical instrument, color will add to the instructional value of the medium used.	_____	17, 25, 33
3. In explaining the operation of a machine, use arrows to indicate each part as it is referred to.	_____	31
4. Slides (still pictures) may be as effective as a motion picture for presenting a school's program orientation to students.	_____	23, 32
5. To demonstrate how a woman sews an intricate stitch by hand, film the action from over her shoulder.	_____	1, 31
6. In teaching a how-to-do-it skill like welding, limit the amount of narration and depend on the visuals for the major instructional effect. In narration, use words in the present tense to direct attention ("hold the tool . . ."; "notice the color . . .")	_____	10, 13, 31, 42-44
7. A film that shows action in many locations is more effective if an optical effect like a dissolve (page 202) is used between scenes to bridge distance rather than abrupt cuts from one scene to the next. Also, background music will enhance the presentation.	_____	16, 18, 25, 35
8. To explain for teachers a new method of teaching algebra, present only the essential facts without repetition of any of the concepts. A brief, general summary should be included.	_____	5, 8, 11, 34
9. In describing an industrial process, quickly present only the essential information. The commentary should describe, at length, what cannot easily be visualized. If it is a lengthy subject, plan that the commentary moves along rapidly.	_____	2, 3, 11, 12, 36
10. Picture sketches from storyboard cards (page 40), converted to film, may be as effective as a high-quality polished treatment for illustrating a farming procedure.	_____	26, 32
11. In treating the subject of animal life at the seashore, color should be used and important concepts presented through multiple examples.	_____	5, 17, 25, 33
12. Introduce the demonstration of a laboratory procedure with an explanation of the purpose of the		

demonstration and what the student is expected to learn from it. Include titles that indicate the sequence of steps in the procedure. Describe carefully and visualize new technical terms. _____ 6, 7, 14, 28, 35

13. For learning to operate a piece of equipment, like a laboratory chemical balance, a continuous loop film that can be viewed any number of times may have advantages. Directions for the learner to stop the film, answer questions, and practice steps in the skill should be included. Correct answers to questions should be provided immediately after the questions are answered. _____ 21, 28, 39-41

Part Two

PLANNING YOUR AUDIOVISUAL MATERIALS

4. Getting Started

Start with an idea and from it develop your objectives in terms of the specific audience with which you plan to use your audiovisual materials.

All too often someone says, "Let's make a movie about our school," or, "How about shooting some slides to train salesmen?" or, "We should have some transparencies for our team teaching class."

Unfortunately such thoughts frequently are the signal to start taking pictures prematurely and produce audiovisual materials that are unorganized and ineffective. These proposals are no more than bare ideas; they require further consideration, such as decisions about the specific content and its organization into planned sequences of pictures.

Occasionally pictures need to be made without any prior planning (there are "one-chance-to-get-the-picture" situations), but desirable audiovisual materials are usually attained through careful plans.

START WITH AN IDEA

An idea, a problem situation, or a need is the starting point for your audiovisual materials. An idea may indicate an area of interest you have, but the more useful ideas are those conceived in terms of a need relating to a specific group—an audience's need for certain information, or for a skill, or the need to establish a desired attitude.

So here is the first step: Express your idea concisely. For example:

In my science classes we learn about community health services. As part of our study we consider methods of water purification. I need some pictures (possibly slides) which would help my students to understand better *the methods used in treating our local water supply.* (Note: This example of the water-purification process will serve as an illustration of the planning steps that follow.)

In the instructional-design approach described in Chapter 1, the first step was to *recognize broad general purposes.* Essentially, these are the beginning *ideas* referred to here. They also need amplification before objectives are developed. Stated purposes (as for a social-studies course, "to understand the structure of national, state, and local governments"; or for a mathematics unit, "to learn the advantages of displaying data in tabular or graphic form") are fine as a start, but they do not lead directly and easily to definitive learning experiences.

DEVELOP THE OBJECTIVES

Build upon the idea or generalized statement of purposes. Doing this means translating the general idea into a clear-cut and specific statement of one or more objectives for the planned learning.

Today much attention is given in the literature (references on page 234) to the topic of *Behavioral Objectives;* these have a key role in instructional design as well as in separate learning activities. This focus is an aspect of the shift from teacher- and subject-centered instruction to the emphasis on the student and his needs.

To plan successful audiovisual materials and other learning experiences, it is necessary to know specifically what must be learned. The purpose of formulating objectives is to provide clear guidance that permits an orderly presentation of content.

When learning takes place, a person behaves differently than he did before the learning experience; here the evidence for learning is that he has become able to do something that he formerly could not do. Or, he may have acquired new knowledge—another measure of learning. Again, through learning a person might respond differently in terms of an attitude or an appreciation. The learning may encompass any one or two or all of these kinds of change.

So, the objectives of learning can be grouped into three major categories—the *psychomotor* area, represented by skills and performance; the *cognitive* area, which includes knowledge and information; and the *affective* area of attitudes and appreciations. None of these objectives excludes the others.

The difficult problem is to spell out the objectives so that (1) learning experiences can be developed to satisfy each objective, and (2) tests or performance measurements can be designed to find out whether the learning has taken place.

The military and industry-business training programs have been dealing with objectives for some time. Their emphasis has been on specific *task-analysis* objectives for operational skills. Just as developing instructional design for education is more complex than developing the weapons or communication systems in the military or industry, so likewise educational objectives, with their greater emphasis on the *affective* area, are more difficult to define and put into effect.

The general nonspecific words that are often used to describe instructional purposes—to *know*, to *understand*, to *become familiar with*, to *appreciate*, to *believe*, to *gain insight into*, to *accept*, to *enjoy*, and so forth—are unsatisfactory guide words for objectives. They do not permit verification through specific observable behavior and they are open to many interpretations of how their accomplishment may be measured.

Useful statements of objectives are made up of two grammatical parts. First: a specific ACTION VERB like one of these—to *identify*, to *name*, to *demonstrate*, to *show*, to *make* or *build*, to *order* or *arrange*, to *distinguish between*, to *compare*, to *apply*, and so forth. Second, CONTENT REFERENCE that follows the verb, like—to name the *five steps in the process*, to kick a *football* at least 30 yards, to write a 500-word *theme*, to apply a *rule*, to solve 4 of 5 *problems*, and so forth.

Notice that in addition to the action verb and the content reference, we may add a STANDARD OF COMPETENCY (at least *30 yards, 500 words, 4 of 5* problems). The standard further provides for setting an attainment level that can be measured.

With this awareness of behavioral and measurable objectives, how can we specifically indicate the objectives for the general idea example on *methods of water purification* indicated previously?

It is *not* sufficiently specific to say:

• To know how our local water supply is treated.

It *is* specific to say:

1. To name the five steps in the purification of our local water supply.
2. To select from a list the scientific principles that apply during each step in the treatment process.
3. To practice the conservation of water.

Statements 1 and 2 above specify cognitive (informational) objectives. Statement 3 specifies an attitudinal behavior. It is much more difficult to indicate behaviors and measurements for attitudes and appreciations than to do so for either knowledge/information or skills/performance objectives. Admittedly some objectives must lead to unpredictable outcomes, as opposed to learnings that build up immediate connections between specific stimuli and specific responses. The attainment of other objectives may not be fully measurable until the individual becomes an active member of adult society. But attempts should be made (sometimes very imaginatively) to devise the best measurable ways of stating objectives. To repeat, only when the objectives are stated in terms of an individual's performance is there much guidance for the design of instruction.

Remember that each topic for instruction (like the water-purification topic) requires a number of objectives, each to be considered individually in designing learning experiences. Therefore, it takes time and careful thought to develop and state objectives. Also, as was indicated during the discussion of instructional design in Chapter 1, it is natural to move gradually from general to specific objectives. Finally, realize that some objectives may become clearly evident only when content is being selected or even when specific audiovisual materials are in the planning stage. In such a case, return to this beginning point, the statement of objective, and check how well the content and learning experiences fit the stated objective; you may want to revise the statement.

You might prepare audiovisual materials for many purposes. Here are some major general purposes with specific examples. They are stated in terms of audience changes, from the audience viewpoint.

• *To learn about a subject;* for example, "to recognize the location and the significance of 10 landmarks important in the early history of our community."
• *To apply the steps in a process;* for example, "to locate and use the major reference books in the school library."
• *To exercise a skill;* for example, "to make slides of interior and exterior subjects with a 35mm camera."
• *To practice a certain attitude;* for example, "to form the habit of using safe procedures in operating shop equipment."
• *To respond to a social need;* for example, "to offer our services in a youth recreation program."

In planning materials, limit yourself to no more than one or two concisely stated achievable objectives. However much you feel it necessary *to cover the whole topic,* you will realize eventually that limitations should be set. If you do not set limits, your materials may become too complex and unmanageable. You may maintain limits by aiming at a series of related audiovisual materials, each of which includes a single phase of a large topic.

It is also important to make the learner aware of the objectives of his learning. Inform him what he is to learn from a film, a self-instructional activity, or a correlated program. There is much evidence to show that better results are obtained when students clearly know what they are expected to learn.

Finally, objectives do not stand alone. It is obvious they are dependent on the subject content that will be treated and are influenced by the needs and dispositions of the learner or intended audience.

CONSIDER THE AUDIENCE (THE LEARNER)

The characteristics of the learner or audience—those who will be using and learning from your materials—cannot be separated from your statement or objectives. One influences the other. Such audience characteristics as age and educational level, knowledge of the subject and attitude toward it, and individual differences within the group, all have bearing on your objectives and treatment of the topic. The audience is the determinant when you consider the complexity of ideas to be presented, the rate at which the topic is developed, the vocabulary level for captions and narration, the number of examples to use, the kinds of involvement and degree of participation of the learner, and similar matters that influence the complexity of the objectives and your handling of the topic.

At times more than one audience may fit your plans, but generally it is advisable to plan for *one major audience group.* Then consider other *secondary* ones which also might use your materials. Describe the major audience, explicitly.

For the example, *Our Water Supply:*

The major audience will be ninth-grade general-science classes. The students have sufficient science background to understand the applications of filtration and chlorination in the treatment of water, but other concepts, such as aeration and coagulation, may be new and will require careful development.

A word of caution: If you plan audiovisual materials for use with younger groups, make sure that the subject and the activities selected are appropriate to their interests and their abilities. Your own enthusiasm for a topic may take you far beyond the limited amount of interest that others may have for it. Also, give careful consideration to the complexity of the subject so that your group does not become burdened with too many details and lose interest as a result.

SOME EXAMPLES

The planning steps thus far examined are: (1) start with an idea; (2) from the idea develop your objectives, with due regard for the intended audience and its characteristics.

Examine the following examples. Are the steps clearly stated and easy to follow? Are the objectives stated in behavioral terms? Which of them may not be so stated?

Idea	Purpose	Audience
Plant life common to our community	To recognize and name the 25 most common species of seed-bearing plants in our county	(1) High-school biology classes (2) Nature clubs
Our school library	(1) To use the resources of our elementary-school library (2) To check books out properly and return them when due	Upper elementary grades of the school
Operation of our insurance company	To understand my role in the successful operation of our company	Employees of the ABC Insurance Company
Lettering aids for making displays	To use a variety of lettering resources for preparing classroom displays	All teachers in the district
Support the school-bond drive at the next election	To vote *Yes* for new school construction at the election	General community voting public
Our church's youth program	(1) To take part in youth-group activities (2) To understand how youth activities help to develop sound character and religious understanding among our young people	(1) Children and teen-agers of church members (2) Church sponsors and adult members

Now apply what you have read.

1. The examples on page 25 relate to the five major purposes listed on page 24. Identify each example according to the appropriate category.
2. It has been indicated that the preparation of audiovisual materials may be based upon the feeling that something is needed to do a *better job,* or the belief that something is needed where presently *nothing exists.* Select one topic that you would like to see developed into an audiovisual material and *express it as an idea.*
3. Now write the specific objectives you want such an audiovisual material to serve.
4. With what audience would you use such materials?
5. What are some of the characteristics of the audience you should consider?

5. Getting Some Help

Consider individuals who may assist you with your planning and production. Examine already-made audiovisual materials relating to your topic.

A TEAM APPROACH

You may be capable of planning and preparing your audiovisual materials without the assistance of others. If you are, you have skills in three areas. First, you have a good knowledge of the subject. Second, you know how to plan your audiovisual materials and how to interpret the subject visually. Third, you have the necessary technical skills in photography, graphic arts, and sound recording.

But if you feel inadequate in any of these areas you should obtain assistance or carefully use this book (in the second and third areas). Even so, there is value in getting reactions and suggestions from other people, so plan to involve others during some phases of the planning and preparation processes. In a class or group, specific jobs may be assigned to individuals, but at various stages group interaction is desirable.

In keeping with this team approach, one leader in the field of visual communications has offered a pattern of personnel involvement.[1] Three individuals or three groups might make up the *production team*. The *subject specialist* is the person or persons having broad knowledge and familiarity with the potential audience. The *communications specialist* is the individual who knows how to handle the content (treatment, scriptwriting, camera angles, and the like) and knows the advantages, limitations, and uses of the various audiovisual media so that the resulting materials will achieve the anticipated purposes. Finally, the *technical staff* comprises those responsible for the photography, the art work, the lighting, and the sound recording.

These separately described areas naturally overlap: the communications person may also take the pictures; or, as was mentioned, you may fill all three jobs. The important thing to recognize is that all three jobs exist. Keep them in mind as you consider the stages of planning and preparation that follow. For example:

[1] Adrian TerLouw, Educational Consultant, Eastman Kodak Company, Rochester, New York.

While planning audiovisual materials on *Our Water Supply,* I will consult with the supervisor of the city water department. The supervisor and I in combination will fill the role of *subject specialist*. I will request assistance also from the school's audiovisual coordinator, who will thus function as *communications specialist*. Since I have a good skill in photography I will prepare the visual materials, but I will be assisted by a *technical staff* of three students who have abilities in photography and art.

Within an instructional design you are concerned with more than just the planning and physical production of audiovisual materials. The materials are to arise out of planned instruction, hence evaluation for effectiveness is important. Therefore the instructional staff and those in charge of evaluation must also play roles during the planning of instructional materials.

RELATED MATERIALS

Before carrying the planning of your audiovisual materials to an advanced stage, locate and examine any materials already prepared on your general topic or on topics closely related to it. They may offer you some useful ideas, or you may find that all or part of such materials may fit one or more of your objectives. This may be especially true of the single-concept 8mm films that have, in part, been derived from 16mm commercial films.

Communicate with audiovisual specialists in school systems, universities, colleges, or business and industry for suggestions of other possible materials and also for their reactions to your plans. Check your library for such references as the *Index to 16mm Educational Films* and other educational-media reference volumes compiled by the National Information Center for Educational Media (NICEM) at the University of Southern California and available from McGraw-Hill Book Company. Also check the *Source Directory: Educational Single-Concept Movie Loops in Instant Loading Magi-Cartridges,* available from Technicolor, Commercial and Educational Division, 1300 Frawley Drive, Costa Mesa, California 92626. Also check the *Educator's Guide to Free Films* and the *Educator's*

Guide to Free Filmstrips, published by the Educators Progress Service, Randolph, Wisconsin 53956.

Now apply what you have read.

Examine the topic you had under consideration at the end of Chapter 4. Assume now that you are to continue with the planning and preparation of the audiovisual material related to this topic, and answer these questions concerning the three roles discussed in the section you have just finished reading:

1. Which roles would you fill? What are your qualifications?

2. Which parts of this book (skim it, or look at the table of contents) would you expect to be of greatest value to you in improving your qualifications for all of the three roles? Is any role beyond this book's objectives?

3. Would you ask for assistance in any of the three areas? Whom would you seek to fill the role of subject specialist? the role of communications specialist? the places on the technical staff?

4. How would you learn whether any audiovisual materials have already been prepared on your topic?

6. Expanding from the Objectives

Learn as much as you can about your subject, then develop an outline of the content in terms of the objectives.

In your preliminary planning you defined your objectives and your audience. Now consider the subject matter upon which your audiovisual materials will be based. Consult with your subject specialist, or if you are handling the content yourself, do any necessary research work. Facts about a subject are often found through interviews, during visits to suitable facilities, and in the library. After this background work you can feel confident that your basic facts are correct and that you will include all pertinent information on your topic.

PREPARE THE CONTENT OUTLINE

From the data you have gathered prepare a content outline. This outline becomes the framework for your audiovisual materials. It consists of (1) the basic topics which support your objectives; (2) the factual information that explains each topic.

A word of caution. Remember the people who will be your audience—their interests and their limitations. Decide what information must be included in detail or what can be treated lightly; what you can suggest for additional study; and what should be left out or considered for other audiovisual materials.

In the sequence of the instructional design the examination of content follows the objectives. At this stage you are not as yet concerned about specific materials. There is no gain in asking at this point whether a film or a set of transparencies, a recording, a printed program, or a combination of media will best serve the objectives. You must find out what content is required to support the objectives. Then you can make decisions about specific audiovisual materials.

USE STORYBOARD CARDS

A good way of relating content to objectives is to connect the two visually. In a few pages we will examine the method of preparing a *storyboard* to visualize the treatment of a topic for an audiovisual material. This same technique has value now.

Write each objective on a 4″×6″ card or slip of paper. Tack or tape the cards to a wall for display. Then, from your notes on paper, make a second set of cards listing the content—the factual information related to each objective—and display these cards under or beside each appropriate objective card. At this stage, list all the available content relating to the objectives, without considering what you may use and what will be discarded.

It is advisable to use cards of one color for objectives and of a second color for the content. Later you may add additional cards for specific materials that relate to single objectives and items of content, or to groups of either.

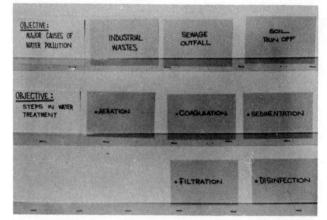

You will find that using cards makes you free to experiment with the order of the ideas until they are in a logical sequence. What you start with as the first point may later become the last one. Additional objectives that occur as you organize can also be added easily at this stage, while anything that apparently disrupts the sequence can also, just as easily, be eliminated or relocated. Later, during the actual storyboarding and scripting, you may find need for further changes, but now you have a simple, natural guideline to follow.

It should be reemphasized that at this stage you include as much as possible about the content—facts, examples, locations, special reminders, and so forth. It will be easier to eliminate some points later than to search for them if needed. While you are listing content, visual ideas may come to mind. Note them also on cards.

Once the content has been listed in relation to the objectives, you may consider this to be a *checkpoint* time—a time when you want to have other persons look over your progress and offer suggestions and help. Even though you may already have a team that includes subject consultants, it is a good idea to bring in other persons, not directly involved in the project, to examine your work objectively. They may find something important left out, or offer a comment that strikes a spark to give a direction you had not considered.

REVIEW WHAT YOU HAVE DONE

Your content outline has been developed in the light of an idea, objectives, and audience. You are now ready to make decisions about the medium or media to carry the objectives and content. Ask yourself such questions as these:

• What medium (media) should be used?
• Is sound (narration, lip synchronization) necessary, or can a silent medium (film, slides, filmstrip) with titles, captions, and directions be used?
• Is motion important or can still pictures convey the ideas and information?
• Is there to be study by individuals or is the emphasis to be on group use?

• Is color important or will black-and-white be satisfactory?
• Will there be any problems in keeping the materials up to date?
• Will I be able to overcome any technical problems in preparation, or do I know where to get help if necessary?
• Might there be problems of duplication, distribution, or storage of the completed materials?
• Will budget and time permit a good job?
• What problems may be encountered when using the materials (facilities, equipment, size of group, and the like)?

Now consider the various media available to you—characteristics, best uses, advantages, disadvantages, and limitations. Then make choices to best serve your purposes.

Now apply what you have read.

1. Develop a brief content outline for the topic you previously selected. Consider the following questions:
   a. What research should you do on the subject?
   b. Have you included all important information, in the light of your purposes and anticipated audience?
   c. Do ideas for additional visual materials concerning other aspects of the topic come to mind for future consideration?

2. Relate the content to objectives on cards of different colors.

An Example of a Content Outline

```
            CONTENT OUTLINE--OUR WATER SUPPLY


    I.  Source of our water

        A.  Initially snow and rain along the western slopes of sections
            of the Sierra Nevada mountains
        B.  Collected and transported as the Mokelumne river
        C.  Held in the upper reservoir

   II.  Treatment at the purification plant

        A.  Aeration
            1. spraying of water into the air
            2. adds or removes oxygen
            3. improves taste

        B.  Coagulation
            1. adding of alum to water
            2. causes small impurities to clump together
            3. takes 10-20 minutes
```

    C. Sedimentation
       1. suspended impurities settle out
       2. removes 85% of all foreign matter
       3. takes about 3 hours

    D. Filtration
       1. passing the water through beds of sand and gravel
       2. strains out unsettled suspended matter
       3. most straining action takes place in top 6 inches of sand

    E. Disinfection
       1. adding of chlorine solution to water
       2. done after filtration is completed
       3. kills bacteria

III. Distribution of water

    A. Transmission pipes
    B. Distribution reservoirs
    C. Gravity flow of water

IV. Conservation of water

    A. Each day 3,000,000 gallons used in our city
    B. Less water collected now than formerly
    C. Need to use water wisely and not wastefully

7. The Kinds of Materials

Consider the specific contributions and special requirements of these seven audiovisual materials: photographic print series, slide series, filmstrips, recordings, transparencies, motion pictures, and television and display materials. Then select those most appropriate to serve your objectives and content.

Notice the sequence that is being developed. First, establish *objectives* and consider your *audience;* then *organize the content* to fit your objectives. Now *select the specific audiovisual materials* and other experiences to carry through your purposes.

Why this sequence? Because audiovisual materials are channels through which content stimuli are presented to the learner—stimuli to motivate, evoke a response, inform, direct attention, evaluate, guide thinking, test for transfer, or whatever. Therefore only after establishing *what it is that you wish to communicate* are you properly able to select the channel or medium through which the content will most likely elicit the proper response that serves the objective.

If motion is inherent in the subject, consider a motion picture; but if motion is not important, then consider materials that demand simpler skills, less time, or less money, and may do the job equally well. To think further: a series of large photographs, which can easily be studied in detail, may be preferable to a filmstrip and less difficult to make. Also, consider using combinations of media to serve your purposes: a series of transparencies that outline a process may be supplemented with a set of slides and the two used concurrently for effective instruction.

On the other hand, perhaps for practice or perhaps because you have certain equipment available, you may wish to prepare a specific material, possibly a series of slides or a motion picture. If this is your starting point, select a subject and establish purposes which will use the medium to its best advantage.

Any one or more of a number of audiovisual materials may be applicable to serve an objective and its content. The decision for selection may be based on your skills, equipment requirements, convenience, or cost. But each of the several types of audiovisual materials makes certain unique contributions to improving communications and subsequent learning. All require careful planning before preparation—some more than others.

When selecting the ones to serve your purposes, examine all of them and become aware of their special characteristics and specific contributions to learning.

PHOTOGRAPHIC PRINT SERIES

A photographic print series may consist of drawings or photographs, in black-and-white or in color. Usually they are enlargements from camera negatives. They may include explanatory captions and they may be accompanied with directions for their use. They lend themselves to display and to detailed self-instructional follow-up study, or they may be part of a programed sequence.

Because photo series are normally used by individuals rather than by groups under direction, they need to be self-sufficient and self-explanatory; brief, concise captions impart this quality.

SLIDE SERIES

Slides are a form of projected audiovisual materials easy to prepare, hence they frequently serve as the starting effort in a local-production program. The pictures are generally taken on reversal color film, which is sent to a film-processing laboratory where the mounted slides are made up. Since they are ready for projection as the laboratory completes them, relatively little time goes into the mechanics of processing and mounting.

For many uses any 35mm camera will make satisfactory slides. But for filming some subjects, for close-up and for copy work, cameras with special attachments are required.

The standard slide dimensions are 2 inches by 2 inches. Since the slides are this small, they are easily handled and stored. Their sequence can be changed, and slides may be selected from a series for special uses. But this flexibility entails some disadvantages. Slides can become out of order, can be misplaced (it is a common occurrence to leave the last slide in the projector!), and sometimes they are accidentally projected upside down or backwards. Most of these disadvantages can be overcome by the use of inexpensive trays and magazines which store the slides and hold them during use. Also, automatic and remotely controlled projectors permit an instructor, while making his presentation, to make slide changes for himself. Tape recordings can be prepared to accompany slides and, with special recording equipment, slides can be shown automatically as the taped narration is played. The development of small, compact viewers also opens many possibilities for using slides with or without taped narration for self-instructional purposes.

Although 35mm and 126 size films are most common for photographic slides, cameras requiring film of other sizes also can be used. In addition, Polaroid transparency film, available in two sizes for Land Polaroid cameras, produces completed slides in a few minutes.

FILMSTRIPS

Thirty-five mm filmstrips are closely related to slides, but instead of being mounted as separate pictures, the film after processing remains uncut as a continuous strip. You can make *double-frame filmstrips* using a standard 35mm camera. Commercial sources usually supply *single-frame filmstrips* with about half the double-frame image area.

Filmstrips have the advantages of compactness, ease of handling for projection, and low cost for duplication when additional copies are needed. Since pictures are always in order, no wrong positioning can occur, as with slides. On the other hand, filmstrips are not flexible since rearrangement of pictures is not possible.

Filmstrips are more difficult to prepare than are slides and they present problems for a beginner. It is not advisable to film subject matter with a 35mm camera and then plan to use this film directly as a filmstrip. To do this would require extreme care to insure the consistency of pictures in composition and exposure. Usually enlarged photographs, drawings, and titles are prepared and then photographed in sequence with a suitable 35mm copy camera. Or, if you desire to prepare a color filmstrip, start with color slides or with color transparencies. Many commercial film laboratories will convert the slides or transparencies into filmstrip form.

Accompanying narration may be in the form of captions, filmed with the pictures, or separate tape or disk sound recording to supplement the projected picture.

TAPE RECORDINGS

With the development of *language laboratories* and then the broadening of their use as *electronic* laboratories or *audio centers* to provide audio experiences in many subjects, tape recordings by themselves have become an important addition to the range of audiovisual materials. Recordings may be prepared for group or, more commonly now, for individual listening. Increasing attention is being given to materials for self-instruction in study areas called *carrels*.

Recordings, for example, can provide brief responsive drill in mathematics or shorthand; can treat English grammar; or can provide language study involving the voice of an expert and allowing opportunities for the student to record his response and then listen to it for comparison with that of the expert. Recordings also can supply information or opportunity for appreciation listening experiences. But care must be exercised that recordings do not become mere oral textbook readings with their limitations of vagueness and abstraction. Correlation with visual materials may be essential for many recordings.

Recordings can reach the student directly as he listens in a classroom or as he handles the tapes and equipment in a study area. Recordings can be brought to him at a simple plug-in station, or remotely on request via dialing, or from a distance over telephone lines at the touch of a button.

In addition to suitable listening and response facilities, tape-duplicating equipment is necessary when recordings will be used extensively.

OVERHEAD TRANSPARENCIES

Transparencies are relatively new in the field of locally prepared audiovisual materials. The growing use of large transparencies is furthered by the development of efficient *overhead projectors* combined with simple techniques for preparing transparencies and by the dramatic effectiveness of the medium.

The projector is used from near the front of the room, with the instructor standing or seated beside it, facing the group. The projection screen is behind him and room light is at a moderate level. Transparencies are placed on the large stage of the projector and the instructor may point to features and make marks on the film. His work appears immediately on the screen. *Progressively disclosing* areas of a transparency and adding *overlay* films to a base transparency are special features that make the use of this visual medium effective in many subject areas.

Overhead projectors are especially useful for instructing large groups on all educational levels. As the projectors become more numerous in schools and in industrial-training facilities, the range of techniques for preparing transparencies should be investigated and the most appropriate ones selected for use. Some methods require no special equipment or training, while for others experience in photography and the graphic arts is necessary.

MOTION PICTURES

Motion pictures, whether 8mm or 16mm, are the most complex and can be the most costly of the audiovisual materials to be considered here. They may require costly equipment,

skilled personnel, much time for preparation, and much money for materials and services. But for some purposes nothing surpasses the motion picture in effectiveness as a medium of communication. The motion picture should be considered whenever motion is inherent in a subject or when you wish to show relationships of one idea to another, to build a continuity of thought, or to create a dramatic impact.

Films need not always be formal and lengthy productions. For some purposes a brief film shown completely in a few minutes is sufficient. It may treat a single concept, a problem situation, or a skill which is to be explained and applied. Such a film may not require titles or special motion-picture effects. If proper projection equipment is available, the film can be loaded into a cartridge as a continuous loop for individual repeated viewing without complex projector threading and operation each time it is used.

Until recently most educational films have been of the 16mm size, but with the development of 8mm silent and sound projectors a new area of inexpensive film production appears possible. The introduction of Super 8 film size brings 8mm quality close to that of 16mm and many educators predict that 8mm film and projectors will cause a revolution comparable to that which the paperback book sparked in the book-publishing field. 8mm films can be used very satisfactorily for individual study, with small groups, or, if Super 8, for regular classes and large groups.

People with limited knowledge of film production can accomplish various effective techniques, such as time-lapse and slow-motion photography, close-ups, photomicrography, and animation. But generally, someone who has experience in making films should be a member of the production staff if advanced techniques are to be used. Such a man can deal effectively and economically with problems of planning, filming, lighting, editing, title-making, and adding sound.

TELEVISION AND DISPLAY MATERIALS

Under this heading we group the audiovisual materials—graphics, photographs, slides, filmstrips, transparencies, and motion pictures—normally used on television. In addition, display boards and their materials are considered here—either for television use or to serve other instructional needs.

Display boards include felt, hook-and-loop, and magnetic surfaces, with materials backed appropriately for adherence and display on the board. They are most often used to progressively build elements of a presentation or to provide opportunities for students to participate overtly by selecting, arranging, or showing relationships among items displayed.

An instructional television program may and usually does employ a combination of visual materials. The success that television has gained in the educational field comes in part from the wise selection of the best aspects of all audiovisual materials and their proper utilization. Audiovisual materials for television are unlike other audiovisual materials in that they are not ends of production but contributions to the total televised presentation; their effectiveness must be assessed in terms of the support they give to the purpose of the entire presentation.

The choice of visuals depends not only upon the purposes to be served by the materials, but also on the ways they will be displayed and used on the program. The method of use will determine whether information should be presented, for example, as a slide for projection or as a large chart for use before the television camera. Ease of preparation, required skills, facilities, time, and material costs are other factors that influence choice.

Finally, the technical requirements of television—format and proportions, size, color, and contrast limitations—must all be considered as materials are selected and prepared.

COMBINED VISUAL MATERIALS (MULTIMEDIA)

If a single visual can do the job satisfactorily, avoid the temptation to try something different simply for the novelty of it. But combinations of visual materials are effective when used together for specific purposes—either concurrently or in succession. Just as the narration on a sound motion picture supplements the pictures, a filmstrip containing local applications may be studied right after a motion picture has shown principles and generalized applications. An audio tape may serve to present information and program a variety of activities and other media for independent study. Or, adjacent screens can be used for

projecting outlines or diagrams as transparencies at the same time with 2″×2″ slides, which describe other details, illustrate applications, or show examples relating to the subject. Side-by-side slides can permit comparisons, relationships, perspective views, or multiple examples. Even television can be combined with other media, as when a transparency of a diagram or outline relates to a technique being shown on the television screen.

These combination uses and others have many worthwhile applications when general principles need to be given concrete meaning through immediate illustration.

SELECTING MEDIA FOR INSTRUCTIONAL NEEDS

Many of us select media for use on the basis of what we are most comfortable with. But, as indicated previously, the choice of a medium should be based on the objectives and content of the learning task itself. No single medium is likely to have properties that make it best for all purposes.

In this chapter we have examined seven categories of audiovisual materials that may be produced locally and have considered characteristics, advantages, and limitations of each one. These summaries may be enough to assist you in making decisions about specific media to serve your objectives and content. But guidelines also are useful which suggest somewhat closer relationships between the various media and instructional requirements.

Two writers have indicated potential contributions of a variety of audiovisual and related media in terms of instructional functions (Robert M. Gagné) and stimulus relationships to objectives (William H. Allen). This is a difficult task as we know from the discussion of learning theory in Chapter 2. There are no clear-cut principles that relate specific media to the service of particular kinds of learning. But the interpretations of these authorities give some basis for your own consideration of this important matter.

The views of Gagné and Allen are presented here in tables taken from their writings.

INSTRUCTIONAL FUNCTIONS OF VARIOUS MEDIA*

Function	Media						
	Objects; Demon-stration	Oral Commu-nication	Printed Media	Still Pic-tures	Moving Pic-tures	Sound Movies	Teach-ing Ma-chines
Presenting the stimulus	Yes	Limited	Limited	Yes	Yes	Yes	Yes
Directing attention and other activity	No	Yes	Yes	No	No	Yes	Yes
Providing a model of expected performance	Limited	Yes	Yes	Limited	Limited	Yes	Yes
Furnishing external prompts	Limited	Yes	Yes	Limited	Limited	Yes	Yes
Guiding thinking	No	Yes	Yes	No	No	Yes	Yes
Inducing transfer	Limited	Yes	Limited	Limited	Limited	Limited	Limited
Assessing attainments	No	Yes	Yes	No	No	Yes	Yes
Providing feedback	Limited	Yes	Yes	No	Limited	Yes	Yes

* From *The Conditions of Learning* by Robert M. Gagne. Copyright © 1965 by Holt, Rinehart and Winston, Inc. Reprinted by permission of Holt, Rinehart and Winston, Inc.

INSTRUCTIONAL MEDIA STIMULUS RELATIONSHIPS TO LEARNING OBJECTIVES*

Instructional Media Type	Learning Objectives		Learning Principles, Concepts and Rules	Learning Proce-dures	Performing Skilled Perceptual-Motor Acts	Developing Desirable Attitudes, Opinions and Motivations
	Learning Factual Information	Learning Visual Identifi-cations				
Still Pictures	Medium	HIGH	Medium	Medium	low	low
Motion Pictures	Medium	HIGH	HIGH	HIGH	Medium	Medium
Television	Medium	Medium	HIGH	Medium	low	Medium
3-D Objects	low	HIGH	low	low	low	low
Audio Recordings	Medium	low	low	Medium	low	Medium
Programed Instruction	Medium	Medium	Medium	HIGH	low	Medium
Demonstration	low	Medium	low	HIGH	Medium	Medium
Printed Textbooks	Medium	low	Medium	Medium	low	Medium
Oral Presentation	Medium	low	Medium	Medium	low	Medium

* William H. Allen, "Media Stimulus and Types of Learning," *Audiovisual Instruction,* January 1967, pages 27-31.

SUMMARY OF CHARACTERISTICS OF AUDIOVISUAL MATERIALS

Material	Advantages	Limitations	Relative Cost to Prepare*	
			Originals	Duplicates
Photographic print series	1. Permit close-up detailed study at individual's own pacing 2. Are useful as simple self-study materials and for display 3. Require no equipment for use	1. Not adaptable for large groups 2. Require photographic skills, equipment, and darkroom for preparation	15¢ per 8"×10" black and white print $3.75 per 8"×10" color print (by processing laboratory)	10¢ $3.50
Slide series	1. Require only filming, with processing and mounting by film laboratory 2. Result in colorful, realistic reproductions of original subjects 3. Prepared with any 35mm camera for most uses 4. Easily revised and up-dated 5. Easily handled, stored, and rearranged for various uses 6. Increased usefulness with magazine storage and automatic projection 7. Can be combined with taped narration for greater effectiveness 8. May be adapted to group or to individual use	1. Require some skill in photography 2. Require special equipment for close-up photography and copying 3. Can get out of sequence and be projected incorrectly if slides are handled individually	20¢	25¢ per color slide
Filmstrips	1. Are compact, easily handled, and always in proper sequence 2. May be supplemented with captions or recordings 3. Are inexpensive when quantity reproduction is required 4. Are useful for group or individual study at projection rate controlled by instructor or user 5. Are projected with simple lightweight equipment	1. Are relatively difficult to prepare locally 2. Require film-laboratory service to convert slides to filmstrip form 3. Are in permanent sequence and cannot be rearranged or revised	65¢ per frame, black and white $1.50 per frame, color (by processing laboratory)	1¢ 3¢
Recordings	1. Easy to prepare with regular tape recorders 2. Can provide applications in most subject areas 3. Equipment for use easy to operate 4. Flexible and adaptable as either individual elements of instruction or in correlation with programed materials	1. May have a tendency for overuse, as oral textbook reading 2. Requires moderate to high equipment costs, complex installation, and continual maintenance for extensive individual facilities	300' — $1.40 600' — $2.50 1200' — $4.00 1800' — $5.50	

Material	Characteristics	Limitations	Estimated cost*
Overhead transparencies	1. Can present information in systematic, developmental sequences 2. Use simple-to-operate projector with presentation rate controlled by instructor 3. Require only limited planning 4. Can be prepared by variety of simple, inexpensive methods 5. Particularly useful with large groups	1. Require special equipment, facilities, and skills for more advanced preparation methods	30¢ 25¢ per single sheet of film
Motion pictures	1. May consist of complete films or short film clips 2. Are particularly useful in describing motion, showing relationships, or giving impact to topic 3. 8-mm film reduces cost for materials and services 4. Are useful with groups of all sizes and with individuals 5. Sound is easily added to magnetic film 6. May include special techniques for handling content 7. Insure a consistency in presentation of material	1. May be expensive to prepare in terms of time, equipment, materials, and services 2. Require careful planning and some production skill 3. A changing field in which some present equipment may become obsolete	$5.50 $6.50 50' 8mm color $8.00 $4.00 100' 16mm black and white $13.00 $10.00 100' 16mm color 2¢-5¢ 2¢-5¢ per 1' of magnetic striping
Combinations of media	1. Combine slides or motion pictures with transparencies; or photographs, slides, or filmstrip for follow-up study after a motion picture 2. Provide for more effective communications in certain situations than when only a single medium is used	1. Require additional equipment and careful coordination during planning, preparation, and use	Refer to each type of material above
Television and display materials	1. Permit selecting the best audiovisual media to serve program needs 2. Permit shifting from one medium to another during program 3. Permit normally unavailable resources to be presented 4. New-type display boards provide flexibility in displaying various kinds of objects and writing on surface	1. Do not exist alone, but are part of total television production 2. Must fit technical requirements of television 3. At times require rapid preparation of materials 4. Some display boards are expensive to make or purchase	Refer to the specific types of material above

* Estimated cost of materials for a single unit. Time and special services would be in addition.

When comparing similar elements from each table some differences will be found. These are probably due to different interpretations of the kinds of tasks certain media can perform and also are indicative that opinions are still dominant over scientific evidence for selecting stimuli to elicit specific responses in human learning.

Study these tables carefully. This is an all-important approach to selecting media for providing meaningful and effective learning activities. Do you agree with all the entries? On the basis of your own experiences and the degree to which you accept the broadening roles of media as presented in Part One of this book, compile your own list of relationships between the various media you might use and the broad instructional objectives they can serve. Also, review the applications and specific examples in subject units described by Briggs and others,[2] and by Mager and Beach,[3] which apply Gagné's conditions of learning to the selection of media.

As illustrated, for many objectives one medium may be as appropriate as another. For example, if it is determined that still pictures are required, then slides, a filmstrip, or transparencies could serve equally as well. Final choice should be on the basis of production capability, available utilization of equipment and facilities, logistics of use, and even student preference.

Finally, media decisions should be made not for a gross entity of learning as large as a *topic,* but rather for individual objectives that collectively make up the topic. Within a given topic, carefully designed combinations of media, where each performs a particular function best and reinforces the learning effects of the others, may be required to achieve the kind of instruction for group or individual that is most effective.

Now apply what you have read.

1. Of the seven types of audiovisual materials described in this section, which are of especial value for: (a) individual study? (b) use with a large group?
2. In question 2 following Chapter 4, you were directed to select a topic and to start planning for the preparation of an audiovisual material. Which material would you now choose for use in developing this topic? Why do you think it the most appropriate?
3. Describe a combination use you might plan to make of two audiovisual materials in presenting the same topic, as was suggested.
4. If you followed the suggestion of making your own list of relationships between the various media and instructional objectives, how does your list differ from those of Gagné and Allen?

The seven types of audiovisual materials—photographic print series, slide series, filmstrips, recordings, overhead transparencies, motion pictures, television and display materials—as well as combinations have different planning requirements and different degrees of complexity in preparation and use. Some require close adherence to all steps in the planning process, while others, such as photographs and transparencies, may be developed without strict procedure. Refer to the appropriate sections in Part Four of this book for guidance as you study the planning steps in Chapter 8, next following this.

---

[2] Leslie Briggs and others, *Instructional Media: A Procedure for the Design of Multi-Media Instruction.*

[3] Robert F. Mager and Kenneth M. Beach, *Developing Vocational Instruction.*

8. Mapping the Way

Prepare a descriptive synopsis of the content; then a storyboard; finally, write the script—a "map" for your production—and from it prepare the necessary specifications.

You have your content organized in terms of objectives and the audience. You are aware of the kinds of audiovisual materials you may consider for preparation, their characteristics and particular contributions, advantages, and limitations. In putting all these together you must decide on which materials can best communicate the content of specific objectives. Your plans may require that a single medium (film, slides, transparencies, or such) carry your message. Or, in the design approach, a number of media may be integrated, each serving one or more specific objectives and content.

Examine the cards you prepared listing objectives and content. Consider the tables in the preceding chapter and the questions on page 29 relating to factors that should be considered for handling the content. Then decide on the medium or media to use.

If more than a single medium is to be employed make cards for each one and organize the objective and content cards with the appropriate medium cards. This plan will give you a visual reference to the flow and relationship of elements within the total topic. Now, start planning for production.

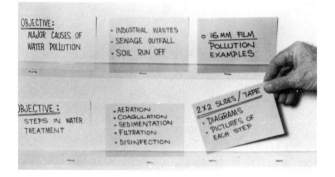

How do you handle the content? Should you start with the first item and plan to go systematically through the whole outline, making a picture for each heading and fact? Is it best to

organize your script logically, or to build from the simple to the complex, regardless of the outline order?

There is no single best manner in which the details of the content outline are transformed into meaningful and related pictures and words. Two approaches have been established through experience, but they are by no means the only sound ones. First, many successful materials carry an audience from the known to the unknown; they start with those things with which the audience is familiar (perhaps by reviewing the present level of understanding) and then lead to as many new facts and new relationships as the material is meant to achieve. Second, many materials are successfully built around three divisions—the introduction, which captures the attention of the audience; the developmental stage, which contains most of the content and in effect tells the story (or involves the viewers in active participation); and finally, the ending, which may summarize or review the ideas presented and suggest further activity.

Recall from Chapter 3 that there is evidence from research to show that detailed introductions and summaries in films and probably in other audiovisual materials do not add much to their effectiveness. This finding may be particularly true of a series of integrated materials, each of which serves a specific objective. The single-concept film, illustrating a process, and the short tape recording of drill material are examples of the latter kinds of materials. A printed study guide or instruction sheet can introduce, relate, summarize, and direct student participation. The material itself contains just the essential facts, explanations, demonstrations, or whatever, without any embellishments.

PLAN FOR PARTICIPATION

A number of investigations of the effectiveness of audiovisual materials have shown the value of having the learner participate in some way during, or immediately after, the study of the material. These experiments, without reservation, have proven that *active participation definitely helps learning.* But most producers of audiovisual materials ignore this principle. Films, filmstrips, and sets of transparencies are designed primarily to present information and, within themselves, provide no opportunity or directions for other than passive activity—mentally or mechanically following the presentation. Hopefully, the treatment of the subject is so motivational that interest is maintained throughout. But often it is not. It is then left up to the teacher or presenter to plan for pre- and post-use activities (possibly with the help of study-guide suggestions).

The way to create participation is to make involvement an inherent part of the material itself. This is a key element of programed materials—the learner is actively doing something as he studies.

Here are some suggestions for developing participation in audiovisual materials:

- Include questions, requiring an immediate written or oral response.
- Direct other written activity (explain, summarize, give other examples, and so forth).
- Require selection from among things shown or heard.
- Require performance related to the activity or skill shown or heard.

These participation techniques often require a break in the presentation—having the student stop the projector to do something, or promoting immediate activity after studying a section of the material.

Also, be sure to plan for evaluation of the participation results and provide *feedback* to the student indicating the correct reply or a comparison of measurement for his level of accomplishment.

WRITE THE TREATMENT

Carefully examine the example of a content outline (page 29) and form an idea of how you might develop the generalizations visually. Form several such ideas. Put them into written narrative form, as you might summarize a book or a motion picture. You will, however, work from the synopsis toward your motion picture or slide series or other material. Two or more treatments that handle the subject in different ways (informational, personal involvement, or dramatic) may be written so as to explore different approaches to the topic.

The treatment may combine the qualities of narration, personal involvement, and drama.

Writing the treatment is an important step as it causes you to think through your presentation, putting it in a sequential, organized form that you and others can follow easily.

MAKE A STORYBOARD

As you develop your story *try to visualize the situations you are describing.* Remember, you are preparing an audio*visual* material—with the emphasis on the word VISUAL. Most people normally think in words but now you may have to reorient yourself and learn to think in pictures—not in vague general pictures but in specific visual representations of real situations. Visualization can be aided by making simple sketches or by taking pictures (instant pictures with Polaroid film are ideal for this purpose) which show the treatment of each element or sequence. These sketches or pictures, along with narration notes, become the *storyboard.* Here is an example of a partial storyboard for *Our Water Supply,* using various techniques.

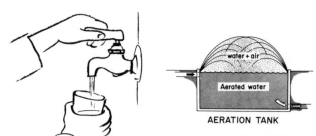

Simple Sketch

Detailed Sketch

**35mm Contact Print
(or 2″×2″ Slide)**

Polaroid Print

Enlarged Photograph

Put the storyboard sketches or pictures on cards as was suggested for the objectives and content on page 28. Use 4″×6″ cards or 8½″×11″ paper. These proportions approximate the format of most visual materials, the pictures being wider than they are high. Use a card with an area blocked off for the visual and having space for narration notes or production comments.

Examples of Treatment

INFORMATIONAL TREATMENT--OUR WATER SUPPLY

Our water supply originates in the Sierra Nevada mountains and flows through the Mokelumne river to a storage reservoir near the city. Then it enters the water purification plant where the water is treated in five steps--aeration, coagulation, sedimentation, filtration, and disinfection. Laboratory tests are made to insure the water's high quality. After it leaves the plant it is sent to storage tanks and eventually to its many uses throughout the city.

PERSONAL-INVOLVEMENT TREATMENT--OUR WATER SUPPLY

What do we know about our water--where does it come from; how much of it is there; and how is it made safe for our use? Two 15-year-old boys became curious about these questions while swimming one day. They checked in the school library and came across a pamphlet describing the city's water supply. They then made arrangements to visit the water purification plant. Here the supervisor took them on a tour. He showed them a large map, indicating that our water originates in the Sierra Nevada mountains and then flows through the Mokelumne river to our city. In the treatment process the boys saw the aeration and co-agulation tanks, the sedimentation basins, and the filter beds. They found out how chlorine was added to water as a disinfectant and also some of the tests made in the laboratory. With the information they read and the things they saw, the boys now were able to answer their own questions about our water supply.

DRAMATIC TREATMENT--OUR WATER SUPPLY

Water is indispensable--without it all living things die; fires cannot be conquered; and many industries cease to operate. Nature provides our source of water. For our community it comes from the Sierra Nevada mountains and reaches us via the Mokelumne river. But the amount is not unlimited. We must conserve it and use it wisely-- otherwise desolation and lifelessness result. And not only must we have water, but it must be pure water, free from disease-causing mi-croorganisms and impurities. Many diseases in man and animal arise from dirty and polluted water. Therefore we purify water. For our community water treatment includes five steps--aeration, coagulation, sedimentation, filtration, and disinfection. Pure water and careful-ly used water contribute to life, growth, and good health for all living things.

COMBINATION TREATMENT--OUR WATER SUPPLY

Water serves us in many important ways. It is essential for all life on earth. Where does our water come from? How is it purified for our use? Our water supply originates in the Sierra Nevada moun-tains and flows through the Mokelumne river to a storage reservoir near the city. Then it enters the water purification plant where the water is treated in five steps--aeration, coagulation, sedimentation, filtration, and disinfection. Laboratory tests are made to insure the water's high quality. After it leaves the plant it is sent to storage tanks and eventually to its many uses throughout the community where conservation and wise use of water are essential.

Storyboard in Use. (Reproduced with permission from the Kodak pamphlet "Planning and Producing Visual Aids.")[1]

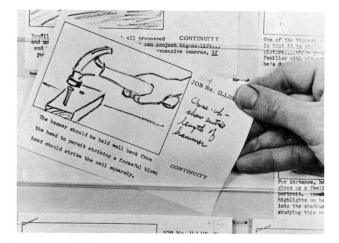

Storyboard Card Containing Visual, Production Notes, and Suggested Narration. (Reproduced with permission from the Kodak pamphlet "Planning and Producing Visual Aids.")

Every sequence should be represented by one or more cards. Include separate cards for possible titles, questions, and special directions (such as indications for student participation). It may not be necessary to make a card for all anticipated scenes. The details, like an over-all picture of a subject followed by a close-up of detail within the subject, will be handled in the script that follows.

The storyboard is another important check-point stage in the development of your audiovisual material. Display it. Make it easy to examine. (See *Planningboards*, pamphlet T-21, Eastman Kodak Company.) Reactions and suggestions from those involved in the project or from other interested and qualified persons are valuable at this point. These people may offer assistance by evaluating the way you visualize your ideas and the continuity of your treatment. Often people studying the displayed storyboard point out things that have been missed or sequences that need reorganization. Rearranging pictures and adding new ones are easy when the storyboard is prepared on sheets of paper or on cards.

DEVELOP THE SCRIPT

Once the treatment and the storyboard continuity are satisfactorily organized you are ready to write your detailed blueprint, the *script*. This script becomes the map which gives definite directions for your picture-taking, art work, or filming. The script is a picture-by-picture listing with accompanying narration or captions. As was indicated for storyboarding, plan *first* what will be seen, then what will be said or captioned. Write the script in a two-column format, placing camera positions and picture descriptions on the left half of the page and narration on the right, opposite the appropriate scene descriptions. (See the example on page 44.)

The placement of the camera for each picture, with respect to the subject, should be indicated. If the subject is to be at a distance from the camera the picture is a *long shot* (LS); if the camera covers the subject and nothing more, a *medium shot* (MS); while a *close-up* (CU) brings the camera in to concentrate on a feature of the subject. Whether the scene is to be photographed from a *high angle* or a *low angle,* or *subjective* (from the subject's viewpoint, as over his shoulder) may also be specified. (For further information on camera positions see pages 194–197 in Chapter 23.

At this stage the narration or captions, indicated along the right-hand side of your script, need not be stated in final, detailed form. It is sufficient to write *narration ideas* or brief statements which later may be refined. Only when an explanation will require that a motion-picture scene be of a specific length must the narration now be written carefully in final form.

Narration is important not only for the part it plays in explaining details as the AUDIO of *audiovisual;* it also may call attention to relationships and indicate emphasis that should be given in some pictures (center of attention or camera position) when filming.

Be alert to problems that may arise with narration. It must be related closely to the visual so as to reinforce the visual, or the narration may interfere or inhibit learning. Review research evidence in Chapter 3 about the relation between visual and audio channels in audiovisual materials. See page 50 for further suggestions concerning writing narration.

On pages 44–45 is an example of a script for *Our Water Supply,* developed chiefly from the informational treatment, with some details adopted from the other treatments.

---

[1] Plastic Planningstrips available from Chicago Box Co., 732 North Morgan Street, Chicago.

CONSIDER THE LENGTH

The content of an audiovisual material affects the time needed to present it. You need to have time in mind as the script takes shape. Any estimate at this early stage is inevitably loose and approximate, but an estimate is necessary.

How are you to forecast the time that will be needed? The following few facts, from experience, may offer some guidance:

- A projected slide or a filmstrip frame can hold attention for about 30 seconds (or it may remain on the screen for only a few seconds).
- A 12-inch disk recording, prepared at 33⅓ revolutions per minute to accompany a slide series or filmstrip, will permit a maximum playing time of 18 minutes on one side (a total of 36 minutes on both sides).
- The average motion-picture scene runs for 7 seconds; it may range from 2 seconds to 30 seconds or more.

You will collect many more such facts as you gain experience.

Even so, how are you to know whether the material, at whatever estimated duration, is too short, too long, or just right? There is no formula. A film or filmstrip or slide series or picture series must be allowed enough time to permit adequate development of the topic, as based on the purposes, but not be so long that it will lose its effectiveness. A single-concept film may run for two or three minutes, whereas an orientation film may require 15 to 20 minutes. A filmstrip for primary-grade children would ordinarily be shorter than one designed for high-school students. Also, available time must be considered—do not come up with a 15-minute film in a 10-minute program spot.

When you (and your team) appraise your script against the amount of time desirable or available, you may need to review it to see whether the needed time can be shortened, or the content divided into two or more outlines for a series of presentations.

PREPARE THE SPECIFICATIONS

You have prepared a map, the script. Now you face the questions: What specific things are to be done now, next, and thereafter until the audiovisual materials are ready to be used? What is to be bought, made, decided? The answers to these are the specifications.

The more complex the projected audiovisual material, the more numerous the specifications. Naturally they need to be organized and classified. Some classes of specifications have no bearing on some kinds of materials, while on others (slide series, filmstrips, motion pictures) all may be needed. Here are some examples of specifications, with detailed and specific points that must be considered and choices that must be made:

- *Type of audiovisual material:* photo series, slides, filmstrip, recordings, transparencies, motion picture, or television or display materials
- *Material and size:* Kodachrome, diazo film, 8mm or 16mm, 5″×7″ prints
- *Length:* approximate number of photographs, slides, filmstrip frames, transparencies; running time for motion picture or tape recording
- *Sound:* tape-recorded narration, synchronous sound, magnetic-strip sound track; silent reading matter; titles, captions, labels
- *Facilities and equipment:* locations for filming, camera equipment and accessories, graphic and photographic supplies
- *Special techniques required:* high-contrast photography, color processing, copy work, time-lapse, animation, microphotography; art work, titles, photocopy, diazo reproduction
- *Special assistance required:* for acting, filming, lighting, graphics, sound recording, film processing, printing, duplicating, secretarial
- *Completion date:* planned for or *must* be completed by when?
- *Budget estimate:* including film and other materials, equipment purchase or rental, film laboratory and other services, salaries (if applicable), overhead charges, and miscellaneous items.

Now apply what you have read.

1. Examine the sample treatments on pages 41–42. Which one or ones do you consider the easiest to visualize as a script? Which treatments are verbally oriented and which ones are visually oriented?
2. Show that there is more than one way of handling your topic's content. Prepare two brief treatments of the topic you selected on page 25, each having a different approach and giving a different emphasis to the topic. Keep in mind your audience and your purposes.
3. Consider the type of audiovisual material you would like to prepare. Does it fit the presentation of the content you have treated?
4. Sketch a few sequences of your storyboard on cards.
5. Prepare a script from the treatment and storyboard. Describe the scenes carefully, using letter abbreviations for camera positions. Write narration ideas if appropriate.
6. List the specifications necessary for your materials.

An Example of a Script

SCRIPT--OUR WATER SUPPLY

Visual	Narration Idea
1. Main Title: OUR WATER SUPPLY.	
2. CU Hand turning water faucet and filling a glass of water.	The water we take for granted --where does it come from? How is it purified?
3. LS Snow-covered mountains	It starts in the Sierra Nevada mountains.
4. LS Mokelumne river.	The Mokelumne carries it west.
5. LS Upper reservoir.	It is held in the reservoir.
6. MS Entrance to the water-treatment plant.	It is purified in our treatment plant.
7. MS Aeration tank. (Overprint: <u>Aeration</u>)	The first step is to spray the water in the air.
8. CU Spraying water.	This is aeration: air is mixed with the water.
9. Diagram of aeration process.	Aeration improves the water's flavor.
10. LS High Angle. Coagulation tanks. (Overprint: <u>Coagulation</u>)	The next step is coagulation, to start the removal of impurities.
11. CU Mixing water in tank.	Here alum is mixed with the water.
12. Diagram of coagulation process.	Impurities coagulate together to form large masses.
13. LS High Angle. Sedimentation basins. (Overprint: <u>Sedimentation</u>).	Third step--sedimentation, the settling of impurities,
14. CU Edge of tank as clear water runs over side into trough.	while clear water flows off at the top.
15. Diagram of sedimentation basin.	Scrapers remove the settled impurities at the bottom.
16. LS High Angle. Filtration beds. (Overprint: <u>Filtration</u>).	Then the water is filtered
17. CU A single filter in operation.	through beds of sand and gravel.
18. Diagram of a filter bed.	Make-up of filter beds--fine sand at top with progressivly coarser gravel below.

19.	MS Chlorine gas tank.	Finally chlorine is added to kill bacteria.
20.	Diagram of chlorination process.	Chlorine is a disinfectant.
21.	MS Two chemists at work in laboratory.	Chemists check the quality of purified water at short intervals.
22.	Diagram. Total purification process--without labels.	Review the steps by questioning what takes place in each step of the treatment process and how each is accomplished.
23.	Repeat diagram in scene 22--with labels.	Review the steps by answering questions in scene 22.
24.	MS Low Angle. Large transmission pipe.	Transmission pipes carry water out of the plant
25.	LS Storage tank on hill.	to storage,
26.	Montage (group of pictures) showing uses of water--washing hands, animal drinking, irrigating field, cooking, fire fighting, etc.	and then to many important uses.
27.	MS A parched field.	Importance of water conservation.
28.	CU Hand turning off faucet with full glass beneath.	Use water carefully and not wastefully.

An Example of Simple Specifications

```
              SPECIFICATIONS--OUR WATER SUPPLY

25 to 35 2" x 2" color slides
2 or 3 titles and 4 or 5 drawings for close-up photographic copy
Tape-recorded narration of 8-10 minutes duration
Materials to be prepared during last 6 weeks of first semester for use
    during second semester
All facilities and equipment available at no cost; most picture-taking
    at water-treatment plant

Budget:
    2 rolls 35-exposure Kodachrome II
      film, with processing ..................................$12.50
    art supplies ...............................................3.50
    1 roll 300 feet x ¼" magnetic recording tape ...............1.50
          Total ...............................................$16.50

Note: $20 was set aside for the project, therefore a duplicate set of
    slides may be prepared.
```

9. Making the Pictures

Prepare a schedule for filming; then complete all art work
and take pictures, keeping a record of all activities.

Now for the actual production.

Production is the point at which some people, unfortunately and mistakenly, start their work on audiovisual materials. It is difficult to convince some people that they need to do some thoughtful planning before making pictures. They may feel they do not have the time to plan, or that they are too knowledgeable about their subject to have to plan. Or they may be so taken with the mechanical phases of production (camera operation, sound recording, film editing, and so forth) that they have an insatiable urge to do something and see results *right now!* If you deal with such a person, you probably will not be able to influence him differently. Let him, then, go directly to production. Most often the results will easily show the fallacy of this approach and the added expense of unplanned production. Experience is sometimes the best teacher!

There is one situation in which unplanned picture taking may be necessary. See the discussion of *documentary* production on page 200.

You will find generally, in contrast to what results from precipitate picture taking, that planning and writing a script will have enabled you to visualize your ideas more clearly and that the final result will serve your purpose better because of its coherence and completeness. In the long run you will probably also save time and money by eliminating errors, reducing the need for retakes, and not forgetting scenes when picture taking.

Detailed graphic and photographic techniques for preparing specific audiovisual materials are presented in Parts Three and Four of this book. Some general practices (especially for making photographic print series, slide series, filmstrips, and motion pictures) are considered here.

SCHEDULE THE PICTURE TAKING

Prepare a list, grouping together all scenes to be made at the same location, those having related camera positions at a single location, or those with other similarities. Then schedule each group for filming at the same time. Preparing and using this list will save you time. You may achieve further economies if you visit locations, check facilities, and gather items (props) for use prior to the time of filming. But remember—if you take pictures out of script order you must be especially careful to edit them back into their correct position and relationship with other scenes.

TAKE THE PICTURES

In general, scene content as outlined in the script should be followed. Sometimes, however, as you prepare to take a picture it is evident that a script change is needed. If a single picture as planned does not convey the intent of the script, two pictures may be necessary. Don't hesitate to take them. Or, if you are uncertain about exposure, make an extra *take* of the same scene with different camera settings. Also, if desirable, repeat a scene, shooting it from a second position or with a change in action. In such cases, the entry on the record sheet (see p. 48) should indicate *take 1*, then *take 2*, and so forth, *all of the same scene*. Be flexible in your picture taking. You spend less time and energy making adjustments at this time than you would spend retaking pictures later if they are found to be unsatisfactory— and you have extra pictures from which to make choices during editing.

When filming a motion picture, rehearse each scene before shooting. Rehearsals permit a check on the action so that the cameraman may "set" his shot and the actor may "feel" the action he is performing. For still pictures, carefully set the scene and check the appearance through the camera viewer before clicking the shutter.

There may be times when a *documentary* approach to all or portions of an audiovisual material is necessary. In such cases pictures are taken of events as they happen, without preplanning or detailed script preparation. It is recommended that this approach be followed only for special cases (athletic events, large-group activities, meetings, spontaneous classroom activity, and other uncontrolled situations). Often two or more cameras are used and coordinated so as to capture all important action (see the suggestions for *multicamera filming* on page 199. Many of these recommendations apply to still-picture taking as well as to motion pictures). The documentary technique puts an extra burden on the photographers and the editing stage becomes extremely important for making decisions which may affect the final treatment of the subject (see page 207 for suggestions concerning preparing a script *after* documenting an activity on film). The producer of a documentary audiovisual needs greater experience and must give more attention to technical details than the producer of a planned and scripted material, since in a documentary production there can seldom be any retakes. The cameraman must think in sequences and not in individual shots. He must recall what went before and anticipate what will be happening and be ready to record it. This in contrast to making a preplanned audiovisual material in which all scenes are thought out in advance and content is controlled.

KEEP A RECORD

Keep a careful record, *a log sheet*, of all pictures taken. It indicates the order in which scenes were photographed and it includes data on exposure settings. This record will be useful to you while evaluating picture quality and content when selecting scenes. These items are important:

• Scene number (according to the script)
• Take number (change each time the same scene is filmed)
• Light intensity (reading from light meter, if used)
• Camera settings (lens, shutter speed, and distance)
• Remarks (notes about the action, scene composition, and reminders for editing)

PERMISSION FOR PICTURES

Almost everyone has the right to control the use of pictures of himself or his property. If you are making audiovisual materials you must respect this right. If you fail to do so, you may expose yourself to personal, professional, or financial embarrassment. Specifically, a person may either permit you or forbid you to show pictures of himself, his children, or his property. It does not matter whether you show them free or for a compensation, to a large or small audience, or whether you show them yourself or turn them over to someone else to be shown.

Most people readily agree to being filmed and to having the pictures used, but you should protect yourself and your associates by having them *sign a release form*. (A suitable release form is shown on page 49.) The release authorizing the use of pictures of a minor child must be signed by the parent.

A special kind of property that must be covered by a signed release is the property in copyrighted materials—commonly books, magazines, other printed matter, and commercial films. In this case you must get the clearance from the owner of the *copyright,* not the owner of the *object.* (You may own this book; but you do not own the copyright in it—see the back of the title page.) You will be wise if you assume that books and the like are copyrighted, and seek clearance before you use pictures of them or parts of them in your audiovisual materials.

Currently the United States Congress is revising the copyright laws that were written in 1909. The draft law permits a teacher to make copies of recordings and other audiovisual materials for purely noncommercial teaching uses as long as the materials are for *use in her classroom,* whereas the 1909 law restricts this use. This is without restrictions. The proposed law does not permit the extension of this right of free reproduction to materials used other than by a teacher in *direct* classroom instruction. This means that copyrighted materials for use in motion pictures, slide series, filmstrips, recordings, or television cannot be reproduced without permission. This applies to materials designed for independent study by students, for use in audio listening centers, to be used by a teacher *other than the one preparing the material,* or whatever.

Since this book will be published before Congress completes its work on the new copyright bill, it is recommended that you check into the final requirements of the bill. Contact the Copyright Office in Washington, D.C. This will give you correct and complete information on copyright.

Now apply what you have read.

All activities discussed in this book up to now have been concerned with the planning phase of your audiovisual production. Now make pictures and prepare drawings. Refer to the how-to-do-it sections in Parts Three and Four.

If appropriate:
1. Make a prefilming schedule.
2. Keep a log sheet.
3. Get clearances.

Example of a Filming Schedule

```
                    FILMING SCHEDULE--OUR WATER SUPPLY

        At Water Plant

        12/14

            Scene    6 -- MS Entrance
                    10 -- LS High Angle Coagulation tanks
                    13 -- LS High Angle Sedimentation basins
                    16 -- LS High Angle Filtration beds
                     7 -- MS Aeration tank
                     8 -- CU Spraying water
                    11 -- CU Water in coagulation tank
                    14 -- CU Edge of sedimentation tank
                    17 -- CU Filter bed
                    etc.

        At School

        12/16

            Scene    2 -- CU Hand on faucet
                    28 -- CU Hand on faucet
                    etc.
```

Example of a Log Sheet

```
                         LOG SHEET

        Title:   Our Water Supply          Date: 12/14
        Film:    Kodachrome II Daylight     Location: Water Plant
        Camera:  Contaflex
        Meter:   Weston IV
```

| | | Light | | | Dis- | |
Scene	Take	Value	f/ stop	Speed	tance	Remarks
6	1	200	10	1/60	15'	
6	2	200	10	1/60	12'	low angle
10	1	400	14	1/60	40'	
13	1	400	14	1/60	30'	poor composition
13	2	400	14	1/60	30'	better
etc.						

A Sample Release Form

```
                              Date: _____

I hereby give permission to (insert name of individual, group, or in-
stitution making the audiovisual materials) to make pictures of me, of
my minor child (insert name of child), or of materials owned by me and
to put the finished pictures to any legitimate use without limitation
or reservation.

              Signature: _____

              Name printed: _____

              Address: _____

              City: _____ State: _____

Project: _____

Director: _____
```

10. Evaluating and Organizing

Examine all drawings and pictures; select and arrange
them into final order and then match narration or captions
to them.

Once the pictures are prepared you are ready for the concluding major step in the production process. During filming the
pictures may have been taken out of script sequence, some
scenes not indicated in the script may have been filmed, and
more than one take may have been made of some subjects.
During preparation of the script, the narration or captions were
written in rough form or noted only as ideas. These changes and
unfinished work give rise to the need for examination, careful
appraisal, selection, then organization of all pictures, and the
refinement of narration and captions. These activities become
the all-important *editing* stage.

THE EDITING PROCESS—PICTURES

Using the script and the log sheets completed while filming,
put all pictures in proper order. Inexpensive *contact prints* or
proof copies of still pictures (page 89) or *workprint* from original motion-picture footage (page 206) may be used for editing.

Now choices must be made from among multiple *takes* of a
scene. Examine all your work critically. You must be imper-
sonal in your judgment and eliminate those pictures which fail
to make a suitable contribution to your specific purposes, and
you must be firm in rejecting pictures that do not meet your
standards of quality.

If you have made changes in the original script (page 44) by
adding scenes or changing the sequence, rewrite the picture side
to fit the edited picture version. Then complete the narration or
caption side of the script as described below.

THE EDITING PROCESS—NARRATION AND CAPTIONS

Since your original script may have included only rough
drafts or mere ideas for narration, there is need for further
developing and rewriting the narration or captions in order to
correlate words with the edited pictures.

As was indicated in explaining the storyboard on page 40,
most of us think in words, and therefore we have a tendency to
attempt to communicate with words more readily than with
pictures. Even so, we comprehend things more effectively and
retain information much longer when major ideas are presented
visually in the form of pictures while being supplemented with
written or spoken words. Words thus have an important part to
play in your materials, but generally they should be secondary
to the pictures. They can direct attention, explain details, raise
questions, serve as transitions from one picture or idea to the
next, and aid in preserving the continuity of the materials. If
you find you have to use many words to explain what a picture
shows, or to describe things not shown in a picture, perhaps the
picture deserves another critical evaluation and possible re-
placement, or you may need to add a supplementary picture.
Let the pictures tell the greater part of your story. If they do
not, you will have a lecture with illustrations and you will fail to
use the audiovisual medium at its best.

Keep in mind your anticipated audience and its background
as you refine the narration. The audience will have bearing on
the vocabulary you use and on the complexity and pacing of the
commentary (page 42). Lengthy narration or long captions are
detrimental to the effects of visual materials. For example, the
average narration should require viewing a slide for no more
than 30 seconds; a filmstrip caption should be no longer than 15
or 20 words. The average length of a motion-picture scene is 7
seconds; individual scenes, depending upon action and. narration required, range from 2 seconds to possibly 30 seconds running time.

Here are some suggestions for developing narration:[1]

• Narration should supplement the picture by making direct
reference to picture content (directing attention, explaining
details, providing transitions) rather than compete with the
picture for attention by describing or discussing things not
shown in the picture.

---

[1] Suggestions adapted from *The Aperture,* monthly publication of the
Calvin Company, Kansas City, Missouri.

• Identify the picture subject being shown (especially if unusual) as quickly as possible with cue words or phrases. Identification that comes late in a written or spoken line may find the viewer lost in his attempt to understand what is being shown.

• Be sure to use proper grammar, words, and expressions. Keep sentences short and avoid multiple clauses. Use simple, straightforward English as in conversation.

• Write enough to carry the picture as necessary—then stop writing.

• Have some pauses in narration, or the audience will stop listening.

• Realize that one bit of narration may cover a number of pictures and that narration may carry over from one scene to the next.

As editing of both pictures and words continues, consider such questions as:

• Does the material satisfactorily serve the original objectives?

• Is there a smooth flow from one picture or idea to the next one?

An Example of a Preview-Appraisal Questionnaire

• Is the material too long over-all, requiring deletions?

• Have important points, not apparent before, been left out?

• Should some of the pictures be replaced or need additional ones be made?

• Is the material technically good?

You may do better than quiz yourself. Here is another good checkpoint for an evaluation of your materials by other subject and audiovisual specialists, or even by a potential audience group. Show the edited visuals and read the narration or captions. A brief questionnaire for reactions and suggestions may be helpful. Responses may reveal misconceptions that are conveyed, shortcomings, or other needs for improvement.

Now apply what you have read.

1. This section mentions a "checkpoint." In what previous sections were other checkpoints suggested? What purposes do such checks serve?

2. What procedures would you follow in editing your materials: (a) the pictures? (b) the narration?

```
                    OUR WATER SUPPLY

 Purposes
 1.  This set of slides is designed principally to explain steps in
     water purification and secondly to encourage conservation of
     water.  How well do you feel these purposes are accomplished?

     _____

 2.  Are there other purposes you believe these slides might serve?

     _____

 Audience
 1.  These slides and the narration are designed for ninth-grade sci-
     ence students.  Is the content appropriate?

     _____

     Are the pacing of the narration and the vocabulary appropriate?

     _____

 Content and technical quality
 1.  Has any important information been left out?
 2.  Are there any errors or inconsistencies in the presentation?
 3.  Would you suggest any reorganization?  If so, specify.
 4.  Is the material technically acceptable?  Would you replace any
     slides?

     _____

     What is your rating of the slides and the narration in terms of
     the purposes to serve the indicated audience?

         Excellent        Good        Fair        Poor
```

Part of a Revised Script, with Pictures for Reference

OUR WATER SUPPLY

Visual	Slide	Narration
1. Main Title: OUR WATER SUPPLY.		
2. CU Hand turning water faucet and filling a glass with water.		The water we take for granted --do you know where it comes from? Is there enough for our continued use? How is it purified?
3. LS Snow-covered mountains.		The story of our water supply begins in the Sierra Nevada mountains. When snow melts or rain falls,
4. MS Mokelumne river.		the Mokelumne river carries the water westward.
5. LS Upper reservoir.		A large amount is collected and held in the reservoir north of the city.
6. LS Entrance to the water-treatment plant.		The water is purified in our treatment plant. Each day 3,000,000 gallons are processed.
7. LS Aeration tank.		The process starts by spraying water into the air.

8. CU Spraying water. (Overprint: <u>Aeration</u>).

This is known as aeration:
oxygen from the air is added
to the water.

9. Diagram of aeration process.

As oxygen mixes with water it
improves its flavor and also
destroys certain types of bacteria.

10. LS High Angle. Coagulation
    tanks.

(and so on)

Now impurities must be removed
from the water. In the coagulation tanks the chemical alum
is added and mixed with water
for 10 to 20 minutes.

(and so on)

11. Completing the Project

Prepare titles and captions; then record narration and reproduce materials into final, complete form.

A few technical tasks remain before your materials are ready for the first formal showing. These include: making and filming titles and captions, recording narration on tape or on magnetic-striped film, and preparing final copies of photographs, slides, filmstrip, transparencies, or motion picture.

PREPARE TITLES AND CAPTIONS

Titles serve to introduce the viewer to the subject. The *main title* presents the subject. *Credit titles* acknowledge contributions of those who participated in or cooperated with the project. *Special titles* and *subtitles* introduce individual sequences and may serve to emphasize or to clarify particular pictures. An *end title* gives your audiovisual material a completed appearance.

A little thought and some care in preparation and in filming will result in neat and professional-looking titles, captions, and labels. They should be simple, brief, easily understood, and large enough to be read when projected. Complex, vague, and illegible titles confuse the audience rather than arouse its interest in an otherwise good production.

Other sections of this book will assist you in the preparation and the filming of titles and graphic materials:

- Making titles (page 100)
- Preparing artwork (page 91)
- Legibility standards for lettered materials (page 99)
- Photographic close-up and copy work (page 82)

Some materials, such as those to be less formally presented by integrated use within an instructional design, should not require extensive, formal titles. Keep these materials as simple as possible with an identifying number or brief title and incorporating captions, labels, questions, and directions as necessary. A formal *End* title may not be needed.

RECORD THE NARRATION

Once the narration has been refined and, if possible, tested along with the visuals on a typical audience group, you are ready to record it on tape or on magnetic-striped film. Type the narration as full-width, triple-spaced pages for ease of reading. Mark places that will require cueing, pauses, and special emphasis (see the example). Then proceed to make the recording.

FINAL PHOTOGRAPHIC WORK

If for your editing you used inexpensive proof copies of photographs or slides or a workprint of the motion picture, now prepare the final materials or have them prepared in the necessary number of copies. (See the appropriate sections in Part Four for instructions.) Then check the final prints with the recorded sound. You are now ready for your first showing.

A final bit of advice: You have spent much time and no doubt have gone to some expense to prepare your audiovisual materials. Protect the time, money, and work against loss by preparing at least one duplicate set of the materials, and file the originals in a safe place for any future need.

A Part of a Narration to Be Read for Recording

NARRATION--OUR WATER SUPPLY

// Point at which cue will be given to start reading.

emphasis   Underlined words are to be emphasized.

••• Brief pause between phrases.

- -

// The water we take for granted •••do you know where it comes from? Is there enough for our continued use? ••• How is it purified?

// The story of our water supply begins in the Sierra Nevada mountains. When snow melts or rain falls, the MO-KE-LUM-NEE river carries the water westward.

// A large amount is collected and held in the reservoir north of the city.

// The water is purified in our treatment plant. Each day three million gallons are processed. The process starts by spraying water into the air.

//This treatment is known as aeration: oxygen

from the air is added to the water. As oxygen

mixes with water it improves its flavor and

also destroys certain types of bacteria.

(and so on)

12. Writing an Instruction Guide

Prepare a teacher's guide or correlated student guide for
use with your audiovisual materials.

MATERIALS FOR CLASSROOM USE

If your audiovisual materials are designed for classroom or
other regular instructional use, an *instruction guide* will offer
the instructor suggestions and reminders for good utilization
practice. Its purpose should be: (1) to help them prepare for
successful use of the materials, and (2) to suggest related activities and problems for instructor and student consideration.

Such a guide may include:
- Information about the materials—type, length, date of prepa-
ration, source for loan, rent, or sale, rental or sale price
- Statement of objectives materials are intended to serve
- Enumeration of intended audience(s)
- Subject area or topic to which materials are related
- Description of content
- Key words, terms, or expressions
- Preparatory questions, problems, and activities for instructor
and students
- Participation activities for instructor and students during ac-
tual use
- Follow-up questions, problems, and activities after using the
materials
- Correlation of the materials with references and other instruc-
tional materials

Also, there are advantages to preparing hand-out materials
for distribution to a group at the time your materials are presented. Such information may relieve members of the audience
of the need to take notes or to copy information that is being
presented, thus permitting them to give all their attention to
your presentation. Such hand-outs, prepared and duplicated in
advance of their anticipated use, may include:

- An outline of the presentation
- Detailed information or how-to-do-it directions concerning
matters being presented
- Sources for items referred to
- Bibliography of references for future consideration by the
audience

MATERIALS FOR USE WITHIN AN INSTRUCTIONAL DESIGN

If your audiovisual materials are designed for use within an
instructional design or in correlation with a series of other
printed and visual materials for students' independent study,
there is little need for a guide of the traditional type. Most of the
elements of such a guide are part of the instructional program
itself.

Students may receive directions that lead from audio and
visual materials to reading materials to activities. Questions,
problems, and other participation activities are introduced.
Evaluations are provided. Therefore the student's general guide
sheet, along with specific correlated instructions, information,
and summaries, serves as a continuous guide for the materials
as they are used.

Now apply what you have read.

1. What elements of an instructional guide for group use of
your materials would you consider using?
2. If your materials are for individual study, develop the student guide sheet.

A Part of an Instruction Guide

INSTRUCTION GUIDE--OUR WATER SUPPLY

A set of 31 2" x 2" color slides with 8 minutes of taped narration.
Available on loan from the Audiovisual Center.

Purposes:
1. To learn the five steps in the purification of our local water
   supply.
2. To recognize the scientific principles that apply during the
   treatment process.
3. To practice the conservation of water (secondary purpose).

Audiences:
Primary: Ninth-grade general-science classes.
Secondary: High-school chemistry classes.

Related topic:
Community health services.

Content: (words underlined represent new vocabulary)

Our water supply originates in the Sierra Nevada mountains and
flows through the Mokelumne river to a storage reservoir near the
city. Each day 3,000,000 gallons are purified in the treatment
plant. Treatment requires five steps: First, aeration as the water
is sprayed into the air. Oxygen mixes with the water to improve its
flavor. Second, coagulation to remove impurities. [and so on]

Questions for group discussion before seeing the slides:

(Instructor or student committee should preview slides and tape
before class.)
1. Do you know the source of our water supply?
2. Do you believe the quantity of water is unlimited?
3. Why must water be purified?
4. How do you think water is purified? [and so on]

Participation during viewing:
Plan to stop the tape after slide 24 and review the details of each
purification step. Slide 25 will review and reinforce the total process.

Follow-up questions and activities:
1. Conduct laboratory demonstrations of each step in the process.
2. Find out how other communities purify their water.
3. Prepare a display to describe health dangers from polluted water.
4. In what ways can water be conserved at home and at school?

Correlation with references and other instructional materials:
Davis, Burnett, and Gross, Science: A Story of Discovery, pages 124-
   127.
Water...(a booklet), East Bay Municipal Utility District, Oakland.
Water Supply, 16mm sound color motion picture, 12 minutes (M 2120).
Wonderland of Science: Purifying Drinking Water, filmstrip, 46 frames
   (F2499).
[and so on]

A Student Study-Guide Sheet

COMMUNITY HEALTH UNIT--ACTIVITY #6

Following the class viewing and discussion of the film Water Purification you are ready for an examination of our local water supply. Be prepared to:

   a. Point out on an area map the source of our water supply and trace how it gets to our city.

   b. List and write a definition of the steps in the purification of our water.

1. For background, read the booklet Water by the East Bay Municipal District.

2. Study the slide series and tape recording Our Water Supply.

3. Complete the diagram of the purification process on the next page.

4. Prepare for the laboratory exercise demonstrating each step in the process.

[and so on]

13. Using Your Materials

Plan your presentation and use by checking facilities and rehearsing; then make your presentation and evaluate the results.

Now . . .

You are ready to use your materials with the intended audience. You—and your team—have spent much time in planning and in preparation, and now, in order to insure a successful reception, it is important that you arrange for the mechanics of the presentation and also make the materials meaningful to the audience whether your materials are for use with a group or for individual study.

Here are some pointers that may make this and subsequent uses successful:

- If you are not familiar with the room in which the materials will be used, try to visit it in advance. Check for electrical outlets, screen placement, seating arrangements, viewing distances, and appropriate placement for the projector. Also, find out how the room lights are controlled.
- Arrange for necessary equipment—projector, tape recorder, stands, screen, extension cord, adapter plugs, and extra projection lamp.
- Provide for the proper physical comfort of the group—ventilation, heat control, light control, and other conditions.
- Provide for distribution of hand-out materials, if appropriate.
- Rehearse your use of the materials (if possible in the setting in which they are to be used).
- If necessary, find out who will assist you with projection and other services, and instruct him accordingly.
- Arrange materials for use in proper sequence and in proper position.

- Prepare the group for viewing the materials. Refer to the instruction guide described in the preceding section.
- Make your presentation, using good projection techniques (centering of the image on the screen, focus, sound level, and the like).
- After the presentation, discuss the materials and, if possible, provide for related activities (see the instruction guide).
- Judge audience reactions and consider any revisions for subsequent presentation.

Evaluate the effectiveness of your audiovisual materials. Encourage reactions from those viewing and using the materials. Determine changes in audience behavior in terms of the purposes originally established (page 23) through observing specific actions by members of the audience, and by administering performance or written tests. These results will allow you to answer the question, "How well do the materials do the job for which they were designed?"

Keep the materials up-to-date by adding or substituting new content when appropriate and eliminating the obsolete. Only by revision will your audiovisual materials be kept timely and maintained at your standards of quality and effectiveness.

Now apply what you have read.

1. Assume you are ready to use your materials. List all the factors you should consider in preparation for use.

14. In Summary

The successful planning and production of audiovisual materials follows a logical sequence. For some types this is a detailed step-by-step procedure; for others it may be simplified and brief. Also, the degree to which any materials are formally completed (including titles, music, duplicates, laboratory services, and the like) is determined by the specific purposes to be served. For example, a short film designed to develop a single concept for direct instruction might be used with limited editing and without titles or special laboratory services.

A check list and outline of steps is given here in tabular arrangement. It covers all possible steps; but your purposes and the treatment you give the subject may permit you to omit some of these steps. The numbers in the various columns refer to pages containing a discussion of the things to be done at each step.

Note: The planning and production of audiovisual materials for instructional television generally follows the recommendations for each category column in the table. The follow-up steps are performed in accordance with the television-program procedures.

Step	Print Series	Slide Series	Film- Strips	Recordings	Trans- parencies	Motion Pictures	Display Materials
Planning							
1. Express your idea	23	23	23	23	23	23	23
2. Develop the objectives	23	23	23	23	23	23	23
3. Consider the audience	24	24	24	24	24	24	24
4. Get some help	26	26	26	26	26	26	26
5. Prepare the content outline	28	28	28	28	28	28	28
6. Select the medium	34	34	34	34	34	34	34
7. Write the treatment	—	40	40	—	—	40	—
8. Make a storyboard	—	40	40	—	—	40	—
9. Develop the script	42	42	42	42	42	42	—
10. Prepare the specifications	43	43	43	43	43	43	—
11. Schedule the picture taking	46	46	46	—	—	46	—
Production							
12. Take the pictures	138	143	155	—	—	193	—
13. Process the film	139	146	156	—	—	205	—
14. Make work copies	139	—	—	—	—	205	—
15. Edit the pictures	139	147	—	—	—	206	—
16. Edit narration and captions	50	50	50	50	50	50	—
17. Prepare artwork, titles, and captions	138	144	156	—	166	205	221
18. Record narration	—	132	132	132	—	210	—
19. Prepare final copies	139	150	157	134	168	210	221
Follow-up							
20. Write the instruction guide	57	57	57	57	57	57	57
21. Prepare for use of the materials	140	60	60	60	60	60	60
22. Use the materials	60	60	60	60	60	60	60
23. Evaluate for future use	51	51	51	51	51	51	51
24. Revise as necessary	60	60	60	60	60	60	60

Part Three

FUNDAMENTAL SKILLS

15. Photography

Photography is based upon light, which first strikes the subject being photographed, then is reflected to the camera, where it passes through the lens which focuses the light on the film to form the picture image. The camera protects the film from unwanted light, and controls the amount of light that reaches the film.

YOUR CAMERA

All cameras are basically similar and include five essential parts:

A. Lens
B. Light-tight enclosure
C. Lens diaphragm and shutter
D. Film-support channel
E. Viewfinder

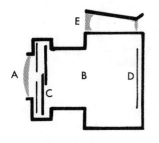

In addition, all cameras except the simplest have some means for changing the distance between the lens and the film in order to focus the image on the film. Some have still other controls and attachments designed to make the camera more versatile—a built-in rangefinder, an attachment for flash lighting, a self-timer, to name a few.

Box cameras are simple to operate because lens setting, shutter speed, and distance setting are preset by the manufacturer to produce satisfactory pictures under good light conditions. Their lenses are generally prefocused so the user does not control them. These cameras therefore cannot be focused sharply on objects closer than 6 feet without supplementary attachments. Such inherent limitations both simplify the operation of box cameras and limit the kinds and quality of pictures that they will take. But box cameras will make satisfactory pictures if these limitations are respected.

Adjustable cameras, as distinguished from box cameras, have numerous and varying features subject to the user's control: methods of changing lens-diaphragm openings, shutter speeds, and focus. Lens quality differs over a wide range. Adjustable diaphragms and shutters are desirable because they can be adapted to changing light conditions and to different kinds of subjects; thus they broaden the possibilities for taking pictures.

The *35mm camera* makes 2″×2″ color slides and low-cost black-and-white or color negatives. These cameras may have either window-type viewfinders or viewers that sight through the camera lens for accurate viewing (called single-lens reflex cameras), especially for close-ups. Lenses and shutters may be adjusted over a wide range of settings. The cameras can be operated quickly and there is an economy with film in that many exposures can be made on a single roll before reloading. For more details on the characteristics of 35mm cameras see page 143.

The twin-lens reflex camera has two lenses, the lower (A) for taking pictures and the top (B) for viewing. The viewing screen is a ground glass, which gives an accurate view of the subject in the same size that will appear on the film negative. The most popular negative size is 2¼″×2¼″ (120 size); such negatives are convenient to handle and are used to make positive slides or enlarged to make prints.

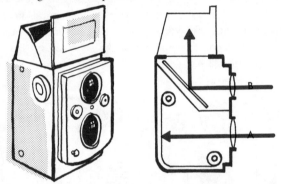

Sheet-film cameras include press- and view-type cameras in many sizes. They use cut sheets of film rather than rolls, thus permitting single pictures to be taken and immediately processed. The larger negative permits extreme enlargement and ease of retouching. These are ideal cameras for copy work and close-up photography since accurate viewing and focusing take place on a ground glass surface directly in line with the lens.

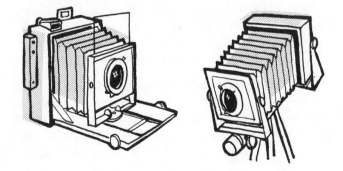

Two other camera types, while similar in structure to the basic forms already described, are recognized separately because of certain unique characteristics. One is the *Polaroid Land* camera. The important feature of all Polaroid cameras is that the film is developed and prints are made in the camera, thus eliminating the need for a darkroom. Prints in both black-and-white and color and slides in black-and-white can be produced quickly.

Polaroid film consists of light-sensitive negative film and a nonsensitive positive stock (paper or film). To the latter are affixed sealed pods, one for each picture, which contain developing chemicals. After a picture is taken, a pull on a paper tab advances the film, rollers squeeze the developer from a pod, allowing the developer to spread between the negative and positive stock. Development takes place immediately and the resulting photograph or slide is removed from the camera in from 10 seconds to 2 minutes, depending on the film used.

The other special camera category is the *automatic-setting* camera. Such a camera includes a built-in exposure meter which measures light intensity at the lens as the rays enter the camera.

The meter is attached to the diaphragm of the lens to automatically adjust the opening according to light intensity and in synchronization with shutter speeds. Once the camera is set for the speed or type of film being used, proper exposure adjustments for almost all conditions are automatically made. Some cameras also include an automatic method of setting the correct focus (distance of camera to subject).

Thus with the automatic-setting camera you are relieved of making adjustments for technical details and can concentrate on picture content, composition, and the relation of one picture to another. Such cameras are available in 35mm and cartridge-loaded 126 film sizes.

The same functions essential in the operation of other cameras are necessary in all *motion-picture cameras*. The differences are in the threading of film, its motion through the camera, and the movement of the shutter behind the lens. (See page 188 for more details on the characteristics and operation of motion-picture cameras.)

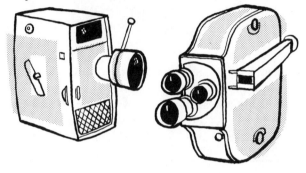

Now, review what you have learned about camera types:

What type of camera might best fit each situation?
1. Used to produce a quantity of color slides.
2. Used to make greatly enlarged close-up pictures of small objects on pieces of film.
3. Simplest for a child to use, as all settings are pre-set.
4. Used to quickly and easily prepare photographs immediately after the pictures are taken.
5. Used as a roll film camera for accurately viewing a subject in same size and appearance as it will be filmed.
6. Aim this camera at a subject and it adjusts its own lens for the immediate light conditions.

CAMERA SETTINGS

The amount of light that enters a camera is controlled by the

[See Appendix A for film correlated with this topic.]
lens diaphragm and the *shutter,* working together. The lens diaphragm limits the area through which light can pass; the shutter limits the time.

Lens diaphragm

Light enters a camera by passing through the lens. The intensity of light entering is controlled by a metal diaphragm which is located either directly behind the lens or between two elements of the lens. The diaphragm acts somewhat like the iris of an eye.

It is always open, but its size can be changed to control the intensity of light passing through the lens.

Lens-diaphragm settings are indicated by a series of numbers —4, 5.6, 8, 11, 16, . . . — called *f/ numbers* or *f/ stops. The larger the f/ number the smaller the opening.* A lens setting of *f*/11 admits only *half the amount of light* passed by an *f*/8 setting.

Thus, adjacent numbers in the series admit light in the proportion of 2 to 1 (permitting the passage of *twice as much light* or *half as much light*).

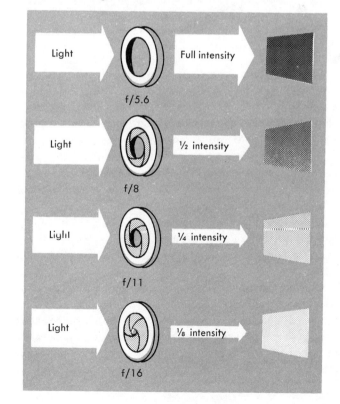

Shutter speed

A second camera setting is the shutter speed. The camera shutter is similar to the eyelid as it closes and reopens rapidly. In the camera the shutter remains closed until opened to permit the lens to "see."

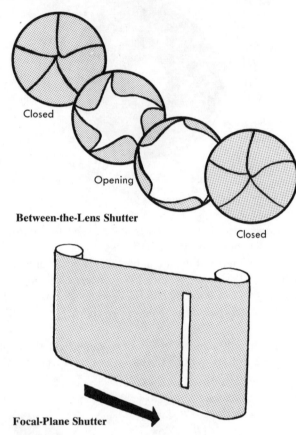

Closed

Opening

Between-the-Lens Shutter

Closed

Focal-Plane Shutter

Generally shutter speeds are measured in fractions of a second—1/2, 1/5, 1/10, 1/25, 1/50, 1/100, ... On the camera they are printed as whole numbers instead of fractions. A shutter speed of 1/50 second is *slower* than one of 1/100 second, admitting light for *twice as long a time.*

Thus adjacent speeds are in the proportion of 2 to 1 (permitting the entrance of light for approximately *twice as much time* or *half as much time*—1/50 twice as much as 1/100; but 1/50 half as much as 1/25).

On some cameras, shutter speeds are graduated in another series of fractions of a second, as . . . 1/30, 1/60, 1/125, and so on. The principle of 2-to-1 proportion holds for these graduations also.

On your camera you may have many speeds from which to select. For general scenes a shutter speed of 1/60 or 1/125 is suggested. But when a moving subject is to be filmed the choice of a shutter speed is dependent on the speed of movement, the distance from camera to subject, and the direction of movement relative to the camera. See facing page.

Since both the adjacent lens-diaphragm settings and the adjacent shutter speeds are in the 2-to-1 proportion, they may be used in various combinations to allow the same amount of light to reach the film. As you will see, the selection of such combinations is important to obtain specific effects.

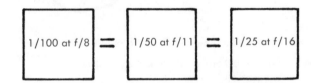

1/100 at f/8 = 1/50 at f/11 = 1/25 at f/16

Focus

The third setting on many cameras is for focus. With your camera you may have to estimate the distance from camera to subject and set an indicator accordingly. Or your camera may include a built-in *rangefinder* coupled to the lens, which, upon proper adjustment automatically sets the lens for the correct subject-to-camera distance.

Distance scale

RECOMMENDED SHUTTER SPEEDS FOR VARIOUS TYPES OF SUBJECT MOVEMENT

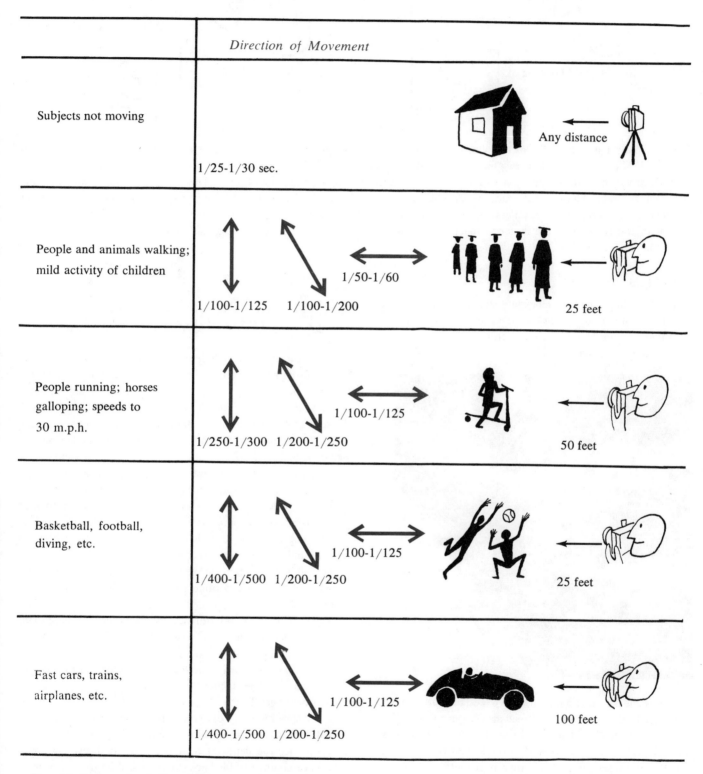

Direction of Movement

Subjects not moving

1/25-1/30 sec.

Any distance

People and animals walking; mild activity of children

1/100-1/125   1/100-1/200   1/50-1/60

25 feet

People running; horses galloping; speeds to 30 m.p.h.

1/250-1/300   1/200-1/250   1/100-1/125

50 feet

Basketball, football, diving, etc.

1/400-1/500   1/200-1/250   1/100-1/125

25 feet

Fast cars, trains, airplanes, etc.

1/400-1/500   1/200-1/250   1/100-1/125

100 feet

For subjects closer than indicated distance, use faster speed.

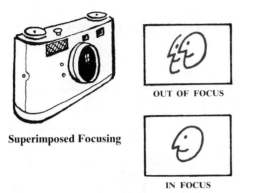

Superimposed Focusing

OUT OF FOCUS

IN FOCUS

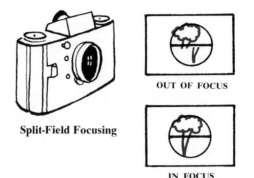

Split-Field Focusing

OUT OF FOCUS

IN FOCUS

The rangefinder may be either of two kinds: *superimposing* or *split-field*. The former will show two images unless the focus is correct, at which point the two images are superimposed to make a single image. The split-field rangefinder will show two half images, one below the other, unless the focus is correct, at which point the two halves are matched together to make a complete image.

Depth of field

While lens-diaphragm openings and shutter speeds work together to admit various amounts of light into the camera, lens-diaphragm openings and distance settings also may be coordinated to get sharp pictures.

out

in focus

Plane of focus

in focus

out

In this scene the camera is focused at 8 feet, but children both closer and farther away than 8 feet also appear sharp. This distance from the closest sharply focused point to the farthest spot in focus is the *depth of field* of the lens at the f/number used. To get a sharp picture a photographer must have his subject in this field.

Of the total depth of field within a scene, about one-third is included ahead of the point of actual focus and about two-thirds beyond the point of focus. Therefore to get the maximum value from the depth-of-field factor, focus your camera lens on a point that is about one-third of the way into a scene. If your camera gives you more exact information, use it.

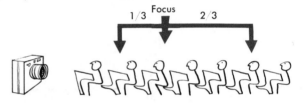

Your camera may include a depth-of-field scale adjacent to the focusing ring. Refer to this scale to determine quickly the depth of field for any combination of lens setting and distance to the plane of focus. The illustrations show how this scale is to be read in combination with the distance scale on the focusing ring. Note that its graduations are like those on the lens-setting scale: 4, 8, 16, 22 (the 2.8, 5.6, and 11 points are omitted for legibility in the scale used in the illustration). It should be easy to observe the two important facts: first, whatever the lens setting, it provides greater depth of field at far distances than at near distances. Second, whatever the distance, it provides greater depth of field at higher-numbered lens settings than at lower-numbered ones. See facing page.

By using this relationship between lens setting, distance, and depth of field, you can often get exactly what you want into your picture.

To get a greater depth of field, use a smaller lens-diaphragm opening (that is, a higher f/ number). The illustration shows how the depth of field, at whatever distance the camera is focused, will be increased by setting the f/ number up from 4 to 16, for example. See facing page.

In order to get the maximum depth of field (for close-up work or for scenes requiring extreme depth) use a large f/ number (small lens-diaphragm opening—perhaps f/16).

To reduce the depth of field (perhaps to throw part of a subject or an undesirable background out of focus) use a small f/ number (large lens-diaphragm opening—perhaps f/4).

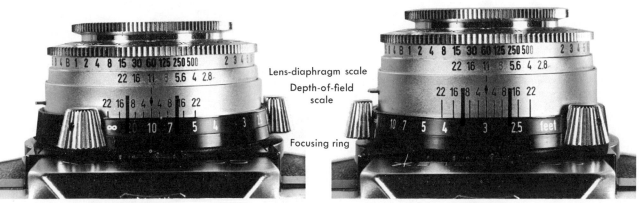

f/11 at 10 Feet   f/11 at 3 Feet

Lens-diaphragm scale

Depth-of-field scale

Focusing ring

The depth-of-field scale is graduated both to left and to right of a zero marker with numbers corresponding to the f/ scale. Some graduations are omitted to permit making the numbers large and clear. At left, the focus (white numbers on black) is set for 10 feet, the lens setting at f/11. Reading the focus scale opposite the two 11 points (between 8 and 16) on the depth-of-field scale shows that the field extends from about 6½ feet in front of the camera to almost infinity. At right, with the same lens setting but with the focus at 3 feet, the two 11 points on the depth-of-field scale indicate that the field extends from a little more than 2½ feet to a little more than 3½ feet in front of the camera.

Depth of Field at Two Possible Lens Settings

The focus is set for a little less than 9 feet. If you change the lens setting to f/16, the field will extend from a little more than 5 feet to something more than 20 feet; if you change the lens setting to f/4, the limits of the field will be about 7 feet and about 10 feet.

Scene with Limited Depth of Field—f/4

Scene with Maximum Depth of Field—f/16

In summary: On adjustable cameras three settings must be made—lens diaphragm opening (f/ number), shutter speed, and distance. Study their relationships carefully and learn how to use them. Also, remember when taking pictures to:

• hold the camera steady
• use a tripod whenever shutter speeds slower than 1/25 second will be used
• squeeze the shutter release, rather than punch it
• keep the light over your shoulder, rather than let it shine toward the camera lens

Now, review what you have learned about camera settings:

1. If a lens setting of $f/8$ permits a certain amount of light to pass into a camera, then how much light does a setting of $f/5.6$ admit?
2. What shutter speed might you select to "stop" the action of a person diving off a board, a car driving past at 25 mph, or a child walking by you?
3. If $f/11$ and $1/125$ second are correct exposure settings, but you want to increase the depth of field by two $f/$ stops, what camera settings would you now use?
4. What is the depth of field indicated on the lens on page 68?
5. Do higher-number $f/$ stops permit *greater* or *less* depth of field as compared to lower-number $f/$ stops?

THE FILM

[See Appendix A for film correlated with this topic.]

Your selection of film is determined by a number of factors:

- Kinds of subjects, such as general scenes, action shots, or close-ups of fine details
- Lighting conditions, such as daylight, floodlights, flash, or low-level room light
- Use for materials, such as enlarged photographs, slides, or transparencies

In addition, choices are based upon characteristics of different films, including:

- Degree of light sensitivity (film speed or exposure index):
  slow films, such as Panatomic-X (index 40) or Kodachrome II daylight (index 25) (see explanation following)
  moderate-speed films, such as Ektachrome-X (64) and Plus-X Pan (160)
  fast films, such as High Speed Ektachrome (160), Tri-X (400), Super Hypan (500)
- Size of film grain
- Useful exposure range to reproduce a range of tones from highlights to shadows.

The terms *film speed, exposure index,* and *ASA* (American Standards Association) *speed* refer to the degree of light sensitivity of a film. They are used interchangeably and are scaled by a number assigned to each film. The number is a relative one; it applies to specified light conditions. A film with a speed of 100 requires less light for proper exposure than one with a speed of 64, and vice versa.

The data about films, as indicated in the accompanying chart, are correct at the time of writing; but changes and new developments are to be anticipated. Check carefully the data sheet packaged with your film for the latest assigned exposure index and other details. See page 74.

Black-and-white film

Black-and-white films are inexpensive, easy to use, and simple to process and print. Their primary use is in making enlargements, as for photographic picture series. Black-and-white films also serve for slides, filmstrips, photographic transparencies, and motion pictures.

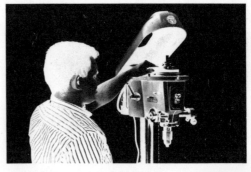

Negative

Black-and-White Slide

Enlarged Print

Color negative film

Color negative film is versatile since it may serve as negative for color prints, for black-and-white prints, and for positive color slides. On a color negative the colors of the subject are complementary to their normal appearance (yellow in place of blue, magenta for green, and cyan or blue-green for red). Kodacolor and Ektacolor are the principal color negative films available. The films, available in sizes for most cameras, are more expensive than black-and-white, but may be processed with prepared kits, thus reducing the cost when a number of rolls are handled. Also, inventions are reported that may simplify the developing and printing of color film.

Color Negative

Black-and-White Print from Color Negative

Color Slide from Color Negative

Color Print from Color Negative

Color reversal film

After exposure and processing, color reversal films become positives—slides, filmstrips, or motion pictures. In processing, the image on the film is *reversed* to make a positive picture.

Color reversal films are supplied in sizes for 35mm and 126 (for Instamatic-type) cameras and for standard roll-film cameras. They are available in a range of film speeds and in various types, each type designed for a specific light condition— daylight or photoflood. The light supplied by these sources dif-

fers in "color temperature," a characteristic measured in degrees Kelvin (°K). Therefore, each film type has an emulsion for a specific color temperature, such as 6,000°K (daylight) or 3,400°K (photoflood). Frequently correction filters can be employed to permit use of a film under lighting conditions that differ from its Kelvin rating.

2″ × 2″ (35mm Film)

2″ × 2″ (126-Size Film)

2¼″ × 2¼″ (120-Size Film)

Characteristics of Some Widely Used Films

Film	Exposure index (ASA)	Grain	Light source	Suggested use
Panatomic-X	40	extra fine	any	copying fine detail for extreme enlargements
All Weather Pan	125	fine	any	general outdoor subjects
Tri-X	400+	medium	any	subjects under low light levels
Kodacolor negative	80	fine	daylight, blue flash	black-and-white or general purposes when color is needed
Kodachrome II daylight	25	fine	daylight	subjects under good outdoor light conditions
Super Ansco-chrome tungsten	500	moderate	photo-flood	subjects under low-level artificial light

Now, test what you have learned about film:

1. Most reversal color films are available in two types. The selection of the type to use depends on what major factor?
2. If you wanted to have both color slides and enlarged color prints from the same subject, what film would you select to use?
3. What is the reason for selecting a film with an exposure index of 100 in preference to one with an index of 64?

CORRECT EXPOSURE

[See Appendix A for film correlated with this topic.]

How do you put together information about f/ numbers, shutter speeds, and film characteristics to get correct exposure? The simplest method is to refer to the data sheet packaged with the film, on which a table gives you *general* guides to proper exposure.

OUTDOOR EXPOSURE GUIDE FOR AVERAGE SUBJECTS	Set shutter at 1/200 or 1/250 second and lens opening at:			
	f/22	f/11	f/8	f/8
	BRIGHT OR HAZY SUN* (DISTINCT SHADOWS)	CLOUDY BRIGHT (NO SHADOWS)	HEAVY OVERCAST	OPEN SHADE
	Exposure Values			
	17	15	14	14
	*For back-lighted subjects, use f/11 or EV15.			

But what about situations involving particularly dark- or unusually light-colored subjects or backgrounds? What corrections should you make when the sun is behind the subject rather than over your shoulder? How do you determine camera settings when doing copy work or when using floodlights? These are common problems and their solutions may require more information than that provided by the data-sheet tables alone.

Using a light meter

The most accurate method for determining exposure is with the use of a photographic light meter. All such meters consist of three main parts: a photoelectric cell, a light-level scale, and a camera-setting scale. See facing page.

Light is measured by an exposure meter in either of two places: at the place where the subject is or at the place where the camera is. The *incident-light method* measures the light where the subject is, with an *incident-light meter* at or near the subject's position and pointed toward the camera. The *reflected-light method* measures the light where the camera is, with a *reflected-light meter* at or near the camera's position and pointed toward the subject. Another way of describing the two methods is to say that the *incident*-light method measures the light that *falls on* the subject whereas the *reflected*-light method measures the light that *comes off* the subject. See facing page.

Some meters measure light by only one of these methods; many have attachments or components which permit measurements to be taken in either way.

The exposure meter measures light through its photoelectric cell and electronic circuit. You then use this measurement to compute lens opening and shutter speed, employing scales on the instrument. Follow these steps:

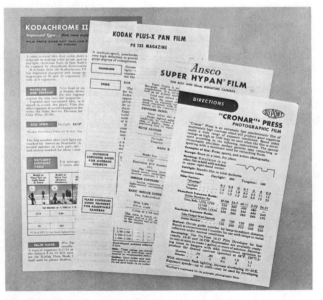

Typical Film-Information Sheets

Light strikes a photoelectric cell which converts the light energy into electrical energy.

The light level is shown by the movement of a needle over a scale.

Then proper camera settings are indicated on the dial scales.

The Incident-Light Method

2. Take your light-level reading and note the light level indicated by the needle.
3. Adjust the movable scale until its pointer points to this light level.
4. You will now find lens openings and shutter speeds matched on two dials. Select the pair you will use.

The two illustrations present examples of the appearance of exposure meters after they have been set as directed above.

The Reflected-Light Method

1. Note the exposure index of the film you are using (as 500 for Super Anscochrome) and set the meter's exposure-index scale at this number.

Incident-Light Meter

Reflected-Light Meter

f/22 at 1/15 Sec.

Since shutter speed and lens opening work together, as has been explained, to admit the proper amount of light to the film, correct exposure is shown by any paired values for *f*/ number and shutter speed. Can you read the paired figures in the two illustrations? If you find *f*/16 paired with 1/30, then other pairs will be *f*/11 at 1/60, *f*/8 at 1/125, *f*/5.6 at 1/250, and so on.

Now, which pair to choose? Your selection is based upon answers to two questions:

1. How much movement is there in the scene? (Recall the examples of shutter speed selection on page 69; the faster the motion the higher the necessary speed.)
2. How much depth of field is desired? (Recall the discussion of depth of field, pages 70–71; for greater depth of field use a setting with larger *f*/ number).

Now apply some of these relationships. Can you explain why the particular exposure settings were selected for these three examples?

f/11 at 1/60 Sec.

A good exposure meter is a worthwhile investment. Use it *carefully* for correct exposure determinations.

- When using an incident-light meter, hold it in the center of the scene and aim the white cone toward the camera.
- When using a reflected-light meter, aim it at the subject, especially for exterior scenes. Do not tip the meter and record too much light from the foreground or from the sky.
- Average the readings of a reflected-light meter taken from various objects in a scene; avoid taking readings with reflected-light meter from very bright or very dark parts of the scene.
- With an incident-light meter, when a subject is back-lighted (that is, when the sun or other light source is behind the subject and parts of the subject facing the camera are in shadow), open the lens to one additional *f*/ number beyond that indicated on the meter.
- When filming under photoflood lights, follow the additional suggestions for using a meter that you will find on page 79.
- When doing close-up and copy work, make use of the exposure information on page 85.
- Follow other suggestions found in the instruction manual accompanying your light meter.

Keep a careful record of light and subject conditions, choice of exposure, and the quality of resulting pictures. From this record you can judge how well your meter is serving you and establish the modifications you must make in using it.

A word about electric-eye cameras. On such cameras an exposure meter is coupled directly to the lens and as light strikes this meter it automatically sets the lens opening (*f*/ number) to correspond to a preselected shutter speed. This lens-opening setting will be satisfactory *provided two requirements are fulfilled:*

- The light must come over your shoulder as you take the picture.
- The meter must not be measuring any bright areas unimportant to the picture (these could cause underexposure).

Electric-eye cameras are almost foolproof—but your own experience may guide you to vary the camera setting under certain conditions.

f/4 at 1/500 Sec.

Now, test what you have learned about determining exposure:

1. What three numbers, relating to exposure, can be determined from a film-data sheet? Which two can be used directly to make camera settings and which one is for a setting on a light meter?

2. What two settings are required on a light meter before determining exposure?

3. When these two settings are made on the meter what pair of numbers result?

4. According to the setting illustrated on the incident-light meter on page 75, if a subject requires extreme depth of field what camera shutter speed would you use? (First, would you select f/4.5 or f/32?)

5. The type of light meter on which the measurement of light intensity is not affected by the color or other characteristics of the subject itself is the _____.

ARTIFICIAL LIGHTING

Good exposures can be made, even under unfavorable lighting conditions, on the high-speed films that are available—some of them with an exposure index greater than 1,000. Even so, it is necessary at times to provide lighting in place of or in addition to the normal light in the area. Such artificial light is either flash light or flood light.

Photoflash lighting

Notice the difference in brilliancy and in shadow detail between two otherwise identical photographs, one taken with the natural available light and one with added photoflash light.

WITH NATURAL LIGHT   WITH FLASH LIGHTING ADDED

Flash bulbs or electronic flash units are one way of creating your own light. Even in sunlight, flash lighting may be used to add light to shadow areas. A flash is most useful for lighting relatively small areas or for lighting larger ones that have light-colored backgrounds. The light fall-off from flash is so great that the background, if it is too far behind the subject, will appear undesirably dark.

The exposure for taking pictures under flash lighting is determined by referring to tables in the literature and using a formula. The tables appear on the film-information sheet, on the flashbulb box, or in the instructions with your electronic flash

unit. There may be some discrepancy in the recommended *guide number* among these sources. In such a case, use the information on the flashbulb box or electronic unit in preference to that on other sources.

In using the tables you take into account the film, the flash source, and the shutter speed to be used; these enable you to find the *guide number*. Then, using this number and the *flash-to-subject distance,* you compute the lens setting from the formula:

$$\text{lens setting} = \frac{\text{guide number}}{\text{distance}}$$

Note the data with the sample picture, and the use of these data in computing the f/ number.

Verichrome Pan film, exposure index 125
No. 25 flash bulb
Shutter speed 1/125 sec.
Guide number 80
Distance 10 feet (flash to subject)

$$\text{lens setting} = \frac{80}{10} = 8$$
$$\text{lens setting} = f/8$$

When using other lighting you may adjust exposure by increasing the shutter speed and the lens setting, but you are less freely able to make such changes when using flash lighting because the duration of flash is brief and is not controlled; hence the shutter speed is substantially fixed and is a component of the exposure guide number.

DISTANT BACKGROUND—DARK   NEAR BACKGROUND—LIGHTED

Flash Lighting and the Background

For unusual flash techniques (bounce lighting, use of multiple flash, reducing flash intensity for extreme close-ups), see the special references for flash photography on page 234.

Photoflood lighting

[See Appendix A for film correlated with this topic.]

Classrooms, offices, and many other areas are usually well illuminated by fluorescent lights. Frequently this light is sufficient for many filming purposes, even with moderate-speed black-and-white films. Because color films respond differently to various light sources, fluorescence may cause unusual effects. Test your film to determine any variations in color rendition and film speed (for example, tests show that High Speed Ektachrome daylight-type film, under certain classroom fluorescent lights, at an exposure index of 80, gives highly acceptable results).

If supplementary or controlled lighting is necessary, consider using photographic floodlamps. They may be essential for motion-picture photography; even for still photography floodlights are often better than flash since you see exactly what effect the lights are creating (reflections, heavy shadows, or uneven lighting) and can make corrections before taking pictures.

Two major types of photoflood lamps are available. The traditional incandescent-filament lamp with wattages of 250, 500, or 1000 in a hemisphere-shaped reflector is widely used. Recent advances in lamp technology have made available small tubular units consisting of quartz filaments and filled with iodine vapor. These quartz-iodine lamps provide a very bright, narrow ribbon of light and project an extremely even illumination. People appearing in scenes in which the quartz-iodide lamps are used should be warned not to look directly into the light as the brightness of the source can cause eye discomfort.

Floods placed close to the camera will light the subject only from the front side. Such lighting results in a flat, shadowless subject with heavy background shadows, usually undesirable.

It is better to place one light about 45° to the side of the camera, somewhat closer to the subject, and higher than the camera. This become the *main or key light*. It substitutes for the sun which shines on an outdoor scene. Therefore it should be the brightest light source (either by wattage or closeness to the subject).

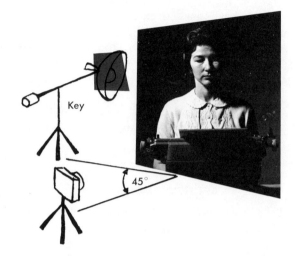

Place a second light (or two) beside the camera (on the side opposite the main light) and at camera height. This light serves to soften shadows created by the key light, thus bringing out more detail in the subject. It is called the *fill light*.

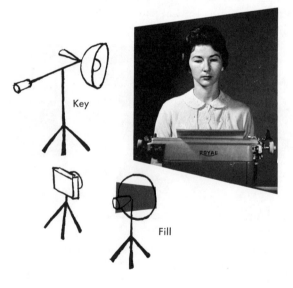

Some light from the key may fall on the background, but a third light (or two), aimed evenly at the background, will illuminate it, thus separating the subject from the background and giving the scene some depth. This is the *background light*. Always keep the subject at least 2 or 3 feet away from the background to minimize heavy shadows created by any lights.

These three lights—key, fill, and background—form the basic lighting pattern for good indoor lighting. The key as the brightest one is often *twice* the light intensity of the fill light (key-light to fill-light ratio 2 to 1); for example, light-meter readings of 100 for key light and 50 for fill light. (For close-up scenes, to soften shadows, the intensity of the fill may equal that of the key light—key to fill ratio 1 to 1.) One or more background lights may be set to illuminate the background evenly with a meter reading one-half to one stop lower than the general reading within the scene. Sometimes a spotlight (or photospot) is used as an *accent light* to highlight a person or an object in the scene.

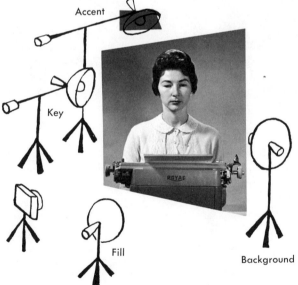

Use your light meter for balancing lights and determining exposure. You can use one or more of four methods:

- Move an incident-light meter through the scene (aimed at the camera). Adjust lights by changing positions until the lighting is even, then determine the exposure.

- Take readings with a reflected-light meter held at various parts of the scene and average them.
- Take a reading with a reflected-light meter from a neutral gray card (Eastman Kodak's neutral test card) held in the scene.
- Take a reading with a reflected-light meter from a face or hand in the scene and then use twice the indicated exposure (that is, a lens opening one f/ number lower, since the flesh tone is somewhat brighter than the over-all scene should be. (For example, for a reading from the face of f/8 at 1/60 second, use f/5.6 at 1/60).

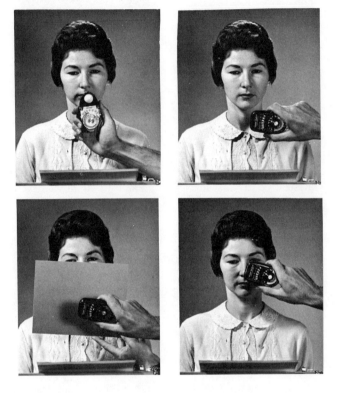

Now, test what you have learned about lighting:

1. Are flash bulbs effective for lighting *small* or *large* areas?
2. Apply the correct formula to determine f/ number: flash-bulb guide number for film is 100, distance of camera to subject is 6 feet.
3. In a scene including people and large objects, what are some disadvantages of using lights placed only right beside the camera?
4. What is meant by the expression, "key to fill ratio is 2:1"? Is this an acceptable ratio to create moderate but not harsh shadows?
5. What method would you use for determining exposure under flood lighting?
6. Explain the positioning and purpose served by each light—accent, background, key, and fill. In what order is each set for use?

PICTURE COMPOSITION

[See Appendix A for film correlated with this topic.]

The effectiveness of your visual materials is strengthened by careful arrangement of elements within each picture, be it a still or motion picture. Although composition may be a matter of personal choice, some principles should be kept in mind:

• Have only one major subject or center of interest in a scene. Do not clutter a picture or make it tell too much. Eliminate or subordinate all secondary elements and focus attention on the main one.

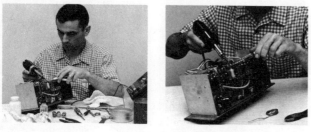

• Place the center of interest near to but not directly in the physical center of the picture area. By making the picture slightly unsymmetrical you create a dynamic and more interesting arrangement.

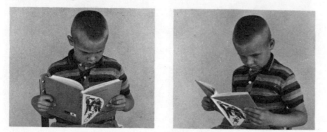

• Try not to be static from one scene to another by shooting from the same relative camera position or angle. Plan to vary camera positions. Changing angles creates a dynamic impression and gives variety to composition.

• Keep the background simple. Eliminate confusing background details by removing disturbing objects, by putting up a screen to hide the background, or by throwing the background out of focus (using a smaller *f*/number, thus controlling the depth of field).

• Include some foreground detail to create an impression of depth (principally in long-shot exterior scenes). Foregrounds help to balance the picture and to make it interesting.

• If action or movement is implied in a picture, allow more space or picture area in the direction of the action rather than away from it.

• In black-and-white photography similar tones may blend together. Have the color of the center of interest contrast with the background and surrounding objects.

• Because viewers have no way of judging the size of unknown objects in pictures, it is important to include some familiar object for comparison.

- Most visual materials normally have a horizontal format. If possible, plan your content for this format. Try not to mix vertical photographs or slides with horizontal ones in a series.

- Finally, use common sense in composition. Ask yourself

"What am I trying to accomplish with this picture or scene?" Then pick what appears to be the best angle and the best distance for the camera. If necessary, view the scene from two or three positions and make pictures from each one for future selection.

Study the suggestions for composition of graphic materials on pages 92– 94. Many of these principles also apply to photographs, slides, and motion-picture scenes.

Now, test what you have learned about picture composition:

Following is a group of six pictures (scenes); each one composes the same subject differently. Which one do you prefer? Why?

1 2 3

4 5 6

CLOSE-UP AND COPY WORK

[See Appendix A for film correlated with this topic.]

In photography it is often necessary to photograph subjects closer than a camera is normally used, such as for titles, reproductions of charts and pictures, and for close-ups of subject details.

Your camera may be unsatisfactory for such close-up work unless you can make adjustments and allowances in two respects: focusing and viewfinding. Most adjustable cameras will not focus if nearer than 2½ or 3 feet to a subject; most view finders become inaccurate because of *parallax* when the subject is close to the camera. And close-up work often requires you to have your camera a foot or less from the subject.

Viewfinding and parallax

The viewfinder on some rollfilm cameras is located above the picture-taking lens. In such cameras the viewer and the taking lens do not see exactly the same area; the difference is of the kind that you perceive when you look at a book with each eye alternately closed. But your eyes can move individually to compensate for some of the difference; the two lenses on your camera cannot do so. This is the phenomenon of *parallax*. The different areas that the taking lens and the viewfinder see are illustrated in two pictures.

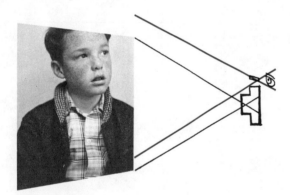

Camera with Window-Type Viewfinder—Parallax Results in Cutting Off a Portion of the Subject

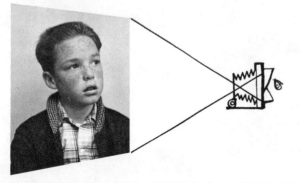

Camera with Ground-Glass Surface behind the Lens—No Parallax Problem

View cameras and single-lens reflex cameras permit through-the-lens viewing of the subject. It is viewed directly through the taking lens and focused on a ground glass. These cameras are preferred for close-up and copy photography.

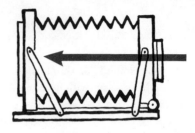

View Camera

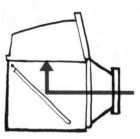

Single-Lens Reflex Camera

If your camera does not have such built-in features or special attachments to deal with the parallax problem, it is difficult but not entirely impossible to do close-up and copy work. You can use framing and copying aids to be described shortly. Using them, however, requires some understanding of the problems of close-up focusing and exposure determination.

Focusing and exposure

Cameras are adapted for close-up photography by one of three devices:

- The camera is built with bellows that can be used to lengthen the lens-to-film distance.
- The camera permits the use of separate extension tubes or bellows that lengthen the lens-to-film distance.
- A close-up attachment can be mounted on the lens to change the optical character of the lens system.

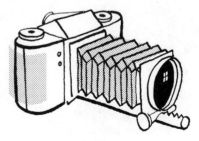

Bellows

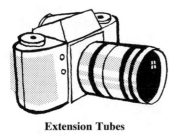

Extension Tubes

When you use bellows or extension tubes for close-ups, you are using the same lens that you would use to take pictures at normal distances. But exposure calculation must be adjusted because of the increased distance between lens and film. The exposure for close-ups under these conditions is found by the usual exposure-meter procedure plus an additional computation. The additional computation takes into account the focal length of the camera lens (which is printed or engraved on the lens housing) and the amount of extension of the bellows or tubes. The formula may be used for measurements either in inches or in metric units. It is:

$$\text{increased-exposure factor} = \frac{(\text{length of extension})^2}{(\text{focal length of lens})^2}$$

The application of this formula to a specific problem is illustrated:

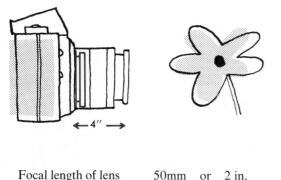

Focal length of lens	50mm	or	2 in.
Length of extension	100mm	or	4 in.
Normal exposure	$f/8$ at $1/60$		

Using the formula with the distances in inches gives:

$$\text{increased-exposure factor} = \frac{4^2}{2^2} = \frac{16}{4} = 4$$

Therefore exposure must be 4 times the normal exposure. This increase can be accomplished by opening up the diaphragm of the lens 2 $f/$ stops (to give exposure of $f/4$ at $1/60$ second) or by reducing the shutter speed one-fourth (to give exposure of $f/8$ at $1/15$ second.

To insure best focus and maximum depth of field when working close, use a larger $f/$ number where possible. Select camera settings with a shutter speed faster than 1 second to avoid the unusual reactions of some films to longer exposure times.

The majority of cameras can be adapted for close-up work with one or more supplementary lenses (close-up attachments) placed in a retaining ring and attached over the regular lens. With this method no compensation for exposure is required as with tube or bellows extension.

Retaining ring

Close-up lens

Adapter ring

Camera lens

To illustrate the effectiveness of close-up attachments, here is a table used with some adjustable cameras:

Width of subject, inches	Distance, camera to subject, inches	Power of close-up lens	Distance setting on camera, feet
26½	39	1+	infinity
11½	15½	2+	6
6	8	3+	2

Using a copy stand

It is difficult to do copy work if you are using a camera without built-in parallax correction features. But with patience and some skill, simple devices can be constructed or purchased and used to insure proper viewing for close-up work.

A series of home-made or commercial focal frames simplifies framing and focusing. For details on constructing and using focal frames see *Kodak Portra Lenses and a Technique for Extreme Close-ups,* pamphlet AB-10, Eastman Kodak Company.

Focal Frame in Use

Portable Slide-Production Copy Kit from Eastman Kodak Company.

An adjustable copy stand, which holds your camera at various heights for different-size copy materials, is very versatile. Vertical stands are more serviceable than are horizontal ones because of the difficulty of securing books in a vertical position.

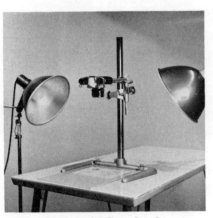

Commercial Copy Stand

Constructed Wooden Stand Made According to Directions on Page 20, "Producing Slides and Filmstrips," Publication S-8, Eastman Kodak Company.

Here is a method for establishing camera and subject positions for filming flat materials of various sizes, using a copy stand with a camera that does not include through-the-lens viewing:

1. Attach the camera to the stand.
2. Open the camera lens fully (to the smallest $f/$ number).
3. Open the shutter (use the T or the B setting).
4. Open or remove the camera back.
5. Place an appropriate close-up attachment over the lens.
6. Set a piece of ground glass, frosted plastic, or tracing paper in the camera at the film position. Make certain the material is cut to fit over the opening and will lie flat. You will view and focus on this surface. See the illustration.

7. Set the material to be copied on the stand under the camera and switch on the lights.

8. Fill the image area with an image of the subject by moving the camera up and down on the stand. Focus, as necessary, by adjusting the distance setting on the lens. The image will be *upside down* as compared with the copy position.

9. When the picture is framed properly and sharply focused, mark the camera position on the stand and make a record of the distance setting indicated on the focusing ring for the close-up attachment used. See the illustration for marks of camera position; letters or numbers may be used.

10. On the base of the copy stand outline the area being photographed and relate it (by letter or number) to the camera position and the distance setting.

11. Repeat steps 7 to 10 for subjects of various sizes. Thus you rule on the stand platform a series of areas and you relate them to corresponding camera positions, distance setting, and close-up attachments.

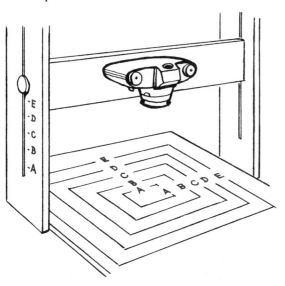

glass (available from photo-supply, art-supply, or hardware stores).

- For close-up filming of three-dimensional subjects, avoid most shadow areas by using *flat lighting* (that is, use a key-to-fill light ratio of 1 to 1).

- Use a meter to determine exposure. An incident-light meter gives a direct reading when placed in the position of the subject or material. If you use a reflected-light meter, read either from a gray card (Eastman Kodak's neutral test card) or from a sheet of white bond paper held against the main portion of the subject. Because such paper reflects a large portion of the light, a reading from it will be *5 times too high*. To correct for this high reading, divide the exposure index of the film by 5 and set your meter at the closest value (example: Kodachrome II Type A, exposure index 40, set meter at $40 \div 5$, that is, at 8).

- Select camera settings with lens-diaphragm opening of $f/11$ or $f/16$ to insure adequate depth of field (but note the exception on page 83 in order to keep the shutter speed faster than 1 second).

- *Remember:* You must have the copyright holder's permission to reproduce copyrighted materials (see page 47).

12. Return the camera to normal (remove the material for focusing, close the shutter, and replace the back).

13. Thereafter, with film in the camera, use the marked positions and the recorded distance settings for copying flat materials of various sizes; it will not be necessary to use the viewfinder.

Suggestions for close-up and copy work

- Use a tripod or a sturdy stand to steady your camera.
- Use either photoflood lamps in reflectors or lamps with built-in reflectors. For copying set the lamps evenly at 45-degree angles to each side of the camera and at a sufficient distance to avoid uneven lighting or "hot spots." Check for evenness of lighting with your meter.
- When copying from a book or other source that does not lie flat, hold the material in position with a sheet of non-reflecting

Filming titles

Titles are handled as is other copy work.

If a mask was used to frame the original art work, align the camera on the copy stand to take in the open area of the mask (see page 91). Remove the mask. Then proceed with routine copying of materials made to its size and format.

If a mask was not used to prepare the lettering, adjust picture size by raising or lowering the camera. Keep in mind that acceptable legibility requires lettering size to be a minimum of one-fiftieth the height of the projected area. (See pages 99–100 for description of legibility standards.)

Titles to appear over a special background as *white-letter overprints* may require double exposure (see page 109 for preparation of art work). First film the background slightly dark (one-half to one *f/* stop underexposed). Then on the same negative without advancing the film, expose the lettering. Many cameras permit double-exposing, but check yours before trying this technique.

Now, test what you have learned about close-up and copy work:

1. Of the cameras described at the beginning of this chapter (pages 65–67), with which ones would you expect to have a parallax problem in viewing?
2. If a close-up lens is used over the regular camera lens, need there be a calculation for change in exposure? Would this also be true if a bellows extension was used?
3. In close-up work is a *larger* or *smaller f/* number desirable? Does this mean that a *slower* or a *faster* shutter speed is used? Therefore, a tripod or stand·is or *is not* essential?
4. Explain how a reflected light meter can be used with a sheet of white paper to determine exposure for copying. In such a situation, what setting for exposure index (film speed) is made on the meter for Ektachrome-X film having a rated exposure index of 20 (tungsten)?

PROCESSING FILM

[See Appendix A for film correlated with this topic.]

You may choose, for convenience, to send exposed film to a commercial film-processing laboratory for developing and even for printing. But in recent years the processing of both black-and-white and color films has been greatly simplified by easy-to-handle equipment and easy-to-follow methods.

Facilities and equipment

- Light-tight room or light-free closet for film loading (a daylight-loading tank eliminates this need)
- Sink with running water and counter-top working area
- Clean, ventilated area for film drying
- Roll-film developing tank with one or more reels for the film

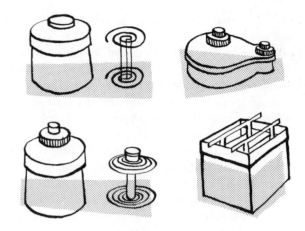

size being used or one or more tanks and film holders for cut film
- Prepared chemicals for processing film
- Graduate or other calibrated measuring container and a funnel
- Thermometer
- Timer or watch with second hand
- 3 to 6 stoppered bottles, preferably of brown-tinted glass

Black-and-white film

Practice loading an old roll of film onto the reel of your tank (see suggestions on the instruction sheet with the tank) until you can do it smoothly. Then, *in the dark,* load and thread the film to be processed. Place the reel in the tank and cap it. From here on do all processing under normal room light.

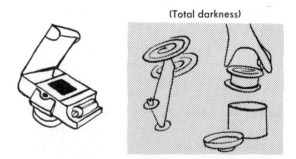

(Total darkness)

Unload camera　　Thread film on reel　　Set reel in tank

The purpose served by each step in the process is:

- *Developer*—acts upon the exposed silver chemicals in the film that have been affected by light during picture-taking, depositing the silver as tiny grains to form the black silver image of the negative.
- *Rinse*—removes excess developer from the film.
- *Fixer*—sets the image by changing the remaining undeveloped silver chemical so that it may be removed.
- *Washing*—removes all chemicals which may cause discoloration of the negative or deposits on its surface.

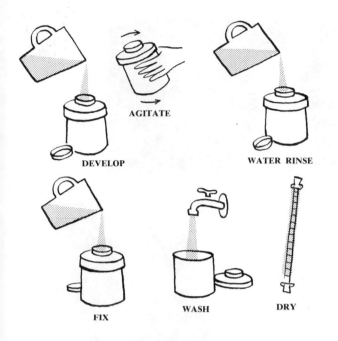

DEVELOP   AGITATE   WATER RINSE

FIX   WASH   DRY

Refer to the information sheet packaged with your film for recommended developer and for specific processing instructions. Follow all directions, especially those for time and temperature controls.

A one-step processing procedure for black-and-white film is available which uses a combined developer-fixer solution called a *monobath*. The developing and fixing actions occur simultaneously, very much as does the processing of Polaroid film. The presently available monobaths are limited to processing only certain emulsions. Therefore this product is, as yet, not widely used.

Judge the quality of your negative by these points:[1]

• A good negative will have a considerable amount of detail, even in its very darkest and lightest portions, unless these portions represent parts of the picture which were themselves entirely lacking in detail.

• A good negative will be transparent enough, even in its very blackest areas, so that you can read a newspaper through it.

• A good negative will have no part of the picture quite as clear as are the borders of the film.

Color negative film

Kodacolor and Ektacolor films can be processed by a film laboratory or with a color processing kit. Processing time in a tank is under one hour with careful timing and critical temperature control (the first step requires a constant temperature of $75°F \pm ½°F$ and the remaining nine steps permit a $4°F$ range).

[1] Adapted from *Basic Developing, Printing, and Enlarging*, Publication AJ-2, Eastman Kodak Co.

The procedure is as follows:

75° F.±1/2°   73 to 77° F.

1. DEVELOPER (14 MINUTES)   2. STOP BATH (4 MINUTES)   3. HARDENER (4 MINUTES)

4. WASH (4 MINUTES)   5   5. BLEACH (6 MINUTES)   6. WASH (4 MINUTES)

7. FIXER (8 MINUTES)   8. WASH (8 MINUTES)   9. WETTING AGENT (1 MINUTE)   10. DRY

Color reversal film

All color reversal films, except Kodachrome, may be "home" processed. Kodachrome is handled only by authorized processing laboratories. As with color negative films, processing kits allow handling of one or more rolls in normal room light with the film in a light-tight tank during the initial part of the process. Here again temperature and timing must be carefully maintained. As an example, the procedure for Ektachrome roll film is illustrated.

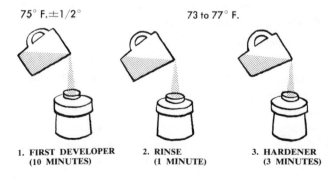

75° F.±1/2°   73 to 77° F.

1. FIRST DEVELOPER (10 MINUTES)   2. RINSE (1 MINUTE)   3. HARDENER (3 MINUTES)

4. WASH
(3 MINUTES)

5. REVERSAL
EXPOSURE

6. COLOR DEVELOPER
(15 MINUTES)

7. WASH
(5 MINUTES)

8. CLEARING BATH
(5 MINUTES)

9. RINSE
(1 MINUTE)

10. BLEACH
(8 MINUTES)

11. RINSE
(1 MINUTE)

12. FIXING BATH
(4 MINUTES)

13. WASH
(8 MINUTES)

14. STABILIZER
(1 MINUTE)

15. DRY

Negative

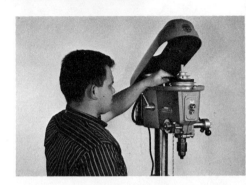

Contact Print

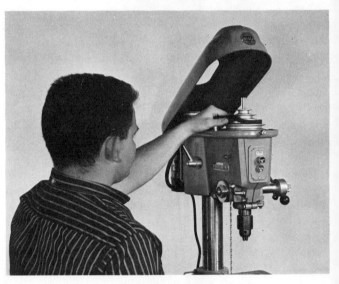

Enlarged Print

MAKING PRINTS

[See Appendix A for film correlated with this topic.]

For successful contact printing and enlarging you may need to know about:

- The selection of contact and enlarging papers (printing papers are classified by speed, weight, finish, contrast, color of image, and base material)
- Exposure—length of time for contact printing; lens-diaphragm opening and length of time for enlarging
- Processing chemicals and times
- Washing, drying, and finishing

More detailed information about printing will be found in the references on page 234. Your photo-supply dealer can advise you on equipment, printing papers, and chemicals.

The negative is used to prepare a positive print on paper or film. *If the print is to be the same size as the negative* the process is *contact printing*, but *if the print is to be larger than the negative* the process is *enlarging*.

After the print material is exposed to light, the photographic paper from either contact printing or enlarging can follow the same general chemical treatment as for film—develop, stop, fix, and wash (for a paper print a paper developer is used in place of the film developer).

A new two-step *rapid processing* method for paper is becoming popular. This method takes only a few seconds for developing and fixing exposed paper. It also eliminates the need for an extensive darkroom and most equipment, other than the enlarger and processing unit. In this method, known as *photo stabilization*, part of the developing agents required are built into the photographic paper. The paper is carried automatically in timed sequence by a system of rollers, first through the developer and then through a *stabilizer* bath. The paper emerges damp-dry. The stabilizer arrests development and stabilizes the image (the chemistry is similar to but not exactly the same as fixing with hypo). Thus, processing is automatically accomplished in a matter of seconds. Although the resulting print will not fade for a long time, it is recommended for greater permanence, that a print processed by this method be fixed in regular hypo and then thoroughly washed and dried. In addition to various kinds of photographic papers, high-contrast and continuous-tone sheet films are available for use in the photo-stabilization process.

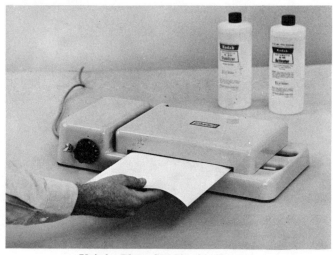

Unit for Photo-Stabilization Process

Printing color negatives is still a relatively difficult and time-consuming process, although new developments can be expected to simplify it. Refer to the instruction sheet packaged with the processing chemicals and the color printing paper for further details.

Facilities and equipment

The standard equipment and materials for a darkroom consist of:

- a darkroom 6 feet by 8 feet or larger, equipped with running water, counter-top workspace, storage, and electrical outlets
- a contact printer or printing frame
- an enlarger with easel and timer
- a print washer or tray siphon
- a print dryer
- one or more sets of trys (3 to a set) in various sizes (8"×10", 11"×14", and so on)
- clock, tongs, and miscellaneous small items
- one or more safelights (with color filter based on printing paper to be used)

- photographic contact and enlarging paper
- prepared chemicals for developer, stop bath, and fixer

Contact printing

This method is particularly useful for rapid preparation of *proof sheets* from negatives. A whole roll of negatives (12 to 36) can be printed at one time on a sheet of contact paper (8"×10"). From these contact prints negatives may be selected for enlargements.

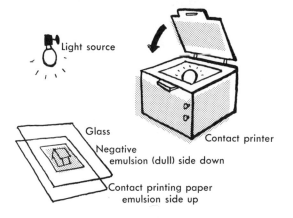

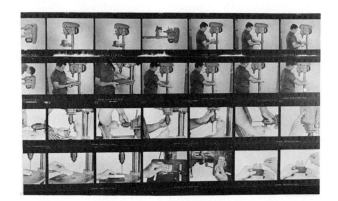

Light source

Glass

Negative emulsion (dull) side down

Contact printer

Contact printing paper emulsion side up

Place the negative (emulsion or *dull side down*) on top of a sheet of photographic contact paper (emulsion or *shiny side up*); cover them with glass and expose the pack to light. Or use a contact printer with a pressure platen and a built-in lamp for exposing. Develop the paper. The resulting print will be the same size as the negative.

Enlarging

Place the negative in the enlarger and project it through the lens onto a sheet of enlarging paper. Make tests on strips of paper before preparing the final prints.

Now, test what you have learned about processing film and making prints:

1. What are the four steps necessary to develop black-and-white film and the purpose of each step?
2. What are some characteristics of a good black-and-white negative?
3. In what ways and with what materials do the four steps in tray processing of black-and-white photographic paper differ from those in developing of black-and-white film?
4. Sketch your own layout for a darkroom, showing location of the equipment and necessary supplies.
5. What purpose is often served by making contact prints of a roll of black-and-white negatives?
6. What are two advantages of using the photo-stabilization process for processing paper over the regular tray process?

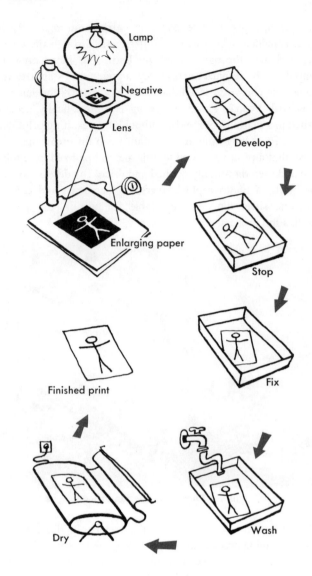

16. Graphics

In preparing your audiovisual materials you may find it necessary to:

- *Plan* art work and titles in terms of size, proportions, and principles of design.
- *Draw* illustrations, diagrams, cartoons, and title backgrounds.
- *Color* art work to clarify details or to give emphasis and add attractiveness.
- *Letter* titles, captions, and labels which comply with recognized legibility standards.
- *Mount* photographs, pictures, and related materials for durability, ease of handling, and attractive display.
- *Protect* the surface of materials to insure long use when handled.
- *Reproduce* materials on paper for distribution, using the most appropriate of a number of methods.

The success of many audiovisual materials can be attributed in large measure to the quality and effectiveness of the art work and related graphic materials. These are achieved through organizing preliminary thoughts, through careful planning, and then through applying the techniques outlined in this chapter.

Many persons who develop audiovisual materials have little or no professional art background. They need not therefore prepare amateurish and poor-quality graphic materials. First, they can consider a number of common-sense practical suggestions and guiding principles, then apply them as the need arises. Second, there are a number of easy-to-use manipulative devices that, with little practice, will insure semi-professional quality results.

PLANNING ART WORK

Your art work must be planned with consideration for the size and dimensions of the working area, for proportions of your visual materials, for design and layout features, for backgrounds, and for the resources, skills, techniques, materials, and facilities that you can employ.

Size of working area

Decide on the size for your art work so it meets these requirements:

- Lettering and drawing can be done easily.
- Parallax and close-up difficulties in the camera, if there are any, can be easily overcome when copying (see page 82).
- The art work is easy to store.

The minimum dimension that is likely to meet these requirements is 10″×12″; therefore use cardboard of this size or larger. You can cut boards 11″×14″ without waste from standard-size 22″×28″ sheets, which may be had in 8-ply or 14-ply thickness. Commonly used working areas, on boards of either size, are 6¾″×9″ and 9″×12″; minimum lettering sizes for these areas are suggested on pages 99–100. Compose within the proper proportions (see below) of your selected audiovisual materials, and provide generous margins around the sides of all work.

The end sheets inside the front cover of this book contain recommended mask sizes for filmstrips and slides. The end sheets inside the back cover have diagrams for masks to use with overhead transparencies and motion-picture formats.

If many scenes require art work and lettering, standardize your size and prepare a mask with a cut-out of the proper working area. The mask will serve as a margin and as a frame when you view the prepared art work and will also be useful as a guide for positioning art work and camera during copying.

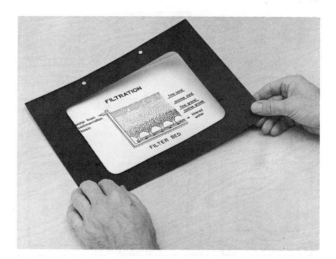

If titles, labels, or diagrams must be placed one over the other or over a background, you need equipment to hold them in *alignment* or *register*. If you need to make only a few such graphics, you may be able to work on an ordinary drawing board with thumbtacks. If you have any quantity of work, a *register board* will save time. Use a two- or three-hole punch to perforate your drawing materials at the edge, and put two or three pegs or pins in the drawing board to fit these perforations snugly while allowing the work to lie smooth and flat. This register board can be used both during preparation of the materials and also when filming the final assembly. A two- or three-ring binder may serve instead of a register board for work that does not require precise alignment.

Proportions of audiovisual materials

• Photographs—commonly 4:5, but may vary depending on size for final use.

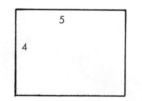

• Slides

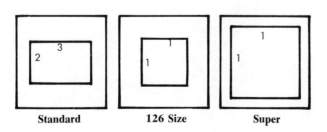

| Standard | 126 Size | Super |

• Filmstrips

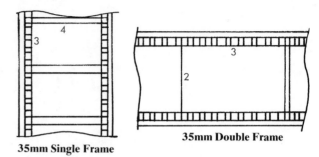

35mm Single Frame   **35mm Double Frame**

• Overhead transparencies—usually 4:5

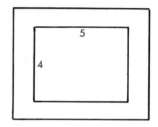

• Motion pictures

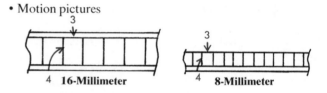

16-Millimeter   **8-Millimeter**

• Television materials

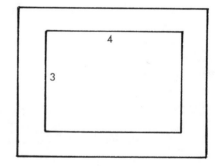

Design and layout

[See Appendix A for film correlated with this topic.]

Examine some of the graphic materials that are a common part of your everyday world—magazine advertisements, outdoor billboards, animated cartoons, television titles and commercials, and so on. You can find many ideas for designing your own materials by studying the arrangement of elements within such commercial displays.

You may be planning a title for a slide series, for a filmstrip, or for a motion picture; or your plans may deal with art work for a chart, a diagram, a poster, or even an instructional bulletin board. In these and other planning situations you should be aware of certain design principles and visual design tools. Then be prepared to apply those that can help you.

Design *principles* include: simplicity, unity, emphasis, and balance.

• Simplicity

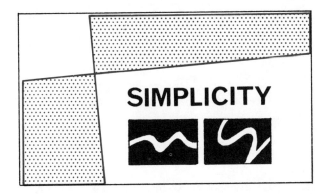

Charts, graphs, and diagrams suitable for page printing may not be suitable for projection. They can include large amounts of information and be acceptable in a printed report or for a manual, but these permit detailed, close-up study which is not usually possible with projected materials. Thus a cutting from a publication, used in a slide, might be so complex it would be confusing. Therefore, evaluate the suitability of all items you consider for inclusion in your visual materials and try to limit your selection or design to the presentation of one idea at a time.

Generally speaking, the fewer elements into which a given space is divided, the more pleasing it is to the eye. Subdivide or redesign lengthy or complex data into a number of easy-to-read and easy-to-understand related materials. Limit the verbal content for projected visuals to 15 or 20 words.

Drawings should be bold, simple, and contain only key details. Picture symbols should be outlined with a heavy line. The necessary details can be added in thinner lines since they should appear less important. Many thin lines, particularly if they are not essential, may actually confuse the clarity of the image when viewed from a distance.

Finally, for simplicity use simple, easy-to-comprehend lettering styles and a minimum of different styles in the same visual or series of visuals.

• Unity

Unity is the relationship among the elements of a visual so they all function together. It can be achieved by overlapping elements, by using pointing devices like arrows, and by employing the visual tools (line, shape, color, texture, and space) described below.

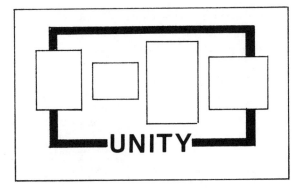

• Emphasis

Even though a visual treats a single idea, is simply developed, and has unity, there is often the need to give emphasis to a single element—to make it the center of interest and attention. Through the use of size, relationships, perspective, and such visual tools as color or space, emphasis can be given to the most important elements.

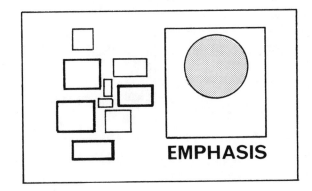

• Balance

There are two kinds of balance—formal and informal. Formal balance is identified by an imaginary axis running through the center of the visual dividing the design so that one half will be the mirror reflection of the other half. Such a formal balance is static.

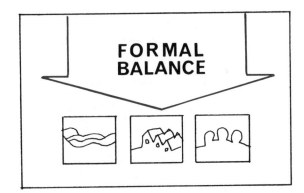

Informal balance is asymmetrical; the elements create an equilibrium without being static. It is a dynamic and more attention-getting arrangement. It requires more imagination and daring by the designer. The informal balance may have an asymmetrical or a diagonal layout.

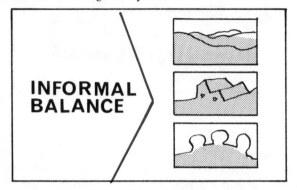

For titles, a symmetrical balance of lettering is formal in effect and is desired for many uses. It requires accurate positioning of letters and extra care when filming to insure even margins (equal side margins, but a somewhat greater area at the bottom than at the top).

Informal arrangements, when appropriately combined with sketches or pictures, make attractive titles. Such arrangements eliminate the problem of centering but not the problem of accurate positioning.

Try various arrangements before doing the final lettering.

The *visual tools* that contribute to the successful use of the above design principles include line, shape, color, texture, and space.

• Line

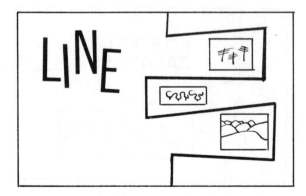

A line in a visual can connect elements together and will direct the viewer to study the visual in a specific sequence.

• Shape

An unusual shape can give special interest to a visual.

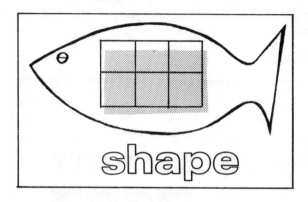

• Space

Open space around visual elements and words will prevent a crowded feeling. Only when space is used carefully can the elements of design become effective.

• Texture

Texture can be used in much the same way as color—to give emphasis or separation, or to enhance unity.

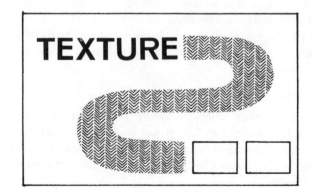

• Color

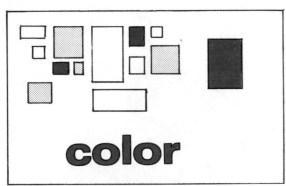

Color is an important adjunct to most visuals, but it should be used sparingly for best effects. Apply it to elements of a visual to give separation or emphasis, or to enhance unity. Select colors that are harmonious together because colors that are dissonant (of equal intensity and complementary on the color wheel, like orange—blue and red—green) create annoyance in the audience and consequently interfere with a clear perception of the message.

Now, review what you have learned about planning art work:

1. What is a satisfactory size for a working surface on which to prepare art work?
2. Which audiovisual materials have a 4:3 proportion? Which a 3:2 proportion?
3. Enumerate the four principles of design and the five visual tools for design.

ILLUSTRATING

[See Appendix A for film correlated with this topic.]

In addition to photographed subjects, your script may require illustrations made as original drawings or as copies of available pictures. If you have an art background you will have little difficulty in preparing such illustrations. If you do not have this ability, you can resort to a number of easy-to-apply methods.

Using ready-made pictures

Pictures from magazines, from free or inexpensive booklets, or from similar sources can serve your needs for some illustrations. If you maintain a file of clipped pictures (*tearsheets*) on various subjects, you may have suitable pictures as called for in your script. At times part of a picture or combined sections of two or more pictures may be needed. Mount pictures on cardboard (see pages 110–116) and add lettering if it is appropriate (see pages 100-108). And remember, always, that such pictures may be copyright and that to use them you may need the permission of the copyright holder (see page 47).

For certain general uses *clip-book* pictures are ideal. Clip books on many subjects are available commercially (see the list on page 238 for sources). Each book contains a variety of black-and-white line drawings, on paper or on translucent material. These may be cut from the page or, frequently, duplicated; pictures or copies are then combined with suitable lettering in paste-ups (see page 121) to make titles or visuals. To use these, reproduce them with a photocopy or similar machine (page 125), or photograph them using high-contrast film (page 181) and print the negative as a slide or transparency on film (page 182) or as a print on photographic paper (see page 90).

If a picture cannot be used directly or easily reproduced, you can place a sheet of translucent tracing paper over the picture and outline the main lines with a pencil. Then transfer the tracing to cardboard or other material by backing the tracing paper with a sheet of carbon paper and tracing over the lines.

Enlarging and reducing pictures

There are a number of machines, simple devices, and hand techniques you might consider using to change the size of available diagrams. We will examine five of them.

A small picture on a single sheet or in a book can be enlarged by using an *opaque projector*. Place the paper or book on the holder of the projector and attach a piece of cardboard to a wall. Adjust the size of the projected picture to fit the required area on the cardboard by moving the projector *closer* to the cardboard (*to be smaller*) or *farther away* from the cardboard (*to be larger*) and focusing as necessary. Then trace the main lines of the projected picture with pencil. After completing the drawing, ink in the lines using pen and ink or a felt pen. This is one of the easiest and quickest ways to enlarge a picture.

If a transparency or a slide of the original diagram is available or can be made by one of the processes to be described later in this book, an overhead projector or a slide projector can be used to make an enlargement.

But also with the *overhead projector,* large pictures can be *reduced* to fit 8½″×11″ or other formats. This technique uses the overhead projector in reverse fashion as compared to its normal enlarging use. The original, large diagram is attached to a wall and a light (floodlight or a slide projector) is aimed at it. Sufficient light must be reflected from the diagram through the lens of the projector to be visible on a white sheet of paper placed on the projection stage. Move the lens up and down to focus the image on the paper. Control the size by moving the whole projector closer to the wall or farther from it. Sketch the visual over the image on the sheet of paper.

Another device, especially designed for enlarging and reducing art work, is the *photo modifier.* It resembles a large view camera (page 66) with a ground-glass back against which tracing paper can be taped. The size of the original picture can be reduced or enlarged in accurate proportion by moving the device and then focusing the image by adjusting the bellows. Perspective can be changed and distortion created by tilting the ground-glass surface or the front lens.

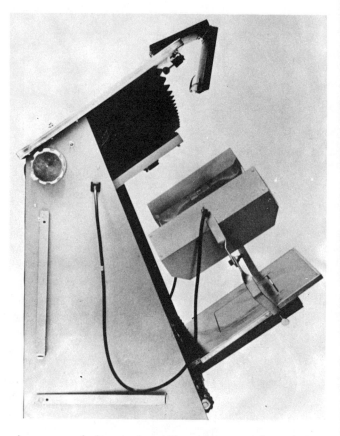

A *pantograph* also may be used to enlarge or reduce pictures. It is operated by setting a fulcrum pin, tracing the lines of the picture with one point, and reproducing them in the desired proportion (larger or smaller) with a pen or pencil at another point.

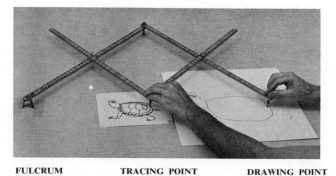

FULCRUM   TRACING POINT   DRAWING POINT

By using *the squaring method,* a picture can be proportionally enlarged or reduced or even elongated and distorted purposefully. First prepare a grid on acetate or translucent tracing paper. The size of each square is determined by the size and detail in the picture (use at least 4 or 5 squares in height or width to cover the picture). Then make a second grid with squares proportionally larger or smaller than the first one (for a 2× enlargement the squares of the second grid should be twice the dimension of those of the first grid). Place the first grid over the picture and copy the relative position of each line onto a piece of translucent paper placed over the second grid.

If you want a copy relatively higher or wider than the original, use rectangles instead of squares on your copy grid—tall or wide according to your wishes for the changed picture.

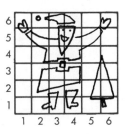

Now, review what you have learned about illustrating for visual materials:

1. What is a "clip-book" and how is it used?
2. List four methods for changing the size of illustrations and compare them as to ease of use, time and equipment required, and probable quality of results.

COLORING AND SHADING

The attractiveness of a black-and-white line drawing is greatly enhanced by the addition of shading or coloring.

Using certain color combinations or coloring selected parts will contribute emphasis and even clarification to a complex diagram. For example, since yellow and orange are colors of high visibility, black lines on a yellow or orange background will command more attention than will black on white.

Those who have art backgrounds may be able to use such techniques as wash drawing and air brushing; even those with limited training may consider using several simple techniques.

Felt pens

[See Appendix A for film correlated with this topic.]

When strips of felt are cut, beveled to an edge, and mounted in a holder, they become printing and drawing tools called *felt pens*. Colored lines of various thicknesses can be made. Some felt pens are refillable and need not be discarded when the ink supply runs out. Inks for use in felt pens may be either permanent or washable and they are available in a variety of colors. Felt pens are useful for coloring small areas. Since the colors are transparent, apply them carefully; each overlapping stroke deepens the tone and may produce uneven coloring in large areas.

Colored pencils and chalk

Ordinary colored pencils, when handled with care, can produce pleasing color effects. Keep the pencil sharp but hold it at a flat angle when stroking, being sure to work back and forth in only two directions. After coloring an area, rub over it with a small piece of blotter or with a stump of rolled paper. Rubbing helps to spread the color evenly over the whole area.

Chalk (often dampened with water) can be used in much the same way as pencils, although chalk adheres better to a coarse surface like construction paper. To prevent smudging of either pencil- or chalk-colored art work, spray a fixative coating over the surface.

Spray-can paints and air brushing

Paint in pressurized cans can be used to apply color to areas on a visual. This technique is also used to color cardboard around three-dimensional letters which are removed, after spraying, to reveal the unpainted image of the letters. By controlling the distance between the spray can and the surface to be sprayed, either a spatter effect or an even paint coverage can be achieved. Protect parts of the visual not to be colored by covering with paper attached with masking tape.

Carefully controlled color spraying can be done with an *air brush* attached to a compressed-air line or to a pressurized-air

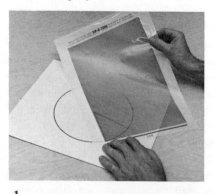

can. By adjusting the air-brush nozzle and depressing the control knob the spread of spray is controlled. As with the spray-can paints, it is necessary to cover parts of a visual around the area to be colored.

Color and shading sheets

[See Appendix A for film correlated with this topic.]

Prepared color and shading sheets are excellent for use on areas of any size. They are available in a wide range of patterns and colors, both transparent and translucent. They will adhere to all surfaces.

Translucent color sheets have an adhesive wax backing which makes them partially opaque. Such sheets should be used to color art work prepared on cardboard. Transparent color sheets are prepared with a clear adhesive backing so the color will project brilliantly when applied to a transparency or to other visuals for projection.

The shading or color is printed on a thin plastic sheet which has an adhesive backing. This in turn is protected with a backing sheet. To work with these sheets, use a razor blade or a very sharp knife and follow the procedure illustrated.

1. Place a sheet of the selected material over the area to be shaded or colored.
2. Lightly cut a piece slightly larger than the area to be colored or shaded. (Try not to cut through the backing sheet.)
3. Peel the cut piece from the backing.
4. Place the cut piece of adhesive-backed material over the area and rub to adhere.
5. Cut to match the area, using lines in the diagram as guides.
6. Peel off the excess pieces of the coloring or shading material.

Now, review what you have learned about coloring and shading:

1. How might the use of felt pens compare to the use of spray paints for coloring moderate-sized areas?
2. When using a color adhesive sheet why is it *not* proper to cut through the color sheet *and* the backing sheet when first cutting the piece for use? Also, why should you *not* cut the piece to be used the exact size at first?
3. Of the coloring methods described, which one might be selected to carefully tint a large, irregular area.

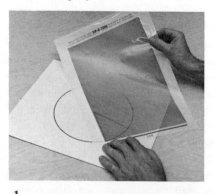

1

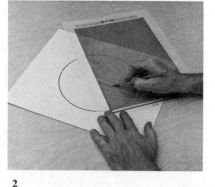

2

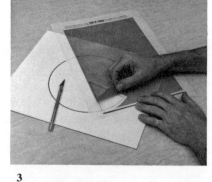

3

4

5

6

LEGIBILITY STANDARDS FOR LETTERING

The legibility of the words, numerals, and other data that an audience is expected to read is frequently neglected during the planning and preparation of visual materials. This neglect is especially common since simple and quick methods have become available for duplicating typewritten and printed materials. But it is very important that planners give proper attention to legibility—hence to methods of lettering, sizes of letters, and styles of lettering. These matters physically control the amount of information that can be presented in one visual unit. Reciprocally, the psychological limits on amount of information affect the choices in respect to lettering. Keep in mind, therefore, the methods for dividing lengthy or complex data into a sequence of visuals; see the discussion of layout and design, page 164.

The suitability of lettering is further complicated by a number of other factors—characteristics of the projection room, such as its shape; the type of screen surface (rear-screen transmitted projection is not as brilliant as front-screen reflected projection and will require larger lettering for legibility); the brightness of the projection lamp to be used; and the amount of ambient or outside light that cannot be controlled.

If your audiovisual materials are designed for use in a specific room, then take into account as many of these factors as possible in deciding on lettering sizes. But no one can predict or be prepared for all eventualities in viewing situations. Often visuals must be presented under less than ideal conditions, therefore it is advisable that *minimum standards* be recognized. As a general guide, select minimum lettering size for *all* materials so that any member of an audience, seated at an anticipated maximum viewing distance, can easily read titles, captions, and labels.

To assist with good legibility, the following guidelines are recommended:

• Select a readable letter style, like a sans-serif or gothic type, in which all letters are easily recognized with a minimum of confusion. Avoid script letter styles because they are difficult to read.

MANY BUYERS	A Sans Serif-Letter
MANY BUYERS	A Condensed Sans Serif
MANY BUYERS	A Modern Letter with Serifs
Many Buyers	A Script Letter
𝕸𝖆𝖓𝖞 𝕭𝖚𝖞𝖊𝖗𝖘	An Old English Letter

Some Common Lettering Styles Arranged According to Their Legibility (Most Legible at Top and Decreasing Downward)

• Use capital letters for short titles and labels, but for longer captions and phrases (six words or more) use lower-case letters with appropriate capitals since the lower-case letters are more easily read.

• Space letters *optically*. Equal measured distances between all letters do not look equal. *Make spaces look equal*, regardless of measurement.

Good   Poor

• Allow 1½ letter widths for the space between words and 3 widths between sentences. Too much or too little space again makes reading difficult.
• Separate lines within a caption so that adequate white space is left for ease of reading—about 1½ times the height of the lower-case letter m, measured from an m on one line to an m (or comparable letter) on the next line.

San Jose State College,
the first public institution
of higher education in
California, was founded
in 1857.   **Too Close**

San Jose State College,

the first public institution

of higher education in

California, was founded

in 1857.   **Too Far**

San Jose State College,

the first public institution

of higher education in

California, was founded

in 1857.   **Good**

Nonprojected materials

For display materials follow these recommendations:

Maximum anticipated viewing distance	Minimum letter height (lower-case letter m)
8 feet	¼ inch
16 feet	½ inch
32 feet	1 inch
64 feet	2 inches

Capital letters, alone or with lower-case, should be correspondingly larger because they are less legible.

Projected materials

For slides, filmstrips, transparencies, and motion pictures, minimum letter size also is based on the maximum anticipated viewing distance. This maximum, as a standard, is accepted as being *six times the horizontal dimension of the picture on the screen* (that is, 6W). Thus, for a screen 6 feet wide, filled with a picture, the maximum viewing distance of 6W is 36 feet.

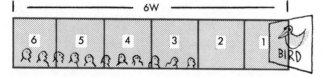

Rear-screen projection does not permit as bright or as contrasty an image as does front projection. For suitable legibility lettering half again as large as for front projection is required for rear-screen projected materials.[1]

The maximum viewing distance for television, in terms of the screen size, is greater, being 12W. As you might expect, minimum letter size for television is therefore greater.

Minimum letter sizes are recommended in a table:[2]

Medium	Maximum viewing distance	Ratio of letter height to height of art-work area	Minimum letter height (lower-case letter m)	
			For area 6¾"×9"	For area 9"×12"
Slides Filmstrips Transparencies Motion pictures	6W	1 to 50	.13"	.18"
Television	12W	1 to 25	.27"	.36"

---

[1] For further discussion see *Space for Audiovisual Large Group Instruction,* University Facilities Research Center, University of Wisconsin, Madison, 1964.

[2] Adapted from *Legibility Standards for Projected Materials,* pamphlet S-4, Eastman Kodak Company.

As the table suggests, captions for slides to be used on a screen 6 feet wide in a room 36 feet or 6W deep, prepared within a 9"×12" work area, would require lettering at least .18" or 1/5" in height. This is 1/50 times the vertical dimension of the working area.

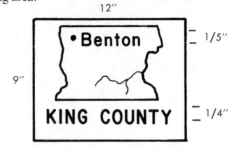

You can make a rough test for the legibility of lettered materials for projection by first measuring the width of the art work in inches, then dividing this number by 2 and placing the material that many feet away from a test reader. If he reads the lettering easily, then for normal conditions the material, when projected, will be legible. But don't trust yourself as a test reader if you prepared the lettering or know how it should read—your memory may help your vision too much.

Now, review what you have learned about legibility standards for lettering:

1. What is the single most important reason why legibility standards must be considered for projected materials?
2. How might you relate the degree of legibility to quantity of information possible in a visual?
3. What are four guidelines that will contribute to good legibility in lettering?
4. What is the minimum letter size for materials displayed at the front of an average-sized classroom—30 feet deep?
5. What minimum-size lettering should be used in the direct preparation of a transparency (7½ inches vertical dimension)?
6. Should visuals for television use be lettered larger, smaller, or the same size as materials for regular classroom use?
7. Does rear-screen projection require larger or smaller lettering than comparable front-screen projection?

LETTERING FOR TITLES

However good the photography and picture content of visual materials, their effectiveness is enhanced by well-appearing titles, captions, and labels. Neat lettering, simple designs, and attractive colors or background patterns all add a professional touch to your materials.

Titles generally require large and bold letters. Since there are relatively few major titles, their letters may be hand-drawn, or set individually in place by hand. But such methods may be too slow for preparing captions that consist of many words; here other lettering techniques are appropriate, adequate, even better. You need to know and select techniques with regard to the results needed and the time available for preparation of your materials.

Some remarks follow concerning nine specific lettering techniques. Many more techniques exist, and still more will be devised by ingenious workers using new ideas and new materials. No one technique is necessarily the best for any lettering job. You need to evaluate as many of them as you can—for your own needs, in respect to availability, cost, ease of use, time required for preparation, and resulting quality.

Boldface typewriter lettering

Lettering typed on a boldface typewriter is good for captions requiring many words. It is satisfactory for titles and subtitles. Its legibility is superior to that of the pica or elite type on regular office typewriters unless the latter is photographed and enlarged. Use paper of good quality, whether white or colored, and a carbon-paper ribbon or a well-inked cloth ribbon. Have the type clean and strike the keys firmly and uniformly to get sharp, even, black impressions.

Three-dimensional letters

Three-dimensional letters are manufactured in cardboard, wood, cork, ceramics, and plastics and are available in plain backs or pin backs. They are excellent for main titles, and when photographed with side lighting they give shadow effects and three-dimensional effects. Costs vary widely according to kind and size. Surfaces can be tinted with paint or water colors. Position the letters against a T-square or on a guide line and adhere temporarily with rubber cement.

Construction-paper punch-out letters

Inexpensive ready-to-use letters, cut out of white or colored paper, in many styles, colors, and sizes, are easy to manipulate and are satisfactory for bold titles. They may be placed over any background. To align them neatly, use a T-square or lightly rule a guide line on the mounting material. Arrange the letters and attach them with a small amount of rubber cement or other adhesive. Finally, erase the guide line.

Gummed-back paper cut-out letters

[See Appendix A for film correlated with this topic.]

Manufacturers supply complete alphabets of cut-out letters with gummed backs. They are similar in effect and method of use to other cut-out letters, and are suitable for titles and labels on many types of backgrounds. Position the letters on guide lines, then fix them on the background after moistening the adhesive on the back with a sponge dipped in water. Be careful not to get water on the front side of letters as some colors run.

Dry-transfer letters

[See Appendix A for film correlated with this topic.]

These letters have sharp, clean edges much like those printed from good type, and are easy to handle. They come in sheets of many sizes, styles, and colors. They are excellent for titles and labels—on many types of backgrounds.

Dry-transfer letters are printed on the back of the sheet and each sheet is backed with a protective sheet of paper. It is important to keep this backing sheet behind the letters except when exposing a portion of the letter sheet for use.

Follow this procedure in using dry-transfer letters:

1. Slip the backing sheet below or above the row of letters having the letter to be used.
2. Position the letter by aligning the printed line under the letters over the guideline drawn on the mounting surface.
3. Burnish (rub) the entire letter to the mounting surface with the round part of a pen, or other blunt object on which you can exert pressure without tearing the paper.
4. Slowly pull the sheet of letters from the mounting surface. The letter will remain transferred.
5. After all letters have been transferred replace the backing sheet behind the letter sheet. Then erase the guideline from the mounting surface.

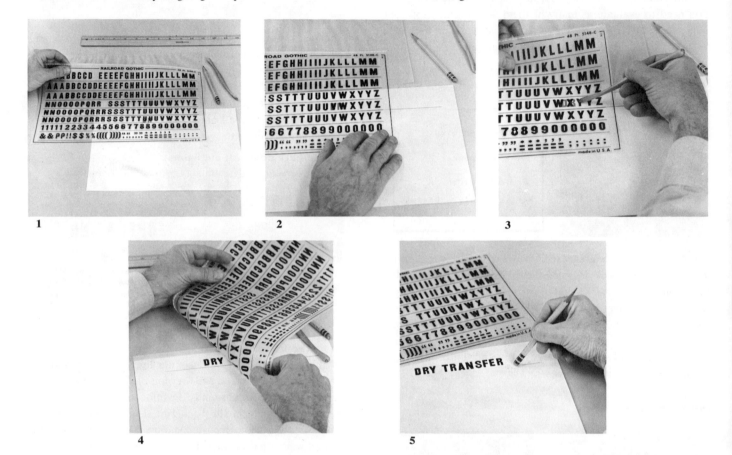

1   2   3

4   5

Dry-transfer letters are available also in transparent colors for direct use on transparencies. When they are adhered to acetate a clean transfer results with no adhesive residue appearing around the letter.

Felt-pen lettering

[See Appendix A for film correlated with this topic.]

The use of the beveled-edge felt pen for coloring has been described on page 97. These same pens can be used for lettering. For successful results:

• Hold the pen firmly in a "locked" or set position in the hand.
• Make no finger or wrist movement. *All* movements consist of arm movements.

Sharp-tipped nylon pens make a thinner mark than do the beveled-felt pens. They are easier to use and are good for quick lettering on all surfaces. The inks in some make permanent marks, but most have water-based inks.

Always replace the cap on a felt or nylon pen as soon as you are done using it. Since their inks dry quickly, uncapped pens will dry out, resulting in a hardened unserviceable tip. If this happens, soak the tip in lighter fluid (permanent-ink pen) or in water (water-based-ink pen).

Stencil lettering guides (Wrico Signmaker)

[See Appendix A for film correlated with this topic.]

Stencil lettering guides are offered in a variety of styles and sizes. The better ones can be used, after a little practice, to produce neat and attractive lettering, even in lengthy captions. They are thus satisfactory, in skilled use excellent, for all lettering needs. Some stencils are designed to be raised off the background and positioned against a metal guide. A special pen is used, which fits and follows the letter outline in the plastic stencil.

Lettering from ½ inch to 4 inches in height can be made with the *Wrico Signmaker* unit. It consists of a *stencil guide,* a *brush pen,* or special *felt pen,* and a *guide holder* to raise the guide from the paper.

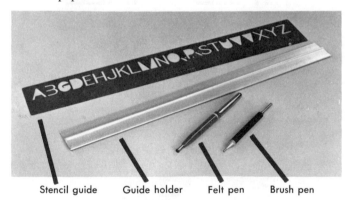

Stencil guide   Guide holder   Felt pen   Brush pen

A stencil guide has this kind of label printed on the lower center part:

(WRICO)
GUIDE No. AVC 100
USE WITH BRUSH PEN C or FELT PEN NCF

These labels give such information as:

AV—letter style (other styles have codes A, D, BF, T, MS)
C—*capital* letters on stencil
L—*lower-case* letters on stencil
N—*numbers* on stencil
Letter size—Wrico Signmaker stencils are based on a code of 100 for 1 inch, 75 for ¾ inch, and the like.
Pen size—Brush pens are coded *A* to *E* with size *A* making the thinnest line. Felt pens are coded *AF* to *EF* with size *AF* making the thinnest line.

1. The letter for the size of a Wrico brush pen is stamped near the tip; on the felt pen the letter is stamped on the barrel. Each stencil guide requires a certain pen size for proper use as indicated on the guide.

2. On the back of the guide holder is an indication of which side to use as based on the pen size the stencil requires. This difference in elevation (look at the edge of the guide holder) is necessary in order to raise the stencil from the paper and avoid the possibility of smearing ink while lettering.

WRICO GUIDE HOLDER No. 18
Use LOW side for guides requiring Brush Pens A and B and Felt Pen BF. ⬆
Use HIGH side for guides requiring all other Brush Pens or Felt Pens.

High side   Low side

3. Align the guideholder on the work. Set the stencil on the guide holder.
4. Hold the brush pen vertically and depress the plunger from the top. You can then see the grooves of the metal "brush" which will hold the ink.

5. Hold the metal collar (located above the black handle shaft) and turn the black shaft so the tip of the brush is flush with the outer tip of the pen. If the brush protrudes

beyond the tip it will scratch the paper. If it is recessed inside the tip ink will not flow to the paper.

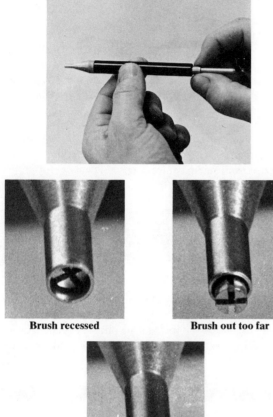

Brush recessed   **Brush out too far**

Brush flush with tip

6. To fill the pen, depress the plunger, then immerse the exposed brush portion so it goes below the ink surface. Then release the plunger. Enough ink is held in the grooves of the brush to make a few letters. Try not to dip the outer tip of the pen itself into the ink but only the extended brush part.

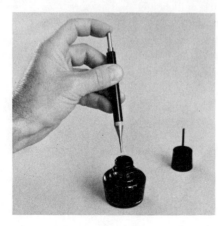

7. Hold the pen in a *vertical position* so the tip is flat on the surface. Move the pen in this position.

8. Go over a letter to make even, crisp lines and get into the corners of the stencil to complete the edges.

ONE   **ONE**

Poor   Good

9. Judge letter spacing according to what looks good. You will improve with practice. When practicing, don't just copy the alphabet; for practice in spacing, letter words.
10. Start near the middle of a stroke and work to the ends. Keep the pen moving to eliminate the globs of ink that collect and fatten ends of strokes and other places where the pen pauses.

TALL   **TALL**

Poor   Good

11. When lettering is completed wash the brush pen under running water. Dry with paper toweling. Do not leave ink in the pen to dry. Always cap a felt pen after use.

Stencil lettering guide (Wricoprint)

[See Appendix A for film correlated with this topic.]

Put drill bit in chuck and tighten with chuck key.

For lettering ½ inch tall and *smaller* use the *Wricoprint* unit. It consists of three parts—a *lettering guide,* a *pen,* and a *lettering pad.* The principle of using the Wricoprint is similar to that of the Signmaker, although the parts are different and the pen is filled in another way.

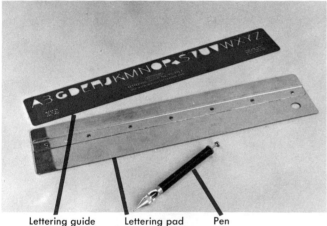

Lettering guide   Lettering pad   Pen

A Wricoprint guide has these labels printed on the lower center and side:

⬭ WRICOPRINT ⬭
LETTERING GUIDE No. VC 1/2 P
USE WITH WRICO LETTERING PAD

FOR USE WITH WRICO PENS No. 3-3A-4-4A-5-5A

These labels give such information as:

V—letter style (the other style is *S* = slant)
C—*capital* letters on guide
L—*lower-case* letters on guide
N—*numbers* on guide
Letter size—Wricoprint-guide sizes are given in fractions of inches, as ½ (inch), ¼ (inch).
Pen size—Wricoprint pens are coded 3 to 7, with size 3 making the *thickest* line.

1. The number for the size of a Wricoprint pen is stamped near the tip.

2. Fill the well near the tip with a few drops of ink.

3. Pull or push the plunger knob at the top of the pen to start ink flowing. Pushing the plunger in reduces the ink flow (the needle end of the plunger fills the flow channel) and pulling it back increases the ink flow (the needle moves back, opening the channel).

4. Test the pen on paper. Adjust the plunger for a *moderate* flow of ink.
5. Hold the pen in a vertical position so the tip is flat on the surface.

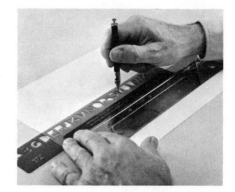

6. Go over a letter to make even, crisp lines.

FOUR   FOUR
Poor   **Good**

7. Follow suggestions 9, 10, and 11 under the Wrico Sign-maker explanation.

Template lettering guides (Leroy)

[See Appendix A for film correlated with this topic.]

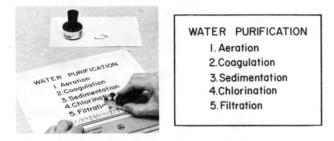

Lettering templates are excellent for all lettering needs, especially for captions of many lines. Although more expensive than stencils, they permit faster work and can give higher-quality lettering. The pens come in ranges from fine to very bold, and are used in a tripod scriber, one leg of which follows the letters grooved in the template.

The most common template equipment is the *Leroy* brand. It consists of a *template,* a *scriber,* and a *two-part pen.*

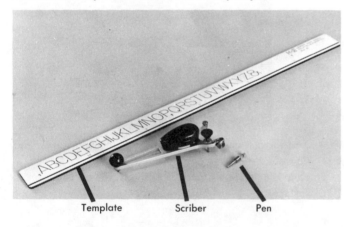

Template   Scriber   Pen

A Leroy template has this label printed in red in the right corner:

The label gives such information as:

3240—letter style

CL—*capitals, lower-case* (and numbers) on the template. Capitals are usually on one side with lower-case and numbers on the reverse side. Larger templates and special ones have only the capitals and numbers or the lower-case on a single template.

Letter size—Leroy lettering templates are coded with 1000 = 1 inch (350 = ⅓ inch)

Pen 4—Both parts (the well and the plunger) are numbered. Lower-numbered pens make thinner lines.

1. Set the template against a T-square (taped to the working surface).
2. Set the pen firmly into the hole in the scriber arm and tighten the screw on the side.
3. Fill the well of the pen with two or three drops of ink.
4. Set the butt end (the arm with the round ball) of the scriber into the long black groove under the letters of the template.
5. Place the scriber arm with the point into the letter groove.
6. Lower the pen to the surface and guide the scriber with little pressure.
7. After completing a letter, lift the pen from the surface and slide the template to position the next letter.

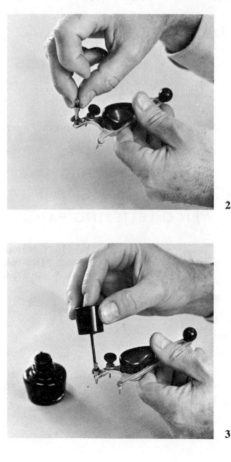

2

3

4

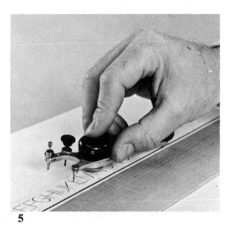

5

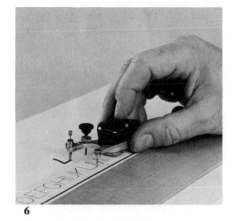

6

The following additional details are useful in proper lettering with the Leroy device:

- Judge letter spacing by eye, according to what looks correct.
- Start ink flowing by stroking the pen on scrap paper. Sometimes it is necessary to raise the plunger part of the pen a few times for ink to reach the tip.
- Adjust the vertical screw on the scriber, just behind the pen, so it touches the paper lightly to permit a steady flow of ink from the pen while lettering.

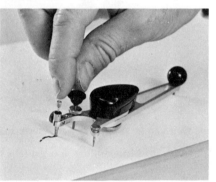

- Start near the center of a stroke and work to the ends. Keep the pen moving to eliminate the globs of ink that collect and fatten ends of strokes and other places where the pen pauses.
- When you complete using a Leroy pen, remove it from the scriber, separate the two parts, and wash them.

- Some Leroy scribers are adjustable. A screw on the underside can be loosened and the two arms spread apart. This permits making slanting letters of various degrees.

- Larger size templates (about or larger than size 500) require the use of a different scriber.

Photocomposing-machine lettering

High-quality professional lettering is often done from type, either by setting metal type or by using a *cold-type* machine to photographically set type on sensitized paper. A photocomposing machine is of the latter type. It is a quick and efficient way to do lettering for titles, transparencies, and publications. Pictured are representative types of photocomposing machines.

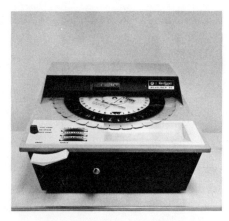

Varitype Headliner

2

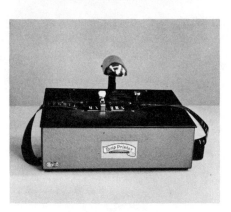

Strip Printer

3

The original letters are on a plastic or acetate alphabet stencil. Many letter styles and sizes are available. Here is how the Headliner is used:

1. Each letter to be made is selected, in turn, and *contact* printed onto photographic paper or film (by exposure to light, in the machine).
2. The paper or film is then processed, either in the machine or in trays in a darkroom.
3. The completed lettering is then ready for use (often for paste-up work (page 121).

1

Now, review what you have learned about lettering methods:

1. What rules guide you for holding and using a beveled-tip felt pen?
2. How do you line up and space punch-out letters?
3. What purpose is served by the backing sheet with dry-transfer letters?
4. What method of lettering might you select to prepare a caption of 12 words?
5. What are the required parts to letter with a Wrico Signmaker unit? How do they differ from the Wricoprint parts?
6. What size lettering will each of these make: Wrico Signmaker 150, Wricoprint ¼, Leroy 240?
7. How does filling a Wricoprint pen differ from filling the Wrico Signmaker brush pen?
8. What is the proper position during use for the brush pen? for the Wricoprint pen?
9. What parts are required to do Leroy lettering?
10. Compare the lettering methods described in this section in terms of best uses, time and skill to use, cost of equipment if required, and quality of results.

BACKGROUNDS FOR TITLES

Select backgrounds that are appropriate to the treatment of the subject in color and design and that do not distract attention from the title or detract from its effect. Such backgrounds will be inconspicuous in color and design, yet will contribute to the mood or central idea of the topic. Cool colors (blue, gray, green) are preferred for backgrounds and warm colors (red, orange, magenta) for titles and visuals over the background.

For backgrounds you may consider plain, colored, or textured papers; cardboards of various finishes and colors; cloth, wood, or other unusual materials; or pictures and photographs. Rich colors give maximum contrast in black-and-white and pleasing effects in color. But do not let the background design or extremes of color interfere with legibility or with the purpose of a title or diagram.

Special techniques

For most uses, prepare simple titles directly on the background material. But for special purposes, you may make *overlays* and place them over the background before filming. Overlays are particularly useful when several titles or diagrams must appear over the same background. Lettering for overlays may be in black, in white, or in color.

Black overlay lettering

• Adhere punch-out letters, cut-outs, or dry transfer letters directly to the background (page 101).
• Make regular black-line transparencies by heat process (page 172), diazo method (page 169), or photography (page 181) and overlay them on the background.

White overlay lettering

Prepare white letters on black nonreflecting cardboard. Then, during filming, double-expose the film to record first the background and then the white title (page 86).

Color overlay lettering

• Use colored dry transfer letters on clear acetate.
• Make single color diazo transparencies (page 169).
• When more than one color is needed on a title, prepare multicolor diazo transparencies or paper copies (page 172).

For applications of these techniques for titles see the section on Titling for Slides on page 144.

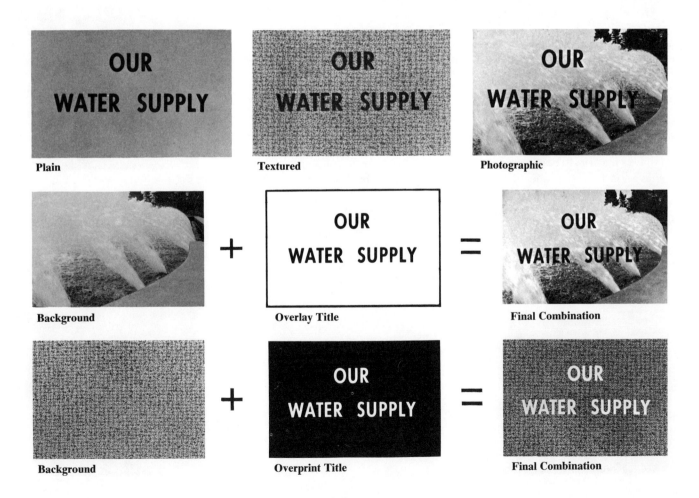

Plain   Textured   Photographic

Background   +   Overlay Title   =   Final Combination

Background   +   Overprint Title   =   Final Combination

MOUNTING

A variety of techniques can be considered for mounting art work and for preserving finished visual materials. Some of these techniques are temporary, others permanent. Materials can be put on cardboard or on cloth.

RUBBER-CEMENT METHODS

[See Appendix A for film correlated with this topic.]

Mounting with rubber cement is a simple procedure that requires no special equipment. It will accomplish temporary or permanent mounting.

Rubber-Cement Mounting Requires These Tools and Materials: Trimmer or Scissors, Cardboard Backing, Pencil, Rubber Cement in a Dispensing Jar, Wax Paper.

Temporary mounting is useful for making paste-ups (page 121) of line drawings and accompanying lettering that are to be photographed rather than used directly. There are four steps:

1. Trim the material to be mounted.
2. With rubber cement, coat the back of each piece to be mounted.
3. Place the coated pieces cement-side-down on the cardboard, while the cement is wet. They can be moved as necessary to get exact position and alignment, or picked up and repositioned.
4. Allow the cement to dry before using the paste-up. Rub away any visible cement.

1

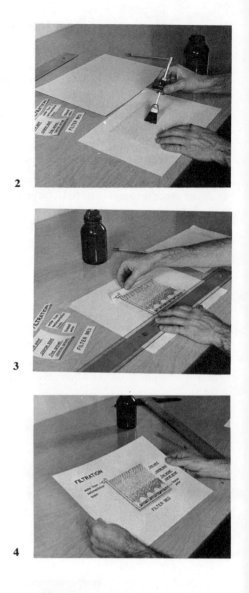

2

3

4

Permanent mounting is not truly permanent, but materials thus mounted with rubber cement will adhere for long periods. There are twelve steps in the procedure.

1. Trim the picture or other piece to be mounted.

1

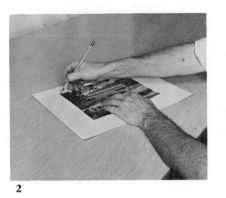

2

3

4

2. Place the picture on the cardboard backing; make guide marks for each corner.
3. Coat the back of the picture with rubber cement.
4. Coat the marked area on the cardboard with rubber cement.

5

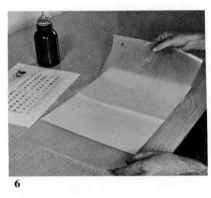

6

7

5. Allow the cement to dry on both surfaces.
6. Overlap two wax-paper sheets on the cement-covered cardboard after the cement is dry.
7. Align the picture on the guide marks as seen through the waxed paper.

8

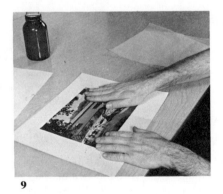

9

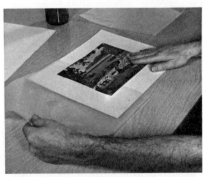

10

8. Slide out one sheet of waxed paper.
9. Smooth the picture to the cardboard on this exposed cement.
10. Remove the second waxed sheet.

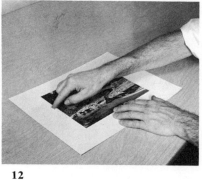

11   12

11. Smooth the remainder of the picture to the cardboard.
12. Rub excess cement away from the edges of the picture.

Consider these additional details when using the rubber-cement methods of mounting:

• Make guide marks in corners on mounting board lightly in pencil so they are not noticeable after the mounting is completed.
• Make sure the brush is adjusted in the lid of the cement jar so the bristles are below the cement level in the jar.
• Cement should flow smoothly from the brush. If it thickens it will collect on the brush and fall in lumps. Add a small amount of rubber-cement thinner and shake the jar well.
• If colored cardboard is to be used, test the cement on a sample, as rubber cement may stain the surface.
• Apply cement with long sweeping strokes of the brush. Move moderately fast as cement dries quickly.
• Keep the lid on the dispenser jar tightly closed when not in actual use.
• In the permanent method, the cemented surfaces can be considered dry when they feel slightly tacky.
• The sulfur in rubber cement may react with the silver in a photograph to stain the face of the picture a yellowish-brown color.

DRY-MOUNT METHOD (ON CARDBOARD)

[See Appendix A for film correlated with this topic.]

This is a fast method, resulting in permanent and neatly mounted materials. It is particularly useful when a number of pictures are to be mounted. The mounting material is *dry-mount tissue*—a tissue paper coated on *both sides* with a heat-sensitive adhesive. When heat and pressure are applied the adhesive is activated. Upon cooling the adhesive forms a strong bond between the picture and the cardboard. Either an electric hand iron or a dry-mount press is used to provide heat and to exert pressure. (The Masterfax unit, shown on page 120, can also be used to dry mount smaller materials.)

The Seal product *Fotoflat* should be used with a hand iron set at *rayon* or *low*. With the dry-mount press use Eastman Kodak's dry-mount tissue or Seal's *MT5* and set the thermostat at 225° F and the tacking iron on *medium* heat.

A shortcoming of the dry-mount method is the possibility that bubbles of steam may form under a picture when heat is applied. Most bubbles can be eliminated by predrying the cardboard and picture. If bubbles do appear after mounting, puncture them with a pin and then reapply heat and pressure. Unfortunately, when bubbles do form, the paper may stretch, resulting in a wrinkle.

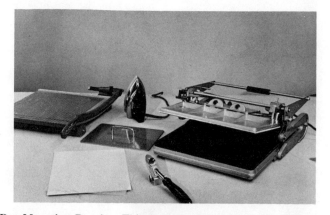

Dry Mounting Requires This Equipment and Materials: Trimmer; Cardboard Backing; Sheets of Dry-Mount Tissue; Hand Iron or Dry-Mount Press and Tacking Iron; Metal Weights.

Here is a comparison of the hand-iron and dry-mount-press methods for dry mounting:

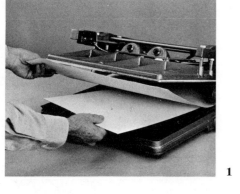

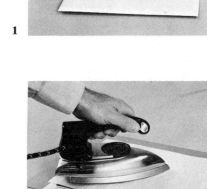

1. Preheat both the picture and cardboard for 10 seconds to remove moisture from them.

2. Adhere the dry-mount tissue to the back of the picture by touching the iron directly to the tissue. Always protect the table top with paper.

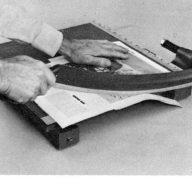

3. Trim the picture and the tissue together on all sides.

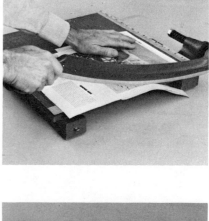

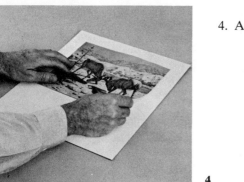

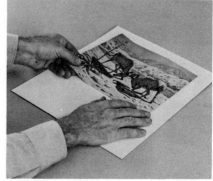

4. Align the picture on the cardboard.

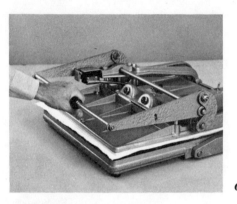

5

5. Tack the tissue to the cardboard in two corners.

5

6

6. Cover the picture with a clean sheet of thin paper. Seal the picture to the cardboard with heat and pressure for 5-10 seconds. With the hand iron, maintain a slow circular motion.

6

7

7. Cool the mounted picture under a metal weight.

7

The Completed Mount

Consider these additional details when dry mounting:

- If more than one sheet of tissue must be used, butt the edges together; do not overlap them.
- If a mounting is too large to be sealed in the dry-mount press at one time, seal it in sections. Make sure successive areas in the press are overlapped so none of the picture is missed.
- When using the hand iron there is a tendency to move the iron quickly across the paper covering the picture. Properly, a moderate amount of pressure should be exerted with the iron and it should be used from the center of the picture outwards with slow movements so all parts receive heat and pressure for about five seconds.
- When pressing is completed place the mount *quickly* under a weight for cooling. This is when actual sealing takes place. A metal weight, which absorbs heat quickly, is preferred.

In addition to mounting complete rectangular pictures, cut-outs around picture can be made to eliminate unnecessary details. Be sure to tack tissue to back of the picture before cutting it out. Then follow the same procedures as described for regular dry mounting to mount a cut-out picture.

Pictures that extend across two pages in a magazine require special handling. Follow these steps:

1. Remove the picture from the magazine by cutting or take out the staples.

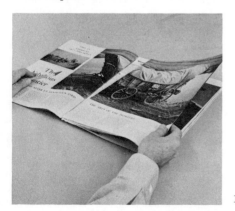

1

2. Trim the edge to be joined on each part of the picture. Remove as little paper as possible.
3. Tack dry-mount tissue to the back of one part, leaving part of the sheet of tissue overhanging the edge to be joined.
4. With the picture face up, align the edges to be joined and touch them together tightly. Make sure there is protective paper under the picture and tissue.

2

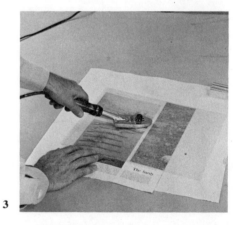

3

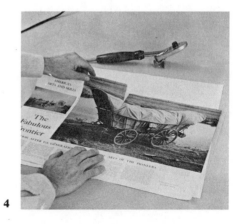

4

5. With a small piece of paper over the joined splice, tack the second part of the picture to the tissue in two or three places. Remember, the picture is face up.
6. Tack additional tissue if necessary to the back of the picture to cover it entirely. Always butt pieces of dry mount tissue together, do not overlap them.
7. Then finish the mounting as with a regular dry-mounted picture—trim, tack to cardboard, seal with the press or iron, and cool immediately under a weight.
8. If a slight white line shows at the joined splice, darken it lightly with soft lead or colored pencil.

5

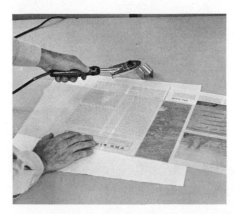

6

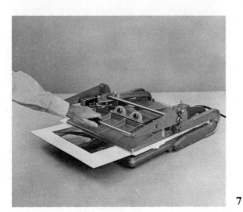

7

8

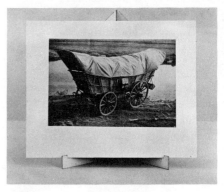

**Completed
Two-Page Mount**

DRY MOUNT METHOD (ON CLOTH)

[See Appendix A for film correlated with this topic.]

For some purposes, as booklets or turnover charts, photographs or visual materials may require a pliable backing. In such cases a dry-mount cloth (Chartex) can be adhered to the back of the materials to give them durability and still maintain flexibility. The adhesive is a coating on one side of the cloth, which is ironed on the back of the materials or applied with a dry-mount press. Larger materials can be mounted so as to be rolled or folded. Follow these steps:

1. Set the dry-mount press at 225°, the tacking iron at *medium*, and the hand iron at *rayon*.
2. Dry the chart in the press or with the hand iron. Besides removing moisture from the paper, this treatment will flatten folds in the chart.
3. *Chart to be rolled:* a. Place the chart face-down on a sheet of clean paper.

3a

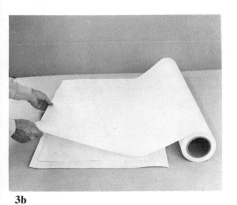

3b

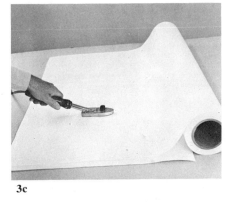

3c

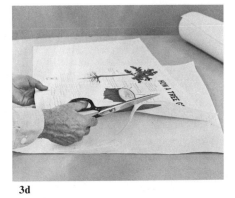

3d

b. Cover the back of the chart with sufficient cloth. Place the adhesive coating (smooth side, on inside or roll) against the back of chart.

c. Tack the chart to the cloth in one large spot.

d. Cut the cloth to match edges of chart or leave excess cloth all around for a cloth margin. Plan for 2 or 3 inches of extra cloth at the top edge for grommets or eyelets.

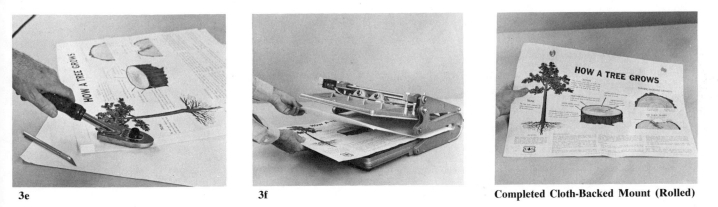

3e

3f

Completed Cloth-Backed Mount (Rolled)

e. If you have left a margin, fold the cloth and tack it to the edge of the chart along the full length of each side. Slit the cloth at the corners so adjacent pieces can be overlapped. *Do not* leave any cloth exposed or unfolded, as the adhesive side will stick to other surfaces during sealing.

f. Cover the chart with paper and seal in the dry-mount press or with the hand iron. Apply heat to each section for at least five seconds. Cool under a weight.

g. Check for bubbles or wrinkles. Re-iron or re-press as necessary.

h. Add gummed eyelets or grommets to the upper cloth margin. Place them 3 inches in from the outer edge. Add an additional one or two toward the center of the margin for large charts.

i. If it is difficult to get a rolled chart to open fully for use, attach a wooden strip to the lower edge of the cloth as a weight.

4. *Chart to be folded:* a. Cut the chart into suitable sections.
   b. Dry each section in the press or with the hand iron.
   c. Spread the cloth on sheet of clean paper with the adhesive coating (smooth side, on inside of roll) placed upwards.

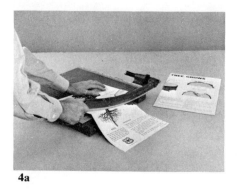

4a

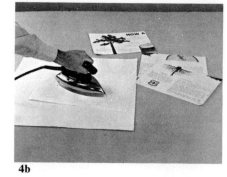

4b

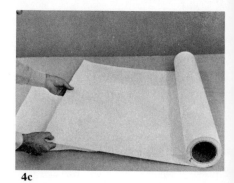

4c

d. Arrange the cut sections of the chart on the cloth. Leave ⅛ inch (or less) between the sections.

e. Tack each section to the cloth from the top side through a piece of paper.

f. Follow steps *d* through *h* as above.

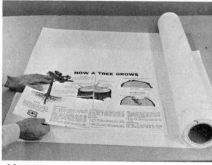

4d

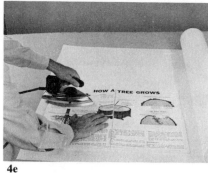

4e

Completed Cloth-Backed Mount (Folded)

PROTECTING THE SURFACE

[See Appendix A for film correlated with this topic.]

The face of a photograph or other mounted material to be handled a great deal needs protection. A clear plastic spray may be applied but an even better and permanent protection is achieved by sealing a clear plastic laminating film over the face of the picture. A dry-mount press set at 270°F. adheres this film to a mounted picture in a few seconds. To get satisfactory results may require some practice, and it may be necessary to increase the pressure by putting cardboard or a sheet of thin masonite into the press.

The following steps apply to laminating a previously dry-mounted picture.

1. Set the dry-mount press at 270° and the tacking iron on high.

2. Dry the mounted picture in the press for 10 seconds.

3. Extra pressure is required for laminating. Put a piece of heavy cardboard or masonite (smooth face to the mount) on the rubber pad of the press.

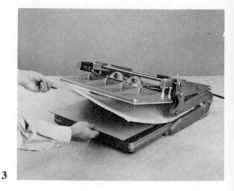

3

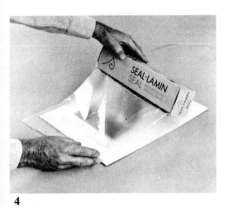

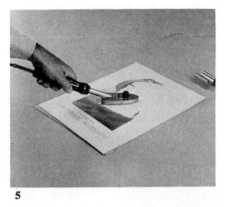

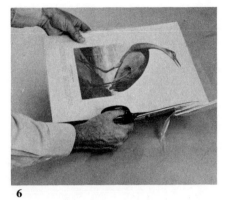

4

5

6

4. Cut a piece of laminating film (Seal-lamin) to cover the entire mount surface (front and back if desired).
5. The adhesive side of the film is on the inside of the roll. Tack the film to the mount in one spot with a piece of paper placed between the film and the tacking iron.
6. Trim excess film so none overhangs the mount edge.

7

8

Completed Laminated Mount

7. Smooth the film over the mount. Cover it with a sheet of paper. Seal the assembly in the press for at least 15 seconds.
8. Immediately after removing the picture from the press cool it under a metal weight for one or two minutes.

Consider these additional details when laminating:

- If bubbles appear under the lamination film they are due to moisture in the picture or cardboard expanding to form steam. Place the mount back in the press for about 45 seconds and cool again.
- It may be helpful, instead of cooling under a weight, to rub firmly over the affected area with a wadded handkerchief.
- If bubbles persist, break them with a pin and press again or rub by hand again. Because of bubbles, the film may stretch, resulting in a wrinkle.
- If unmounted pictures are laminated (to protect and display both sides of a sheet), seal one side with film, as above. Then repeat the process on the second side.

- If materials to be laminated are wider than the roll of film to be used (11″, 20″, and 22″ rolls are available), butt adjacent pieces together. Seal each piece in turn, in the press.
- Thin three-dimensional objects such as leaves can be laminated easily to cardboard. Before starting, secure the object in place with rubber cement.
- When laminating glossy photographs, follow the above procedures, but with these changes:

    Set the thermostat on the press at 325°.

    Wipe the surface of photograph with cotton moistened in rubbing alcohol. Allow thorough drying before laminating. Preheating the photograph is unnecessary.

    Apply additional pressure in the press with an extra piece of cardboard or masonite.

Protect face of picture with a sheet of thin paper.

Maintain pressure in the press for at least one minute. Cool immediately under a weight.

In addition to the dry-mount press, other units are used for laminating. The one pictured below is typical of those that will handle unmounted pictures. Another kind is described in the following section.

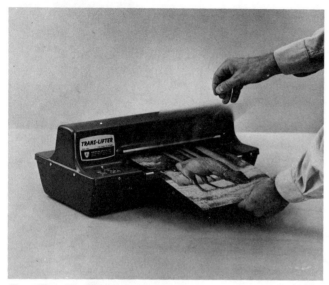

Translifter (National Adhesive Co.)

Now, review what you have learned about mounting and surface-protection methods:

1. What are two differences between *temporary* and *permanent* rubber-cement mounting methods?
2. For what two reasons is wax paper used in the rubber-cement permanent method?
3. What is the principle of mounting with dry-mount tissue?
4. Why is tissue tacked to the back of the picture *before* the latter is trimmed to size?
5. What procedure is used if bubbles appear under a completed mount?
6. Compare three methods—rubber-cement permanent, hand iron, and dry-mount press in terms of: speed of process, ease, equipment, cost, and quality of mount.
7. What two variations of the regular dry-mount procedure are used when a two-page picture is mounted?
8. How do you decide whether to mount a map on cardboard, on cloth to be rolled, or on cloth to be folded?
9. Why should cloth either be trimmed flush with the chart edge or turned as a border before sealing it to the chart?
10. What are two variations of the regular dry-mount procedure when covering a mounted magazine picture with laminating film?

MULTIPURPOSE EQUIPMENT

[See Appendix A for film correlated with this topic.]

It is an accepted axiom that a piece of equipment should be designed to serve only one primary function. When it is adapted to perform a number of functions, it may not do any of them very well. But because of the interrelation of various graphic techniques, certain pieces of equipment can very satisfactorily do a number of things.

As was shown previously, the dry-mount press can be used to dry mount, to laminate, and (as will be seen on page 177), to make picture transfer transparencies.

Another unit, the Masterfax, can perform five important reproduction and production functions—make paper copy reproductions of printed sheets, prepare spirit masters for further duplication (page 124), dry mount, laminate, and make transparencies.

Masterfax (Ditto/Bell & Howell)

The Masterfax is a flat-bed thermal unit, similar in method of use to the equipment described for heat-process transparencies on page 172. Two features of this machine are important and both contribute to good-quality reproductions. First is the infrared lamp that provides the heat and exposure by moving past the stationary materials, rather than having the materials rotate around the lamp. Second is the "vacuum blanket" in the lid, against which a pump creates a vacuum guaranteeing extremely tight contact between the original material and the paper or film for reproduction.

Materials are assembled on the glass surface of the Masterfax unit in the following ways (and they must not extend beyond the glass), to prepare:

• Paper copies—original sheet (image down) on reproduction paper (sensitive side down) on glass surface.

- Spirit masters—original sheet (image down) on carbon sheet (carbon side down) on master sheet on glass surface.
- Mounting—cardboard on dry-mount tissue on picture on black bonding sheet on glass surface.
- Laminating—laminating film (adhesive side down) on picture on laminating film (adhesive side up) on black bonding sheet on glass surface.
- Laminating—dry-mounted picture (face down) on laminating film (adhesive side up) on black bonding paper on glass surface.
- Transparency—original sheet (image down) on heat sensitive film (coating down) on glass surface

For the mounting and laminating procedures set the exposure dial at the red mark (for the longest possible exposure). For other procedures, adjust exposure setting as instructed or according to experience.

MAKING PASTE-UPS

When materials are prepared for offset printing, or sometimes for photographic print series, slides, or transparencies, the lettering and the visuals (in the form of black-ink line drawings) are made separately. Each part is then *pasted* onto paper or cardboard in proper arrangement. The result of this procedure is termed a *paste-up*. For example, prior to printing, a paste-up was made for each page in this book.

Pasting-up is done by putting rubber cement on the back of each piece, as in temporary mounting (page 110). This method permits moving the piece for alignment before the cement dries and the piece adheres firmly.

Wax may also be used as a backing adhesive for paste-ups. It is applied with a hand-operated roller or a mechanical coating unit. Wax backing permits ease of alignment, a tight seal between copy and paper, and elimination of some of the clean-up problems that rubber cement presents.

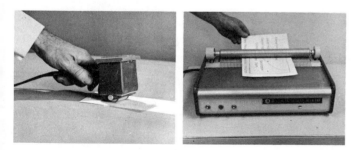

Paste-ups are useful in preparing titles and diagrams for all types of visual materials. Use high-contrast film to photograph the paste-up (page 181). Print the resulting negative in the visual form you need. See next page.

REPRODUCING PRINTED MATTER

When audiovisual materials are prepared there is often the need for accompanying reading matter for use by teachers and students. Also, for individual learning activities, duplicates of programs, photographic print picture series, and instructional sheets may be required. A number of reproduction processes can be utilized. Each one serves a particular need and has certain requirements, advantages, and limitations. We will examine eight commonly used methods.

Spirit duplication

[See Appendix A for film correlated with this topic.]

A master is prepared with colored carbon sheets placed in contact with the back side of the master paper. Impressions are made on the front side of the master by writing, typing, or drawing. At the same time a carbon impression is deposited on the back of the master sheet. Up to five carbon colors may be used to prepare one-color or multi-color paper copies.

The carbon transferred to the back of the master is an aniline dye, soluble in methyl alcohol. In the spirit duplicator, alcohol is spread over the duplicator paper. When the master comes in contact with paper some of the dye is deposited on the paper, producing a printed copy.

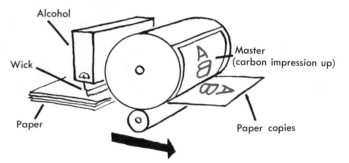

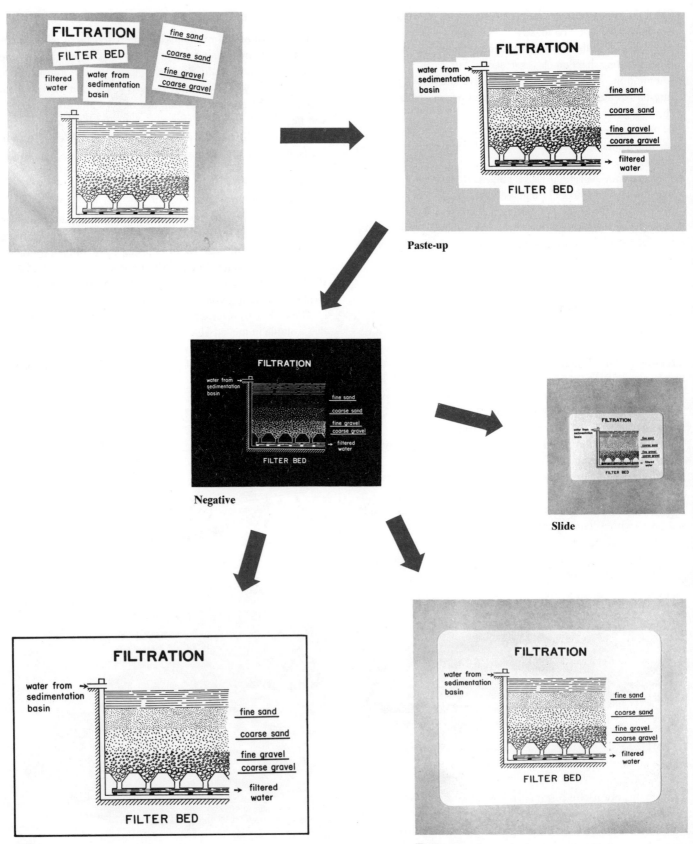

Paste-up

Negative

Slide

Print

Transparency

Stencil

One printing application of the stencil process is *mimeograph.* The stencil consists of a sheet impregnated with a wax-like substance that does not allow ink to penetrate unless the coating is broken or pushed aside by a stylus or by the force of a typewriter type, thus leaving openings for ink to pass through.

In the machine, ink flows through a cotton pad onto and through the stencil wrapped around a rotating cylinder. Blank paper, pressed against the stencil by a rubber cylinder, absorbs the ink. By using separate stencils and reruns of the paper, more than one color can be put on the same sheet.

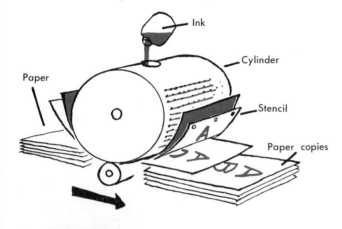

Care must be exercised in preparing the stencil and the operation of the machine takes some special experience. Quality is similar to good reproduction by the spirit method, but somewhat less than that from offset printing since in mimeographing the ink is absorbed by the porous paper and has a tendency to spread.

Electronic scanning machines are sometimes used to reproduce printed sheets onto stencils without any hand work. The resulting printed copies from such stencils are of textured quality.

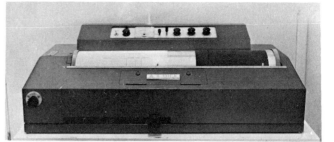

Electronic Scanning Mimeo

Diazo

[See Appendix A for film correlated with this topic.]

Inexpensive paper copies can be made from translucent master diagrams by the same process described for making transparencies (page 169). The paper products of this process are called *white prints* and have blue or black lines on white paper, as opposed to *blueprints* with their white lines on blue background. The latter are still widely used for making large plans and engineering drawings on paper. The diazo method requires a translucent (tracing paper or matte film) or transparent (clear film) master sheet with opaque markings for reproduction. The diazo machine has two separate sections. In the first, light-sensitive paper is exposed through the master to ultraviolet light. In the second section, fumes of ammonia develop the exposed image on the paper.

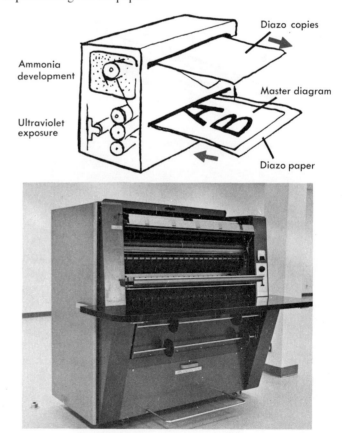

This method is essentially a hand operation, as the master comes out of the machine after each exposure for reinsertion with a new sheet of diazo paper. Some diazo machines will reproduce masters up to 42 inches wide and of any length. Except for large sheets, the process is not efficient for runs of more than ten copies. Exposure of printed sheets to direct sunlight will cause some fading of the image. Reproductions of halftone printed pictures and continuous-tone photographs can be made satisfactorily on certain diazo papers.

Thermal

[See Appendix A for film correlated with this topic.]

This process is represented by the Thermo-fax (3M Company) equipment and materials. It requires a master drawn or typed sheet (on any kind of paper) exposed in contact with thermal paper to heat generated by an infrared lamp. The processing time is only a few seconds and no development time is required. The thermal paper costs about three cents a sheet. This process is widely used to prepare transparencies as well as paper copies (page 172).

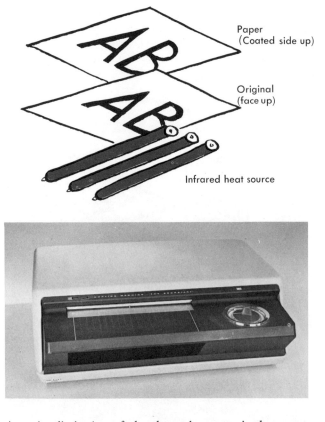

Paper
(Coated side up)

Original
(face up)

Infrared heat source

A major limitation of the thermal process is that master drawings or printing must consist of heat-absorbing material (pencil, black ink, or other carbon-depositing items); markings made by dyes (spirit copies, ordinary ball-point pens, colored inks) are not reproducible. The average thermal paper used is not durable and the image is not very sharp. But for quickly

making a few copies for temporary reference, this process is fine.

The thermal process is also useful for making *spirit masters* from printed sheets for normal spirit duplication (as with Masterfax machine page 120). A special backing sheet with a waxed carbon surface, attached to a thin master sheet, is fed through the thermal machine with the original printed sheet. The resulting master will permit up to 100 paper copies. Prepare the thermal master in this way:

1. After removing the thin separating sheet, place the master on the original printed sheet with the thin master sheet on top.
2. Put the sheets into a plastic carrier.
3. Set the thermal copy machine as instructed.

1

2

3

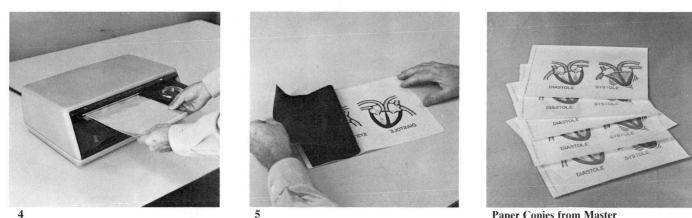

4   5   **Paper Copies from Master**

4. Run the carrier through the machine.
5. Separate the carbon sheet from the master sheet. A strong impression on the back of the master will insure good reproduction copies.

Photocopy (diffusion transfer)

This process, also used to make transparencies, is described on page 174. First a sheet of negative paper is exposed to light while in contact with a printed sheet. Then the negative and a positive sheet of photocopy paper are passed together through a fluid developer. The resulting copy of the original sheet is damp dry. While this is the basic photocopy process, other machines use heat for developing and thus produce dry rather than damp copies.

Negative paper

Paper positive

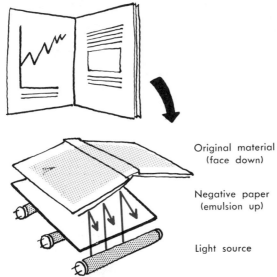

Original material (face down)

Negative paper (emulsion up)

Light source

By this process *all* colors and kinds of markings will reproduce in black-and-white. The image is of good quality and durable white paper is used. Photocopy machines are simple to use and certain ones will reproduce pages from books as well as single sheets.

Book Copier

Electrostatic

There are two related processes under this category. Both require charged surfaces that are effected (discharged) by light. The charged area will hold a substance to create the image.

In *xerography,* a selenium-coated plate, which is photoelectrically sensitive, is given an electrical charge. The original to be duplicated is exposed to light, with the white area (and gray portions of photographs) reflecting light to the charged plate. The light that reaches the selenium-coated surface dissipates the electric charge, leaving a charge only in the image area. The copy paper (any ordinary paper) is charged and a toner (a fine black powder) is transferred to it from the selenium surface. Finally, the copy paper is heated to fix the powder permanently to the image area.

1. Positive electric charge is placed on selenium-coated plate.
2. Image of original is projected onto plate to form latent image.
3. Negatively charged powder *toner* is dusted onto selenium plate.
4. Sheet of paper is placed over plate and receives positive charge.
5. Final copy is heated to fuse image into paper.

A related method, the *electrofax* process (RCA trade mark name), requires the use of a special copy paper coated with zinc oxide, discharging of the coating by light, and collection of charged toner on its surface.

1. Uniform electric charge is placed on copy paper.
2. Image of original is projected onto charged paper to form latent image.
3. Powder *toner* is brushed onto paper, where it adheres to image area.
4. Toner is fused to paper with heat.

The electrostatic machines are easy to operate but expensive to purchase (some are leased on a per copy charge). Copies are of fair to good quality.

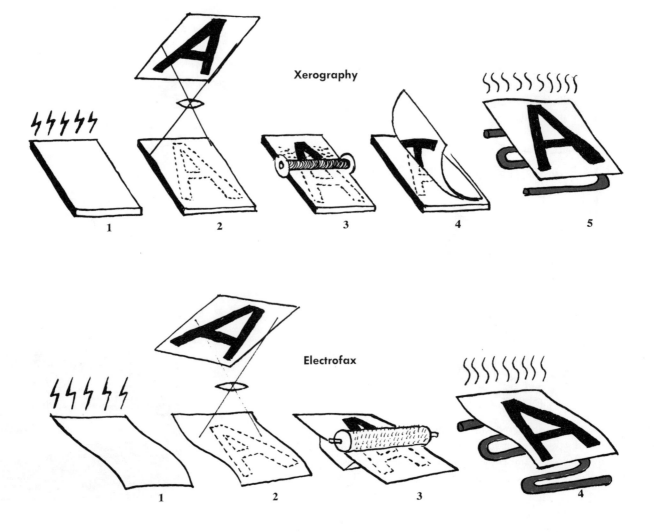

Xerography

Electrofax

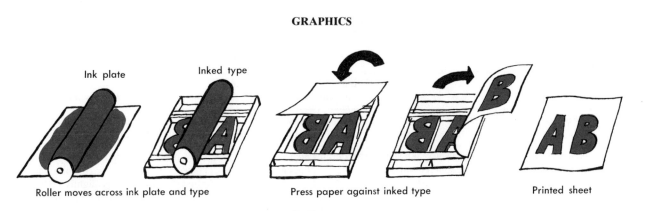

Ink plate   Inked type

Roller moves across ink plate and type   Press paper against inked type   Printed sheet

Letterpress

Letterpress printing

The most widely used form of *relief printing* is letterpress. This method transfers ink from a raised surface (the image areas) to the paper. The raised surface may range from an artistic woodcut, to metal type, to fine photoengravings. The paper normally used has a very smooth finish and can hold very fine detail. Letterpresses range from small hand-fed units to those that print in multicolor at up to 800 feet per minute.

A print shop or duplicating department must set the type or prepare the plates and operate the equipment.

Offset printing

The basic principle of offset is that grease (ink) and water do not mix. The printing plates have ink-receiving (greasy) image areas and ink-repelling (watery) nonimage areas. Plates are prepared directly on paper or aluminum with special pencils and typing ribbons, by thermal or photocopy methods, by the electrostatic process, or photographically using the same high-contrast film as for transparencies (page 181). A water roll on the press coats the plate with a thin layer of water; where there is an image the grease in the image repels the water but allows the ink, which is oily, to adhere. The ink is then *offset* or transferred to a cylinder covered with a resilient rubber "blanket." The ink image from the blanket is then transferred to paper.

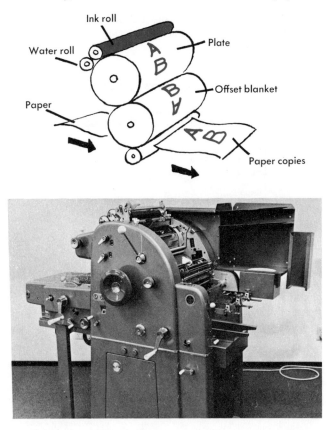

Ink roll

Water roll

Plate

Paper

Offset blanket

Paper copies

The offset process is extensively used for educational and commercial printing. It requires expensive equipment and trained personnel.

Summary of Reproducing Processes

Method	Principle	Reproduction Speed and Approximate Material Cost		Evaluation
Spirit	Carbon impression on master transferred to paper with alcohol.	Moderate	Master 5¢ Paper $2.00/ream	Master easily prepared; operation simple; good for up to 200 copies in multicolor.
Stencil	Ink passes through openings in waxlike stencil and is picked up by paper in contact with stencil.	Moderate	Stencil 20¢ Paper $2.50/ream	Care needed in making master; machine more complex than spirit; each color requires separate operation; quality slightly better than spirit; long run easy; clean-up takes time.
Diazo	Expose sensitized paper to ultraviolet light through translucent master; develop in ammonia.	Slow	Paper 3¢ per 8½″×11″ sheet	Easy operation; good for few copies; image affected by sunlight; duplication of photos possible; translucent master required.
Thermal	Expose sensitized paper with master to infrared light.	Fast	Paper 5¢	Rapid, easy reproduction for few copies; quality fair; won't copy all colors; image affected by heat; produces spirit masters.
Photocopy	Expose negative paper in contact with original to light; develop negative and positive together.	Slow	Paper 10¢ (sets)	Can copy anything; good quality; some processes give damp copy; requires periodic cleaning machine.
Electrostatic Xerography	Charged selenium drum discharged by light; toner powder collects on charged paper for image.	Moderate	Paper 5¢	Can copy anything; fair to good quality; machine cost high; operation simple after adjustments.
Electrofax	Charged, coated, light-sensitive paper discharged by light; collects charged toner to form image.			
Letterpress	Ink from raised type transfers to paper.	Fast	$3.00 per 100 copies	Excellent reproduction of fine detail and tone gradations; typesetting can be time consuming.
Offset	Ink adheres to image on plate; transferred to blanket and then to paper.	Very fast	Plates: 12¢ to $3.00 Copies: $3.00 per 100	Inexpensive plates and rapid preparation of plates of some types; quality excellent; operation requires technician; clean-up time lengthy.

17. Recording Sound

On Tape　　　　**On a Record**　　　　**On Film**

Recorded sound may be used as individual tape recordings, or in conjunction with the visuals when a slide series, a filmstrip, or a motion picture is prepared. The recording may be on tape, on a disk record, or on the motion-picture film.

Plan to make your recording when picture editing is completed and after the narration has been refined (see pages 50–51). (For detailed information on selection of equipment and on all phases of recording, see "Sound Completes Your Picture," by Leendert Drukker, *Popular Photography,* vol. 49, November, 1961, pages 113-128.) First typewrite the narration in a form that will be easy for the narrator to follow. The illustration on page 55 with its narrow page and marks for cueing and special attention is recommended.

THE NARRATOR AND THE SCRIPT

Choose one or more persons who speak clearly and who can read the script in a conversational tone while still communicating with proper feeling and expression. Generally men's voices are more easily understood on a recording than are women's. Have the narrator study the script carefully. The script should have markings indicating where points are to be emphasized. You should verify the pronunciation of proper names and special terms, and indicate it in the script. The script should have all cueing places plainly marked.

MUSIC AND SOUND EFFECTS

Research evidence indicates that background music is not essential to effective communications with audiovisual materials. In some instances, indeed, it interferes with the message.

But for other purposes it may help in creating a desirable mood and in building continuity. Music as background for titles will assist projectionists to set the volume level for the narration which follows. When music is used under narration, maintain it at a low enough level so it does not interfere with the commentary or compete with the picture for the viewer's attention.

Select musical recordings carefully. Semiclassical pieces that are descriptive and maintain an even tempo and volume are more desirable than are popular or classical selections which may dominate the picture. If your audiovisual materials are to be distributed and sold, permission must be obtained for the use of copyrighted music. A number of commercial music libraries, for a fee, make available selections of all types for recordings. (See page 241 for a listing.)

Sound effects, which add a touch of realism, also are available commercially. If you do not want these commercial effects or cannot find them, you may record actual sounds on tape, or create sound effects (see page 235 for a book on this subject). Sound effects on tape can later be transferred to the final tape or to the magnetic film recording.

RECORDING FACILITIES

Good-quality recordings are made in an acoustically-treated and soundproofed room. Where possible use a room having some wall drapes and carpeting. Do not try to "deaden" the room entirely, as it would be difficult for the narration to sound vibrantly alive in such a room. When desirable facilities cannot be found, improvise a recording booth in a corner of a room with some drapes or blankets to reduce sound reflections. Then

record after normal working hours to eliminate extraneous noises.

When you record sound on magnetic-striped motion-picture film the projector is the recorder and the microphone is attached to it. Thus particular care must be taken to eliminate as much projector noise as you can. The narrator and microphone must therefore be separated from the projector. To achieve this separation, use the most effective of several methods that may be feasible:

- Put the projector and the narrator in separate rooms, preferably with a glass window or door in the partition between them.

- If no transparent partition is available between two rooms, project the picture through an open doorway and use the wall as a sound barrier between the projector and the microphone.

- If only one room is available, make a partition to shield the microphone from the projector, using a blanket or other sound-absorbing material.

RECORDING EQUIPMENT

[See Appendix A for film correlated with this topic.]

A tape recorder of average quality and price (about $200) or slightly better may be used to make the recordings for slides or for a filmstrip. The operating principles of all recorders are the same, whether their controls are actuated by buttons, by knobs, or by levers.

If you have a choice of microphones, select one of good quality. The dynamic microphone is capable of reproducing a wider range of tones and is thus preferable to the crystal or ceramic types included with most tape recorders.

Check the instruction manual that should accompany your recorder if you encounter any questions about the way to operate it.

If only voice is to be recorded, a tape speed of 3¾ inches per second (ips) is satisfactory. Music, however, requires higher fidelity than voice; if it is to be included, the tape should be run at 7½ ips.

Music or sound from a disk can be transferred to a tape in either of two ways. The better of the two methods avoids the use of the microphone and produces sound of superior quality.

In the preferable method a *patch cord* is used to connect electronic components of the record player and the tape recorder. If the record player has the necessary jack, the cord can be run from the record player's *speaker output* to the tape recorder's *phono input*. If there is no speaker output, use *alligator clips* to connect the record player's *speaker terminals* to the recorder's *phono input*. See facing page.

The alternative and inferior method is to record through the microphone; undesirable room noises may be picked up by this method. If you must use the microphone, set it on a pillow or a blanket in front of the speaker of the record player, at a distance of 1 to 2 times the diameter of the speaker.

Music, sound effects, and voice may be mixed during the original recording by setting the microphone beside the speaker

From the Speaker Output to the Phono Input

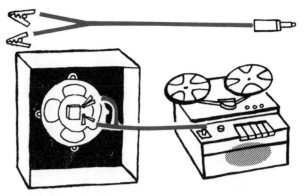

With Alligator Clips on the Speaker Terminals to the Recorder Phono Input

of a record player as the voice recording is made. Control the volume on the record player to bring the music in or to fade it out.

Better quality and control are obtained by using an electronic *mixer* to add music and sound effects after the original voice recording is completed. A *dubbing* (a copy) of the narration is made, through the mixer, onto a second tape. Recordings also are added to the second tape through the mixer and in this way voice and music can be blended by controlling volumes and fading one in and the other out or under. The use of a mixer is particularly important when adding music to a voice recording being made on magnetic-striped film. (See *Magnetic Sound Recording for Motion Pictures,* publication P-26, Eastman Kodak Company).

MAGNETIC RECORDING TAPE

There are many kinds of magnetic tape for use in making recordings. Which type is best to use?

Your tape choice depends largely on how you plan to use your recording. The best guidepost is recording time per reel (at your chosen recording speed).

For comparatively short programing, 1½-mil acetate tape offers the advantages of low cost, low print-through (signal transfer from layer-to-layer), and long life. It provides recordings of excellent quality.

For longer programs, a 1-mil tape is preferred. It provides 50 per cent more recording time than the 1½-mil tape on a reel of the same size. Tapes of this thickness are available in both acetate and polyester (mylar) backings. Acetate is recommended for economy, while polyester provides extra strength and protection against breakage, especially for repeated uses.

The longest available playing time is provided by ½-mil polyester tape. Tape this thin usually is *tensilized,* a process which protects it from excess stretching during use. Some tape recorders will not handle this extra-thin tape; consult the instructions with your machine.

The following table shows maximum recording time for two-track tape recorders *recording in both directions* at 7½ and 3¾ ips. Use half of the time shown for a recording made on only one side.

Tape	Reel size, inches	Tape length, feet	Recording time, minutes	
			At 7½ ips	At 3¾ ips
Standard	3	150	7.5	15
1.5-mil	5	600	30	60
acetate	7	1200	60	120
Long-play	3	225	12	24
1-mil acetate or	5	900	45	90
1-mil mylar	7	1800	60	180
Extra-long-	3	300	15	30
play 0.5-mil	5	1200	60	120
mylar	7	2400	120	240

PREPARATION FOR RECORDING

The quality of a recording depends primarily on proper microphone use and on regulating volume level. Follow these practices:

• If possible, attach the microphone to a stand so it cannot be handled or moved during recording.

- If a stand is not available set the microphone on a table with a sound-absorbing towel or blanket under the microphone.
- Determine by test the best distance from the narrator's mouth at which to place the microphone (about 10 or 12 inches) and have him speak across the front of it rather than directly into it.
- Make a volume-level check for each voice to be used. Select a moderately high volume setting, but one below the distortion level. This setting permits greater flexibility for controlling volume during playback.
- Be sure to turn off fans and other apparatus that make noises which may be picked up by the microphone.
- Set the script on a music or other stand so the narrator will not have to handle the script too much or lower his head while talking.
- Have a glass of water nearby for the narrator to "lubricate" his throat if necessary.

RECORDING PROCEDURE

Three people may be necessary to make a recording: the narrator, a cue giver—someone familiar with the timing of the narration in relation to the pictures, and a person to operate the recorder or projector.

Seat the narrator at a table with microphone and his narration script before him (each sheet separate so it will not make shuffling noises when moved). Stand the person to give cues behind the narrator ready to watch the projected pictures. He will indicate when each section of the narration is to start by tapping the narrator on the shoulder. The third person operates the recorder and the projector.

Experience shows that the best recording takes place in the first one or two tries. As the narrator repeats he loses spontaneity and may make more frequent errors. Rehearse the presentation and then make the recording. Then play the recording back, checking the narration with the script to make sure that nothing has been left out, that no words are mispronounced, and that there are no extraneous noises.

During recording, it is possible to include music, sound effects, or even a low tone, a brief buzz signal, or tap to indicate slide or film changes. The best source for a controlled tone or signal is an electronic audio "sync" generator. The frequency (a high, middle, or low tone) can be selected and the unit attached to the input of the tape recorder and activated with a button.

As was indicated earlier, it is preferable to make a dubbing from the original narration and mix necessary sounds at that time. If automatic filmstrip or slide-tape equipment is to be used (page 151), the inaudible control signal to change slides is recorded on the second track after the sound recording has been made on the first track. But with magnetic-sound motion-picture recording, music and other effects must be recorded at the same time with the original narration.

TAPE EDITING

After the recording is completed, tape editing may be necessary to remove slight imperfections, to add tape for lengthening pauses, or even to substitute a corrected bit of narration. Follow these steps for successful tape editing:[1]

1. Listen to the recorded tape, listing spots to be edited (use the index counter on the recorder to note locations on the tape).
2. Replay the tape and stop at the first spot.
3. Pinpoint the spot to be edited by moving the tape manually back and forth across the playback head.
4. Carefully mark cutting points on the base or shiny side of the tape. Use a fine-tipped felt pen or a china-marking (grease) pencil.
5. Cut the tape; remove the felt pen or grease-pencil marks; then splice the ends together or add tape as necessary.
6. Repeat the same procedure at the next editing spot.

The editing procedure is impractical for magnetic-striped motion-picture film which cannot be cut without damage to the picture area. For film it is necessary to re-record until the sound track is correct.

TAPE SPLICING

[See Appendix A for film correlated with this topic.]

Splicing is best and most conveniently done with a tape-splicing unit. Most of the inexpensive ones are used as follows:

1. Set one piece of tape, with shiny (base) side up, firmly in the splicing channel so it just passes the cutting groove.
2. From the other side, do the same with the second piece.
3. Draw the razor blade across the 45° cutting groove to cut both pieces of tape at the same time. Remove the top waste end of tape.

---

[1] Adapted from *The How To Do It Book of Tape Recording*, Minnesota Mining and Manufacturing Co., St. Paul, Minn., and from *Tape Tips from Capital Audio Engineers*, Capital Recordings, Los Angeles, California, 90028.

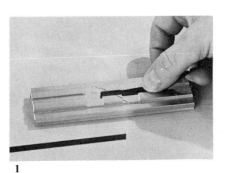
1

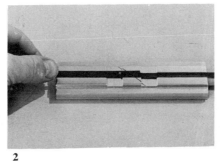
2

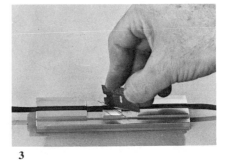
3

4. Cover the cut with a one 1-inch piece of splicing tape.
5. Rub firmly with a fingernail or nonmetallic burnisher.

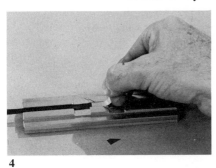
4

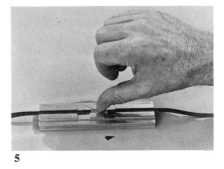
5

6. Draw the blade along both edges of the splicing channel to trim any excess splicing tape extending beyond the edges of the magnetic tape.
7. Examine the splice for strength.

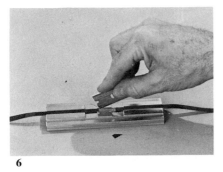
6

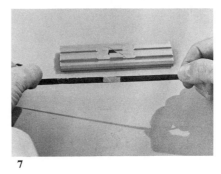
7

If you have no splicing unit, follow this procedure:

1. Line up the tape ends, shiny sides up and overlapping, then cut through both tapes at a 45-degree angle.

2. Butt the cut ends exactly together.
3. Cover the cut with splicing tape and rub firmly with a fingernail or nonmetallic burnisher.

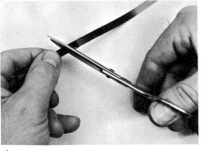
1

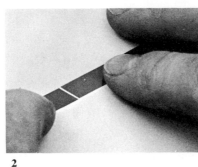
2

3

4

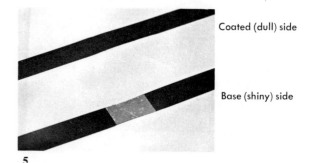

Coated (dull) side

Base (shiny) side

5

4. Trim off the excess splicing tape.
5. Examine the splice to see if it is properly and soundly made.

PRESERVATION AND DUPLICATION

When your editing has been completed, with all sound and signals on the tape, it becomes the *master* recording. Make a dubbing of it, and file the original.

When a slide series or a filmstrip is to be duplicated in quantity, the recording must also be duplicated. A commercial recording laboratory can prepare the required number of 10- or 12-inch disk recordings from the final tape. Disk recordings are the least expensive method of quantity duplication.

TIME-COMPRESSED SPEECH

A recording device is available that will appreciably change the rate of playback of a tape recording.[2] The unit will increase the playback speed of an ordinary recording up to twice normal without changing either pitch, volume, or comprehension. Thus the term *time-compressed speech*. This is accomplished by dropping parts of syllables and shortening the silent period between words.

This device offers potentials for saving time when an individual wants to scan a recording rapidly (like leafing through pages) or for reviewing a recording. It may find extensive use with audio materials designed as part of independent learning activities.

Now, apply what you have learned about recording sound:

1. Consider the recording facilities available to you. What arrangements would you make to insure the best possible tape recording?
2. How would you prepare a recording so as to include music from a disk, along with the narrator's voice?
3. What are the most desirable practices for proper microphone placement and use?
4. What method would you use to add an audible signal to a tape recording for indicating slide changes?
5. Explain the procedure for removing a portion of a tape recording and inserting a substitute part.
6. What equipment, materials, and procedures would you use for splicing tape?

---

[2] Called the Iltro Information Rate Changer, and available from Gotham Audio Corporation, 2 West 46th Street, New York, N.Y. 10036.

Part Four

PRODUCING YOUR
AUDIOVISUAL MATERIALS

18. Photographic Print Series

Individual Study

Ready Reference

Small-Group Viewing

Television Use

Display

A photographic print series consists of photographic prints prepared from black-and-white or color negatives. The preparation of photographic prints involves four main steps: (1) taking pictures, (2) processing film, (3) editing and making prints, and (4) preparing prints for use.

A print series may convey information, teach a skill, or affect an attitude through individual study, small-group viewing, ready reference, display, or television use.

Before taking pictures always consider this planning check list:

- Have you clearly expressed *your idea* and limited the topic? (page 23)
- Have you stated the *objectives* to be served by your print series? (page 23)

- Have you decided that a photographic print series is the *best medium* for accomplishing the objectives? (page 34)
- Which of the five methods of use shown above fits your plans?

  (Perhaps your print series supplements other audiovisual materials for follow-up detailed study.)
- Have you considered the *audience* which will use the print series and its characteristics? (page 24)
- Have you prepared a *content outline?* (page 28)
- Have you sketched a *storyboard* or prepared a *script* as a guide to picture-taking (page 40)
- Have you considered the *specifications* necessary for your print series? (page 43)
- Have you, if necessary, selected other people to assist you with the preparation of materials? (page 26)

The information in Part Three, Chapters 15 and 16, on photography and graphic techniques is basic to the successful preparation of photographic print series. As necessary, refer to the page references indicated with the following topics.

TAKING PICTURES

Your camera

You can prepare a print series successfully with any camera—from the box type to the press type. For enlargements 8″×10″ or greater, a camera with a good-quality lens is preferable because the negatives prepared with some box cameras are incapable of producing good enlargements. If you are selecting a camera for purchase, consider the characteristics and advantages of each category described on pages 65–67.

Carefully study the three settings that are made on adjustable cameras—lens diaphragm, shutter speed, and focus. Understand the purposes for each, the relation of one to another and to depth of field; then determine how each setting is made on your own camera. These settings have been discussed and explained in this book on pages 67–72.

Accessories

You may find need for:

- A photographic light meter to determine exposure accurately (page 74)
- A tripod to steady the camera (When filming at shutter speeds slower than 1/25 second *always* use a tripod.)
- A flash gun or photoflood lights for indoor scenes (page 77)
- A close-up attachment to photograph subjects at close range and to do copy work (page 82)
- A cable release to eliminate any possibility of jarring the camera during long exposures

Film

Factors pertinent to your choice of film are discussed on page 72.

Many photographers limit themselves to using a few general films, or even to one, for most purposes. This practice enables a photographer to become familiar with the behavior of his film. Some of the most useful black-and-white films are briefly described in the table on this page.

The variety of color negative films from which photographs can be made is limited. Kodacolor and Ektacolor are the most common. From them not only color prints but also color slides and black-and-white prints may be prepared.

Exposure

Correct exposure is based on proper camera settings for the film to be used and on the conditions under which pictures are to be taken. Box cameras require good light conditions, as the settings are limited or the lens and shutter are pre-set. For other cameras, film-information sheets indicate general exposure for average conditions. (page 74)

Film	Exposure index (ASA)	Characteristics
Panatomic-X	40	Slow speed, fine grain; for copying detail and making extreme enlargements
Plus-X Pan	160	Moderate speed; all-purpose
Super Panchro Press Type B	125	Moderate speed; all-purpose; sheet film
Tri-X	400+	Fast; medium grain; for use under low light levels
Super Hypan	800	Extremely fast, medium grain; for use under very low light levels

Lighting

The proper use of artificial light is essential for many good photographs. Over-all, even, almost shadowless fluorescent light found in many areas is ideal for black-and-white pictures, even with films of moderate speed.

To boost the light level striking the subject and then reflecting to the camera, photoflash bulbs in reflectors or electronic flash units may be used. They are handy and easy to operate, especially when small areas must be illuminated. Make sure that your camera is synchronized with the flash (at the recommended shutter speed); then apply the information on page 77.

For more carefully controlled lighting and for larger areas, use photoflood lamps. They are available in various sizes and are used with separate metal reflectors unless they have built-in reflectors. In place of regular photoflood lamps, consider using the highly efficient *sealed quartz lamp* of approximately 1000 watts.

Avoid flat lighting created by placing lights beside the camera only. Instead, establish a lighting pattern involving a key light, fill lights, and supplementary background and accent lights. Study the purposes and placement of these lights and exposure determinations as described on page 78.

Close-up and copy work

When a picture series requires a large or enlarged view of a subject, it is not necessary or always advantageous to take the picture close up; a negative or a portion of a negative can be enlarged in making the print. (This flexibility is an advantage of having negatives.) But close-up picture-taking may give sharper images or better perspective. Close-up photography presents problems of parallax, viewfinding, focusing, lens diaphragm setting, exposure timing, and lighting; solving these problems may require knowledge and use of special equipment and attachments. The problems and solutions are discussed and explained on page 82.

When copying flat materials with either a single-lens reflex or a view camera you view the subject directly through the camera lens. Materials can be placed on a stand, the camera set on a tripod, and lights adjusted as shown on page 83. But with other cameras, in order to overcome the problem of parallax when copying, use a focal frame or a simple copy stand. Suggestions for constructing and using such a stand are on page 84.

A reminder—remember to obtain a release when preparing to use copyrighted materials. See the form on page 49.

Titles and illustrations

Since most print series are designed for study by individuals, there is need for explanatory titles, captions, labels, and possibly diagrams in addition to photographs. Titles should serve the purposes noted on page 54 and captions may need refinement according to the suggestions. Then:

1. Word each one so that it is brief and communicative.
2. Select materials or aids for appropriate lettering. (pages 101–108)
3. Prepare the lettering, keeping in mind the final proportions of your photographs, using simple yet effective design features and appropriate backgrounds. (pages 92–94)
4. Use close-up copy techniques to photograph each completed title. (page 86)

Prepare captions, labels, and *overprint* titles by first making an 8″×10″ or larger print from the subject negative (page 88). In planning the composition be sure to provide light areas where black lettering will appear or darker areas to support white lettering. Then select an appropriate method for doing the lettering from among the special techniques described on pages 108. Film the final title according to suggestions on page 86. Print each title negative along with others in the picture series.

When preparing illustrations:

1. Plan the artwork. (page 91)
2. Select suitable backgrounds. (page 109)
3. Use appropriate illustrating, drawing, and coloring techniques. (pages 95–98)
4. Use close-up copy techniques to photograph each illustration. (page 86)

Composition

A well-composed picture tells one story or points out only one specific detail. Plan for simplicity of composition and clarity and sharpness of detail.

The actual size and placement of a subject within the picture frame can be decided during enlargement printing. But as you

plan and photograph each scene keep in mind the general suggestions for good composition on page 80.

Scheduling and record keeping

As you plan to take your pictures, make a list of scenes that can be filmed conveniently together. Then schedule each group. Organizing the work thus will save time and facilitate your picture-taking. See the example on page 48.

Then, as you prepare to shoot pictures, consider the suggestions on page 47. Keep a record of the scenes filmed, the number of times each is taken, the camera settings used, and any special observations. Develop a form similar to the sample log sheet on page 48.

Be alert to the matter of copyright limitations as explained on page 47. Remember to obtain a release from those persons appearing in your pictures. See the sample form on page 49.

PROCESSING FILM

It may be desirable to send exposed film to a processing laboratory for developing. Frequently color negative film is handled in this way since the procedure is long, requiring careful time and temperature controls. But processing black-and-white film is easy and fast, requiring a minimum of equipment and facilities. The procedures are outlined on page 86.

EDITING AND MAKING PRINTS

Selections must be made from among the many pictures taken —some are in addition to those called for in the script or are substitutes; others are multiple takes of the same scene but differ in composition and exposure. First make *contact prints* or small enlargements (up to 4″×5″) of all usable negatives (page 89).

Examine the prints, choosing those of highest quality that fit or supplement each scene in the script. Refer to the log sheet prepared during picture-taking for assistance in making choices. Make your final selection and assemble the prints, titles, and illustrations in sequence.

Now complete final or master enlargements of proper size and number.

Regular darkroom tray processing may be satisfactory for one or a few copies. If a number of prints will be needed, consider using the photo stabilization method with its processor as described on page 89. For a large quantity of prints here are alternatives for duplication:

- Diazo paper copies from translucent master photographs (page 123)
- Commercial reprints for volume above 250 copies (source, page 239)
- Screened negative and plate for offset press run (page 127)

PREPARING PHOTOGRAPHS FOR USE

The final task is to prepare your picture series for attractive display or for ease of use by individuals and for durability.

Protecting

Protect the surfaces of photographs and other mounted materials that will be handled a great deal.

- Coat them with a clear, fast-drying plastic spray
- Seal a mylar laminating film over the face of the picture (page 92)

Mounting

Mounting photographs on cardboard protects them and assures long service. Use the dry-mount method described on page 112.   If a flexible backing is desirable, as for a turnover chart or a small booklet, mount the photographs on a cloth backing as shown on page 116.

In a series for use by individuals, separate photographs should be attached together. Cloth sheets may be stapled (cover staple points with tape), while cardboard pieces may be bound with inexpensive plastic loops (punch the cardboard and insert the loops—sources on page 239).

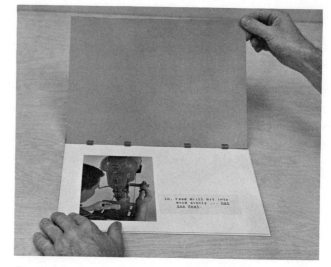

Plastic Loops

Then press the tape to the picture backing, *on the back side.* Three or four such tape-tack units can hold fairly large and heavy display materials to a wall.

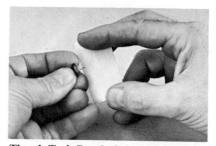

Thumb Tack Punched through Masking Tape

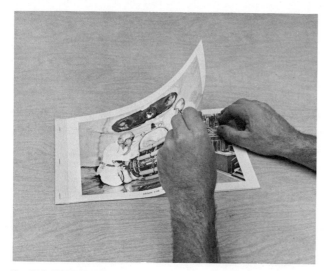

Stapled Cloth Booklet

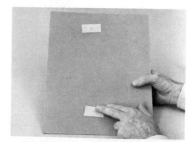

Tape-Tack Units on Back of Mounting

Displaying

If your picture series is to be displayed for ready reference, or will be part of an exhibit, make use of the principles of design and the suggestions for layout on page 92.

Photographs can be attached to the display surface with a variety of adhering aids, some of which are not visible from the front side when applied to the back of each corner.

One of the most effective techniques is to use masking tape through which thumb tacks are punched from the adhesive side.

Other useful adhering aids, not visible from the front side of a display, are:

- Double-sided tape (Base-Tape) that has pressure-sensitive waxed surfaces on both sides
- Regular masking tape cut in 1-inch strips and looped on itself with the adhesive-side out
- A puttylike adhering plastic (Plasti-tak) that is activated by stretching and kneading

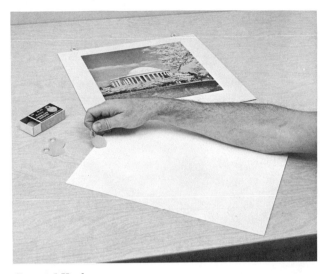

Gummed Hooks

Eyelets

If the same materials are to be displayed over and over again, consider using gummed-back cloth hooks or setting eyelets in the cardboard (available from art-supply or dry-goods stores). These may be used with straight pins or hooked to small nails permanently set in the display board.

Now, review what you have learned about producing a photographic print series:

1. What minimum planning is necessary as you prepare to make a print series?
2. What picture-taking equipment would you use?
3. How will you process the exposed film?
4. What is meant by "editing the contact prints"?
5. What is your procedure for making photographic enlargements?
6. In what form will you prepare the photographs for use?

19. Slide Series

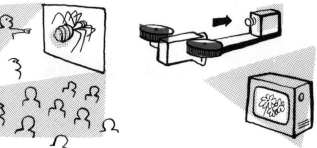

Individual Study   **Group Viewing**   **Television Use**

A slide series consists of transparencies, usually in color for projection, all mounted in square frames, usually 2″×2″.

A slide series may convey information, teach a skill, or affect an attitude through individual study, group viewing, or television use.

Before making slides always consider this planning check list:

- Have you clearly expressed *your idea* and limited the topic? (page 23)
- Have you stated the *objectives* your slide series should serve? (page 23)
- Have you considered the *audience* which will use the slide series and its characteristics? (page 24)

- Have you prepared a *content outline?* (page 28)
- Have you written a *treatment* to help organize the material and then sketched a *storyboard* to assist in your visualization of the content? (page 40)
- Have you decided that a slide series is the *best* medium for accomplishing the purposes? (page 34)
- Have you prepared a *scene-by-scene script* as a guide for your slide-making? (pages 42)
- Have you considered the *specifications* necessary for your slides? (page 43)
- Have you, if necessary, selected other people to assist you with the preparation of materials? (page 26)

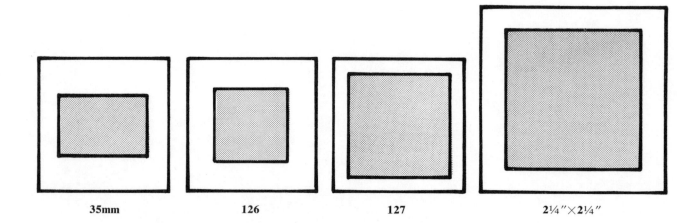

35mm   **126**   **127**   **2¼″×2¼″**

The preparation of a slide series involves four main steps: (1) taking pictures, (2) processing film, (3) editing slides, and (4) preparing the slides for use.

The information in Part Three, chapters 15 and 16 on photography and on graphic techniques is basic to the successful preparation of a slide series. As necessary, refer to the page references indicated with the following topics.

TAKING PICTURES

Your camera

Most of the cameras described on pages 65–67 can be used to prepare slides. Color films are available for box cameras, for twin-lens reflex cameras (using film sizes 120 or 620), and most popularly, for 35mm and size 126 cameras. Negatives from films used with larger cameras can be reduced by a laboratory to 2″×2″ slides. Those cameras with adjustable lens settings (f/numbers), shutter speeds, and attachments for focusing are especially useful since their flexibility enables you to record various subjects under almost any light and action conditions.

The majority of slide series are made with 35mm and 126 cameras. There are two major types.

- One with a *window viewfinder* through which you see a picture slightly different from the one that the camera will record. This difference becomes greater as the camera gets closer to the subject. (Study the parallax problem described on page 82.)

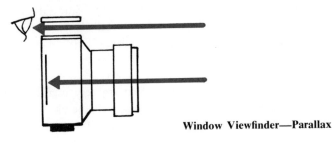

Window Viewfinder—Parallax

- The other (single-lens reflex camera) with a *reflecting mirror* and a prism which permits you to accurately view the same picture that the lens transmits to the film—regardless of the distance from camera to subject.

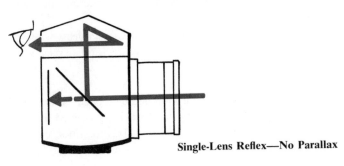

Single-Lens Reflex—No Parallax

The single-lens reflex camera is preferable for picture-taking in which framing is critical, as in close-up and copy work. With some difficulty most other 35mm cameras can be adapted for close-up photography.

Carefully study the three settings that are made on adjustable cameras—lens diaphragm, shutter speed, and focus. Understand the purposes of each, the relationship of one to another and to depth of field, and determine how each setting is made on your camera. These matters have been discussed and explained on pages 67-72.

Accessories

You may find need for:

- A photographic light meter to determine exposure accurately (page 74)
- A tripod to steady the camera (When filming at shutter speeds slower than 1/25 second *always* use a tripod.)
- A flash gun or photoflood lights for indoor scenes (page 77)
- A close-up attachment to photograph subjects at close range and to do copy work (page 83)
- A cable release to eliminate any possibility of jarring the camera during long exposures

Film

Select a reversal film to prepare slides when only one or a few copies will be needed. If many copies will be required, use a color negative film if it is available for your camera. In addition to considering the factors explained on pages 72–74, select film on the basis of:

- The main light source that will strike the subject (daylight or photoflood; see the note about fluorescent lights on page 78)
- The anticipated light level (low, moderate, high)
- The desired sharpness of reproduction
- The desired reproduction of colors
- The expected number of pictures to be taken (based on 35mm 20- or 36-exposure cassettes or rolls)
- The manner of film processing (by film laboratory or by yourself)

Selections can be made from among commonly used color films listed in the table on page 143.

Exposure

Correct exposure is based on proper camera settings for the film used and for the light conditions under which pictures are to be taken. Film information sheets provide general exposure data for average conditions (page 74). For proper exposure, reversal color films permit only a narrow range of camera settings, limited to from one-half to one f/ stop on either side of the correct setting; therefore use a photographic light meter to determine exposure accurately. Follow the recommendations on pages 74–77.

COMMONLY USED 35MM COLOR FILMS

Film	Type	Exposure Index (ASA)		Use
		Daylight*	Photoflood*	
Color reversal:				
Kodachrome II	Daylight	25	12 (80B)	Good color, high resolution,
	Type A	25 (85)	40	and sharpness for slides
Ektachrome X	Daylight	64	20 (80B)	Color saturated; like Koda-chrome in other respects
High-Speed	Daylight	160	50 (80B)	Available moderate light in-doors and outdoors
Ektachrome	Type B	80 (85B)	125 (3200°K)	
Anscochrome 500	Daylight	500	125 (80A)	Available low light
Color negative:				
Kodacolor X	—	80	40 (82A)	For prints and slides; gives strong, true colors
Ektacolor X	Type L	50 (85B)	80	For prints and slides; gives softer colors
	Type S	100	32 (80B)	

* Numbers in parentheses are filters recommended for converting film to use with other than recommended light sources. Note how the exposure index drops.

The data about films, as indicated in the accompanying chart, are correct as of the time of writing; but changes and new developments can be anticipated. Carefully check the data sheet packaged with your film for the latest assigned exposure index and other details.

Lighting

As is indicated in the table of film characteristics (page 144), color films are designed for use with specific light sources. Select your film accordingly, although with a proper light-balancing filter a film can be used under other than the recommended light conditions. When such filters are used, the exposure index of the film is reduced (example: Kodachrome II Type A with exposure index 40 when used outdoors requires a No. 85B filter and the exposure index is reduced to 25). Refer to the film-information sheet packaged with each roll for detailed information about light-balancing filters.

For many slide subjects the use of artificial lighting is necessary. To boost the light level, photoflash bulbs in reflectors or electronic flash units may be used. They are handy and easy to operate, especially when small areas must be illuminated. Make sure that your camera is synchronized (at the recommended shutter speed) with the flash. Then apply the information and formula on page 77).

For more carefully controlled lighting use photoflood lamps. They are available in various sizes and are used with separate metal reflectors or have reflectors built into them. In place of regular photoflood lamps, consider using highly efficient *sealed quartz lamps* of approximately 1000 watts. Avoid flat lighting created by placing lights beside the camera only. Instead, establish a lighting pattern involving a key light, fill lights, and supplementary background and accent lights. Study the purposes and placement of these lights and methods for determining exposure with them as described on pages 78–79.

Close-up and copy work

Close-up and copy techniques often are very useful when preparing color slides. Your script may call for close-ups of objects, for details in a process, or for copies of maps, pictures, and diagrams. For these purposes, as has been mentioned, the single-lens reflex camera is the more suitable by reason of its accuracy in viewing. Refer to pages 82-85 for guidance; these deal with viewfinding, parallax, focusing, lens openings, exposure timing, and equipment and attachments that you may need for this special kind of photography. They also suggest procedures for copying flat materials and for constructing and using a simple copy stand.

A reminder—always remember to obtain a release when preparing to use copyrighted materials; see the form on page 49.

Titles

Titles should serve the purposes noted on page 54. Be sure to take account of the legibility standards for projected materials (pages 99–100) as you select lettering sizes for titles, captions, and labels. Then:

1. Word each title so it is brief *and* communicative.
2. Select materials or aids for appropriate lettering. (pages 100–108)
3. Prepare the lettering and artwork (pages 91–98), keeping in mind the correct proportions of your slides (page 92 and inside front cover), using simple yet effective design features (page 92), and selecting appropriate backgrounds (page 109).
4. Use close-up copy techniques to photograph each completed title on color film (page 82).

You can prepare titles on black-and-white film and then color them quickly and with ease to make negative or positive slides:

To make a negative slide:

1. Prepare lettering and art work in black on white paper or on cardboard (if necessary use the paste-up technique on page 121).
2. Film the title. Use either 35mm Eastman Kodalith or 35mm Eastman High Contrast Copy film. The Kodalith film is preferable and its use is described on page 181.
3. Process according to instructions; when dry, swab the emulsion (dull) side of the negative with transparent water-color dye or with a colored felt pen.
4. Mount the film in a cardboard frame for use.

To make a positive slide, prepare white lettering (dry-transfer letters) on black paper and film as above, or:

1. Follow step 1 as for making a negative slide.
2. Follow step 2 as for making a negative slide.
3. Contact print the negative onto a piece of high-contrast cut film (page 183).

4. After developing, fixing, and washing, dip the positive into concentrated transparent water-color dye, then hang it to dry. The clear film background will absorb the dye evenly.
5. When the positive is dry, mount it in a cardboard frame for use.

Special titles, captions, or labels can be added to prepared color slides. In composing such slides be sure to provide light-colored areas where black lettering will appear and darker areas to support clear lettering:

To add black lettering to a slide:

1. Prepare a high-contrast negative and then a positive on cut film as in making a positive slide. Do not color the background.
2. Seal the slide and this positive in the same mount between glass covers.

To place white or clear lettering on a pictorial slide, double-expose the original subject and the lettering on the same frame

of film. (Check your camera's instruction booklet to determine if double exposure is possible before applying this method.) Then:

1. Prepare lettering in white on nonreflecting black paper or cardboard.
2. Film the subject slightly darker than normal (one-half f/ stop underexposed) so that the lettering will stand out.
3. Then cock the camera *without advancing the film.*
4. Film the lettering with normal exposure and then advance to the next frame.

You can use various methods, according to the materials you have to work with, for superimposing colored letters on a slide.

Here are several:

• Place colored letters directly on an original flat picture, then copy the picture and lettering together as a slide. The letters most useful for this method are the dry-transfer letters described on page 101.
• Place a diazo-colored transparency of the lettering over the original flat picture, then copy the combination as a slide. For information about diazo transparencies, see page 169.
• Make a high-contrast positive of the lettering on film and use this as a master to prepare a diazo-colored 35mm slide (page 183).Then align and seal the diazo slide in the same mount with the prepared color slide.

To put colored lettering on a colored background, prepare the lettering on a color background according to one method described below and film:

• Use colored lettering on colored paper, cardboard, or suitable background material.
• Use a diazo-colored transparency (page 169) over suitable colored background.
• Use the Multicolor diazo process (page 171) to prepare lettering and contrasting background colors on one sheet.

A variation of the *progressive disclosure* technique, used with overhead transparencies (page 162), can be applied to slides. Use this method if a series of titles or a list is to be shown, one at a time, but in cumulative order.

Prepare the total list on white paper, then use the *negative slide* method for preparation as described previously. Frame the entire list, then cover all items but the first one with a sheet of white paper. Film the first item. For the second picture, uncover the second item and film the two that are exposed. Repeat with three items uncovered, and so forth. The result will be a series of slides, each one revealing an additional title or item on the list.

After the slides are completed, use felt pen to color the words comprising the list. Use a different color for each new item introduced on a slide. In this way the new item will stand out and be separated from the prior items on the list.

Illustrations

For preparing illustrations and diagrams:

1. Plan the art work in terms of the slide proportions. (pages 91–92)
2. Select suitable backgrounds. (page 109)
3. Use appropriate illustrating, drawing, and coloring techniques. (pages 95–98)
4. Use suitable copy techniques to photograph each illustration as a slide. (page 82)

Composition

Composition must take place in the viewer of your camera when you film each scene; therefore study the general suggestions for good composition on pages 80–81. As you select subjects, keep in mind the proportions of the slides you are preparing.

If you can, prepare all slides with a uniform format—preferably horizontal.

Scheduling and record keeping

As you plan to shoot your slides, make a list of scenes that conveniently can be filmed together. Then schedule each group. Organizing the work thus will save time and facilitate your picture making. See the example on page 46.

Then as you prepare to make slides, consider the suggestions on page 46. Keep a record of the scenes filmed, the number of times each is taken, the camera settings used, and any special observations. Develop a form similar to the sample log sheet on page 48.

Remember to obtain a release from the persons appearing in your pictures. See the sample release form on page 49.

PROCESSING FILM

One advantage and convenience in using reversal color film is that after exposure, a roll may be sent to a film-processing laboratory (through your local photo dealer). The slides are returned mounted in cardboard frames ready for projection. But, if desired, most color films (Anscochrome, Ektachrome, and color negatives) may be processed with kits of prepared chemicals. Time can thus be saved between filming and seeing the completed slides; moreover, if a number of rolls are ready at about the same time, money also can be saved. The requirements and some of the cautions that must be observed when processing both reversal color films and color negative films are outlined on pages 87–88.

EDITING SLIDES

Selections must be made from among all the slides—some are in addition to those called for in the script or are substitutes; others are multiple *takes* of the same scene but differ in exposure and composition.

Place all slides on a light box or other illuminated area for ease of inspection. Discard those so indicated on the log sheet prepared while filming. Examine the slides; eliminate the poorer ones until the remaining selection is limited to those only of highest quality that fit or supplement the prepared script. Now revise the script as necessary and, if spoken or recorded commentary is to accompany the slides, refine it. Refer to the suggestions on page 50.

With the editing finished, your slide series is nearing completion. It may be advisable at this time to show the series and to read the narration to other interested and qualified persons. For suggestions for developing a questionnaire to gather reactions and suggestions which may help you to improve your slide series, see page 51.

PREPARING SLIDES FOR USE

Slides may be mounted in commercial cardboard frames, in snap-together plastic mounts (source on page 239), or between glass plates. The glass seems advisable for protection when slides are to be handled a great deal or are to be used with older types of projectors that may not preheat the film, resulting in buckling and changes in focus on the screen.

But there are drawbacks to glass-mounted slides:

• They are heavier than cardboard mounts, and more expensive.
• They require more time when mounting.
• The glass may break if slides are dropped.
• Moisture often collects under the glass, or even mildew.
• Glass-mounted slides may not fit into some holders or slide magazines.

Moreover, slides may not need the protection of glass. In modern projectors they are removed from magazines and returned to magazines mechanically during projection, and thus are touched by the hands only when being filed or rearranged in the magazines.

Regardless of whether you mount in cardboard or between glass, always protect the surface of film being handled by wearing thin cotton gloves (generally used when editing motion-picture film).

Mounting in cardboard frames

Use these tools and materials: cotton gloves, hand iron, cardboard mounts, gummed-back thumbspots, scissors—and the film to be mounted.

Materials for Mounting in Cardboard Frames

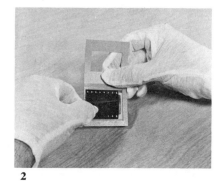

1

3

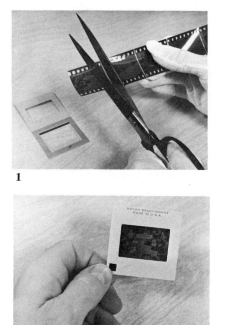

4

1. Cut the film along the frame line between the pictures.
2. Align the film in the mount.
3. Using an electric iron (set at "low"), seal all four sides.
4. Put a thumbspot in the lower left-hand corner (as you view the slide correctly).

Mounting in glass

At one time slides were sealed in glass with slide-binding tape. This preparation required much hand work; eventually, also, the tape might loosen or become sticky. Moreover, some projector trays or magazines do not accommodate tape-bound slides. More recently, with the availability of metal and plastic frames into which the film and glass slip easily, mounting slides in glass can be accomplished quickly and with little effort.

Get together these materials and equipment: soft brush, razor blade or scissors, paper mask, glass plates, frames, and the film to be mounted. The procedure shows the use of the Eastman Kodak metal frame.

1. If the film is in a cardboard frame, cut the cardboard and remove the film.
2. Dust each piece of glass.

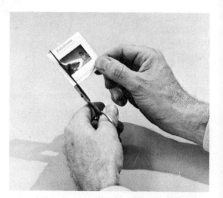

1

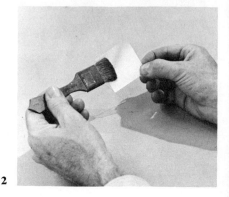

2

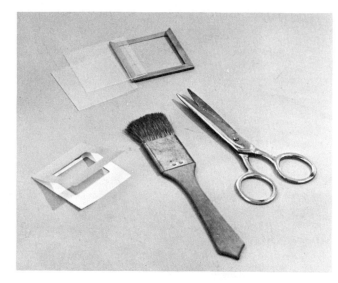

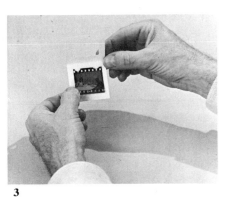

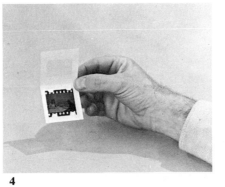

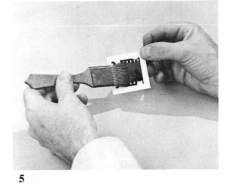

3

4

5

3. Align the film in the paper mask (silver side up).
4. Set the film under the paper tabs.
5. Dust the film on both sides.

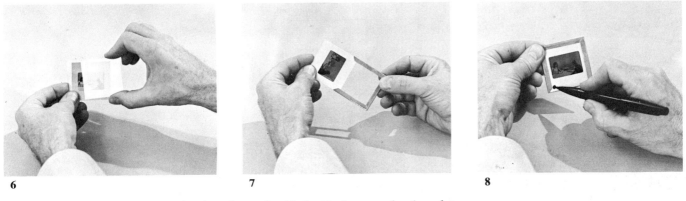

6

7

8

6. Place the mask with the film between the glass plates.
7. Slide the sandwich (upside-down) into the metal frame to complete the mounting.
8. Add a thumbspot to the lower left-hand corner (as you view the slide correctly).

Thumbspots, punched from gummed-back labels, help you to arrange slides correctly for viewing and for projection.

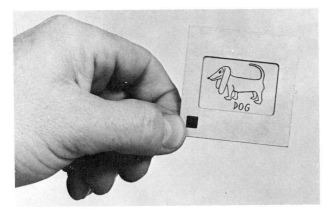

Thumbspot in Lower Left Corner when the Slide Is Viewed Correctly

Thumbspot in Upper Right Corner when the Slide Is Correctly Positioned for Projection in a Manually Operated Projector

Thumbspot in <u>Upper Right Corner</u> when the Slide is Correctly Positioned for Projection in a Carousel Projector Tray

RECORDING NARRATION

Narration may be used with a slide series in the following ways:

- as informal comments while slides are projected
- as formal reading of narration as slides are projected
- as recorded narration with an *audible* signal to indicate slide changes
- as recorded narration with an inaudible signal which electronically controls slide changes (requiring a special programing unit connected between the tape or record sound unit and the slide projector)

If a tape-recorded narration is to be prepared, refer to earlier suggestions concerning the selection and duties of personnel, recording facilities and equipment, and recording and tape-editing procedures. (pages 129–134)

Disk recordings can be made in quantity from the master tape to accompany duplicate slide sets. Sources for this service are given on page 241.

DUPLICATING SLIDES

If the number of duplicate slides that will be needed is known before photographing begins, then all duplicates can be made as high-quality originals when the original subjects or materials are photographed. Should additional sets be required after photography has been completed, a film-processing laboratory can make duplicates of the original slides.

Some people successfully project slides onto a matte-surface screen and then photograph the image to make duplicates. Careful exposure and film-color balance to match the color temperature of the projection lamp are important. (Use film balanced for photoflood light.) A slide made by this latter method

will have more undesirable contrast (deeper and darker shadows and whiter highlight areas) than does the original slide, and some loss of original color.

The most successful method of slide duplication is with a specially designed slide duplication unit. It consists of a camera, with an appropriate close-up lens, mounted vertically over a translucent glass plate that holds the original slide to be copied. Behind the glass plate is an electronic flash unit. Exposure information is printed on the vertical bar holding the camera.

Repronar Slide-Duplication Unit

FILING SLIDES

Initially most slides are stored in the small 20- and 36-exposure boxes in which they are received from the processing laboratory. As quantities of slides are accumulated some type of filing system is advisable so that individual slides can be located easily. Develop a numerical filing system and consider the illustrated filing methods.

Slide Box   **Slide Cabinet**

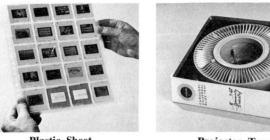

Plastic Sheet   **Projector Tray**

SELECTING A PROJECTOR

Simple slide projectors require the operator to insert each successive slide in a holder, feed it by hand into the projector, remove it by hand, and so continue with each slide in the series. The process is slow and requires much care to keep slides arranged properly. The operator must be alert for focus change as heat from the projection lens causes cardboard-mounted sides to buckle. The operator using such a projector must give undue attention to mechanics and can scarcely conduct a narration or give a lecture in addition.

For most slide projectors, adapters are available for attaching magazines or tray-fed low-cost slide-changing units, either hand-operated or remotely controlled from a distance through an electric cord with a push button (operated by the speaker once the machine is switched on). Newer projector models preheat slides in the magazine maintain correct focus, and are completely automatic, even permitting wireless remote control (including focus as well as slide changing). Such units eliminate all the problems inherent in the hand placement of slides—inversion, wrong sequence, or off-cue changes. Magazines for some projectors have capacities as high as 100 slides, thus permitting a program to be set up in a single loading.

Magazine projectors offer further advantages with respect to the preservation, care, and storage of slides.

• Slides are protected from frequent handling and thus need not be protected by glass.
• Slides may be quickly removed from magazines for examination and resequencing. Unless so removed, they are always in proper order and in proper position for projection.
• Magazines and trays are easily handled and stored.

Automatic slide-projector and tape-recorder combination units offer the added feature of being able to put an inaudible signal on the tape which, at the proper instant, will set off a relay that causes a slide change. Such a unit accomplishes automatic projection of slides, correlated with narration. Separate "programing units" for use with many tape recorders (may require stereo units) and slide projectors (having remote-control outlets) also permit this operation (see the list on page 239).

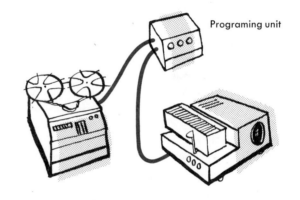

Programing unit

For individual use of slide series, a number of compact viewers that magnify or project the slide image from the rear onto a translucent screen may be used. More sophisticated models include sound playback units using tape cartridges which electronically control slide changes and may permit the viewer to stop the tape while studying the slide image.

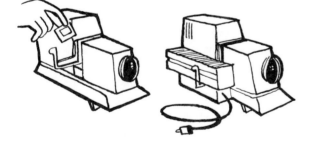

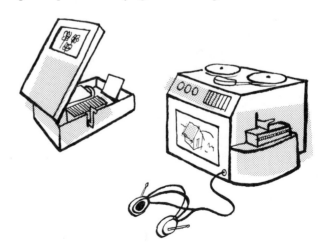

In summary, there are available:

- projectors requiring hand placement of slides—may be used with separately operated tape recorders.
- projectors with hand-operated or remotely controlled changing units having slides in magazines or trays—may be used with separately operated tape recorders.
- combination or separate projectors and tape recorders—with inaudible-signal automatic slide-changing attachments.
- hand or table viewers for individual use—may be used with separately operated tape recorders.
- automatic projection viewers for individual uses—some with sound playback attachments.

TECHNIQUES OF PROJECTION

One advantage of using slides in magazines is the ease with which a showing can be "programed." This means that you decide not only the order of using slides, but also when you want to transfer the attention of the audience to other matters (participation activities, discussion, or whatever) by interrupting the projection. To accomplish the latter insert $2'' \times 2''$ pieces of cardboard in the magazine at places where the screen should be dark with no image. Then when a blank falls into projection position the light rays from the lamp are interrupted and the screen goes dark. When the audience is ready for the next slide, projection can smoothly start—the blank is removed and the next regular slide is shown.

Slides lend themselves very readily to *multiple image* projection (often termed multimedia or cross-media use). Two and in

some cases three screens may be used, each with its own projector. Comparisons, relationships, and examples are effectively shown as two or more slides are projected simultaneously. This type of projection requires careful planning and coordination during use and should be considered only when the technique can make an important contribution to better communication (as opposed to using a single projector and one screen). See references for multiple-screen use on page 232.

Slides also can be used with other media, projected at the same time. Overhead transparencies and motion pictures are examples which, for some purposes, can be effectively correlated with slides.

PREPARING TO USE YOUR SLIDE SERIES

With the completion of the slide series and of your preparations for using it, consider the advisability of developing an instruction guide as described on page 57.

Remember that the success of your slide series will depend not only on its content and quality, but also on the manner in which you introduce and show it to an audience. As you prepare for the first showing, if your materials are designed for group use, follow the suggestions on page 60.

Now, apply what you have learned about preparing slide series:

1. What size film does your slide-making camera use?
2. Is your camera a window-viewfinder or a single-lens-reflex type? What are the advantages or limitations of it?
3. What film or films would you select for use? Why have you made your choice(s)?
4. What method of making slide titles would you use in each situation:
   a. a general main title having black lettering on a colored background?
   b. "overprinting" a word on a prepared slide?
   c. a series of three titles to be shown progressively as negative slides with colored words?
5. What factors do you consider in making choices during editing of slides?
6. Assuming your slides will be handled a great deal, how would you protect them?
7. Describe one use you might make of "multiple image" projection.

20. Filmstrips

Group Viewing

Individual Study

A filmstrip consists of a series of illustrations and photographs on 35mm film, in sequence, prepared for projection.

The filmstrip may convey information, teach a skill, or affect an attitude through individual study or through group viewing.

Before making pictures always consider this planning check list:

• Have you expressed *your idea* clearly and limited the topic? (page 23)

• Have you stated the *objectives* the filmstrip should serve? (page 23)

• Have you considered the *audience* which will use the filmstrip? (page 24)

• Have you prepared a *content outline?* (page 28)

• Have you decided that a filmstrip is the *best* medium for accomplishing the purposes and handling the content (as opposed, possibly, to a series of slides)? (page 34)

• Are you aware of the difficulties that must be overcome in making a filmstrip? (page 154)

• Have you written a *treatment* to help organize the material and then sketched a *storyboard* to assist in your visualization of the content? (page 40)

• Have you prepared a *scene-by-scene script* as a guide for your picture-taking? (page 42)

• Have you considered the *specifications* necessary for your materials? (page 43)

• Finally, if necessary, have you selected other people to assist you with the preparation of materials? (page 26)

TYPES OF FILMSTRIPS

There are two types of filmstrips, both on 35mm film: the single-frame and the double-frame. Most filmstrip projectors will show either.

Single-frame filmstrips

The most common type of filmstrip, standard in commercial preparation, is the *single-frame* filmstrip. It consists of pictures about 18mm × 24mm positioned on 35mm film so that the long dimension runs across the film. The proportion of this single-frame picture is thus nearly though not exactly 3 to 4.

To prepare this type of filmstrip a single-frame 35mm camera is necessary. Two such cameras are sold under the trade names of Olympus and Petri. Single-lens reflex models are available, which, in addition to use for direct filming, are best for copying photographs, art work, or even slides for filmstrip production.

In commercial production of single-frame filmstrips a precisely aligned 35mm motion-picture camera, held on an animation stand to permit rapid changes in position, is used.

Double-frame filmstrips

Pictures on a *double-frame* filmstrip are of the same size as those on 2″×2″ slides, that is, 24mm × 36mm. The long dimension runs in the lengthwise direction on the film. The proportion of this double-frame picture is nearly though not exactly 2 to 3.

A standard 35mm camera is used to prepare the double-frame filmstrip, either directly from original subjects or as a copy of prepared illustrations.

SPECIAL CONSIDERATIONS WHEN PLANNING A FILMSTRIP

During planning, in addition to the usual steps on page 153, consider these special factors that influence good filmstrip results:

- Treat the filmstrip as an entity, with continuity among frames, rather than as a series of separate disconnected pictures.
- A filmstrip need not be limited to a single visual medium. It may consist of photographs, art work, diagrams, charts, or graphs in any combination. Select the appropriate medium to best serve each scene in your script.
- Variety in the pace of a presentation is important. If narration is to be used, vary the timing of it from frame to frame. Captions also should vary from a few words in some frames to as many as 15 or 20 words if required.

DIFFICULTIES TO OVERCOME

There are several ways of making filmstrips, all of which present certain difficulties that must be understood and faced.

Making a filmstrip requires a camera with an accurate film-transport mechanism, extreme care when filming, and a great deal of patience on your part. Most important is the need for accurate alignment and registration so that the film is advanced exactly the same amount from one frame position to the next. Very few cameras, other than expensive professional ones, provide this accurate movement. Minor variations between frames may not be too serious, as slight adjustments can be made in framing during projection, but you should be aware of this problem.

Any error made while filming—wrong picture order, improper composition, or wrong exposure, will require reshooting the entire filmstrip (with the same risks repeated). Therefore you must take care and use a systematic procedure. Follow the script carefully, and keep an accurate record of pictures taken and exposures used.

The length of the filmstrip you can make is limited by the length of the film available for your camera. A normal 36-exposure roll of 35mm film can result in a strip of 30 double frames or 66 single frames, leaving a few frames for leader and trailer. Longer filmstrips require special camera attachments or the services of a film laboratory.

The difficulties extend to duplicating filmstrips as well as to making them. Duplicating an original filmstrip requires special equipment and it is best to leave this reproduction process to a qualified film laboratory.

The information in Part Three, chapters 15 and 16, on photography and on graphic techniques is basic to the successful preparation of filmstrips. As necessary, refer to the page references indicated with the following topics.

MAKING A FILMSTRIP BY DIRECT FILMING

For beginners, the direct-filming procedure is *not* recommended (consider, instead, making a slide series, which can be converted into a filmstrip or projected as slides). But an experienced photographer, if he observes care as to standardized procedure, details, and uniformity of pictures, can prepare a satisfactory color filmstrip by filming scenes directly with a regular or single-frame 35mm camera.

Remember! Direct filming will produce a *double-frame filmstrip* unless a single-frame camera is used. Hence, shoot all scenes with the regular camera in horizontal position—a double-frame filmstrip projector will not properly project vertical pictures. With a single-frame camera all pictures are taken as the camera is held vertically.

For direct filming, use a color reversal film (Anscochrome, Ektachrome, or Kodachrome). Balance for nonrecommended light conditions by using the proper filter. (page 144)

Exposure is a critical factor in direct filming, inasmuch as one poor picture will require refilming of the entire series. Carefully study the three settings that are made on adjustable 35mm cameras: lens setting, shutter speed, and focus. Understand the purposes of each, the relation of one to another and to depth of field; and determine how each setting is made on your camera. Then relate these settings to the determination of exposure. The three settings have been discussed and explained in this book on pages 67–72.

In direct filming, you must shoot titles, close-ups, and copy work at the proper points in the sequence. Prepare the titles and copy work in advance, and make ready for the close-up shots.

Finally, if you send the film to a laboratory for processing, be sure to indicate that it is to remain as a strip and is *not* to be mounted as slides.

MAKING A FILMSTRIP FROM SLIDES

The easiest method for preparing a filmstrip is to prepare slides and copy them onto 35mm film. Make a regular 2"×2" color-slide series, including titles and captions, as explained on pages 142–152.

Remember! All the slides must be in horizontal format.

The time before conversion is the time for editing and also for any tryout or review-evaluation. It may be advisable to show the series and to read any planned narration to other interested and qualified persons. For suggestions about a questionnaire to gather reactions and suggestions, see page 51.

You can transfer your slides to 35mm film for a filmstrip by using a single-frame 35mm single-lens reflex camera equipped with a proper close-up attachment and attached to a copystand. The slides to be copied are placed over a simple light box or other back-lighted surface.[1] Use a reflected-light meter to deter-

---

[1] For constructing a simple light box see page 25 in *Producing Slides and Filmstrips,* publication S-8, Eastman Kodak Company.

mine exposure. You may wish to shoot a roll of test film, exposing for various camera-lens settings, to be certain the correct exposure for your set-up is determined.

If a regular 35mm camera is to be used it is necessary to copy two slides at the same time, as this camera is of the *double-frame* type. The procedure is similar to that described for copying illustrations in the next section. Study the suggestions there and construct a mask to hold *two* pieces of 35mm slide film (remove the film from the cardboard mounts) to be photographed.

At least one commercial slide copy unit (the Repronar, see page 150) includes an attachment for converting 35mm slides to filmstrip form.

Recall that the format of a 35mm slide (3:2) differs from that of a single-frame filmstrip (4:3). Therefore in copying slides *cropping* or loss of part of the slide area must be recognized. To be prepared for this loss reproduce the cropping guide shown. Place the guide under a slide. Within the rectangle is the approximate area (depending on the aperture of your camera) of the slide that will be converted to the filmstrip frame. By examining a few slides you will realize that the subject for each slide must be composed so that important objects or action are not close to the side edges or they may be lost during conversion to filmstrip.

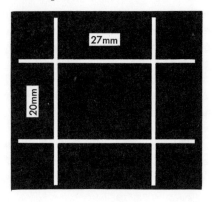

Commercial film laboratories, equipped with special copy facilities, can convert slides into single-frame filmstrips at a cost of $2 to $4 per color slide. For a list of film laboratories offering this service, see page 241.

For high-quality professional filmstrip results, most original materials are filmed on either 4″×5″ Ektachrome sheet film or as 2¼″×2¼″ slides. These larger areas permit sharper reproduction; simplicity in addition of captions, labels, and other markings; easier control of color (through color and contrast masking at the laboratory); and generally better over-all quality as compared to starting from the smaller 35mm slide. The versatility of 35mm originals can be increased by making color prints (4″×5″ size) from each slide, then retouching each print and overlaying lettering. The prints are then copied onto film as described in the next section.

MAKING A FILMSTRIP BY COPYING ILLUSTRATIONS AND PHOTOGRAPHS

One common method for making a black-and-white or color filmstrip from original materials is to prepare the illustrations and photographs in proper size and format and mount each on cardboard. Add titles, captions, and labels. Then send the complete set of these *filmstrip flats* to a film processing laboratory for conversion into a filmstrip, or copy the prepared flats yourself, in sequence, on 35mm film.

Follow the recommendations for preparing a picture series when making photographs (page 137) and the suggestions for making titles and captions (page 54), , in keeping with standards of legibility (page 99).

The size of each enlargement and illustration depends on the type of filmstrip to be prepared or on the 35mm camera to be used for copying:

- For filmstrip flats to be converted by a film laboratory, use the *single-frame mask* size as your guide in composing all illustrations, photographs, and titles. The proportion is 3 high by 4 wide (6″×8″) and an outline of it is printed inside the front cover of this book.
- For filmstrip flats to be copied with a single-frame camera, also use the *single-frame mask* size.
- For filmstrip flats to be copied with a standard 35mm camera to make a *double-frame filmstrip,* prepare your materials to fit within the *double-frame mask size.* The proportion is 2 high to 3 wide (6″×9″) and an outline of it is printed inside the front cover of this book.
- For filmstrip flats to be copied with a standard 35mm camera to make a *single-frame filmstrip,* prepare your materials to fit within the openings of a special *two-illustration mask.* The dimensions of this mask are shown inside the front cover of this book. (This design is recommended in *Photographic Production of Slides and Filmstrips,* publication S-8, Eastman Kodak Co.) The mask permits the placing of two illustrations

under the camera at one time. The proportions of the mask openings are near 3 high to 4 wide (2¾″×4″).

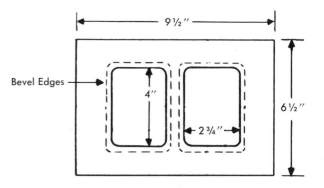

Two-Opening Mask for Copying Single-Frame Filmstrip with Standard 35mm Camera (adapted from "Photographic Production of Slides and Filmstrips," publication S-8, Eastman Kodak Company). See full-scale outline inside front cover.

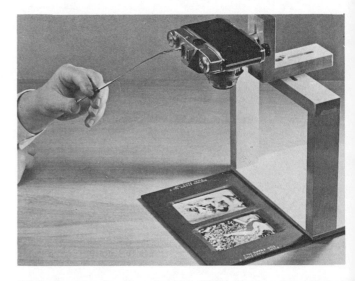

Camera Position for Photographing Single Frames with Standard 35mm Camera. The camera takes two frames on each exposure. (Reproduced with permission from the Kodak pamphlet "Simple Ways to Make Slides and Filmstrips.")

When using the above mask be sure each picture is located at the proper mask opening.

Follow these suggestions as you make ready and film your materials:

1. Before you convert the illustrations and photographs into your filmstrip, be sure to edit them carefully. Also, you may want to try the set out by showing them and reading any planned narration to other qualified and interested people. Revising pictures or captions at this point is less expensive than revising them after the filmstrip has been made. For suggestions about a questionnaire to gather reactions and suggestions, see page 51.

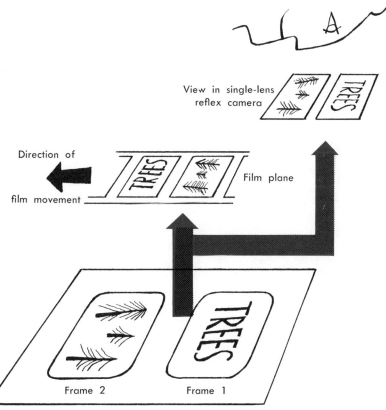

View in single-lens
reflex camera

Direction of

film movement

Film plane

Frame 2   Frame 1

Filmstrip Flats

2. When all illustrations, photographs, and titles have been prepared, using the appropriate mask cut from cardboard as a guide for precise positioning and mounting, number each piece in sequence for filming. Keep the numbers in a corner of the projection area, but have them clear and uniformly placed (the lower right corner is the usual location).

3. Prepare to copy the flats on a copy stand (page 83).

4. For black-and-white use a fine-grain film such as 35mm Kodak Panatomic-X (available in 20- and 36-exposure rolls) or 35mm Kodak Direct Positive Film (available only in 100-foot rolls which must be spooled into cassettes). Shoot five or more frames as a test. Process either film with a Kodak Direct Positive Film Developing outfit to a reversal or positive filmstrip (this procedure is quicker and more satisfactory than making a negative and then printing a positive from it—see the instructions with the film and developing outfit).[2] Examine the test print for exposure, framing, alignment, and focus. Repeat the test as necessary. For color use Ektachrome-X reversal film.

5. Shoot the total picture series to make a master filmstrip. Leave five or six black frames (by clicking the camera shutter with hand held over the lens) at the beginning as leader, and after the end title as trailer. If only a few copies of the filmstrip are needed, repeat the filming and developing procedure. (*Always photograph all filmstrip material in one working period.* Do not be distracted by other activities.)

For a large number of prints, duplicates can be made from the master filmstrip and the services of a film laboratory are recommended to insure quality and consistency. Check the requirements and prices of film laboratories which offer this service. For a list see page 241.

Upon completion, roll each filmstrip with the emulsion (dull) side on the inside to insure proper handling when projected. Store it in a filmstrip can (source on page 239) and label the can with the title.

CORRELATING WITH NARRATION

If narration is to accompany the filmstrip, refine it to fit the visuals (suggestions on page 50). Narration and supplementary comments can accompany filmstrip projection as:

- Informal comments and instructions for participation
- Formal reading of narration
- Recorded narration with an *audible* signal to indicate frame changes—either with a tape or disk sound unit

---

[2] Panatomic X is not a reversal film but is used as such in this method. See *Black and White Transparencies with Panatomic-X Film,* pamphlet F-19, Eastman Kodak Co.

- Recorded narration with an *inaudible* signal which electronically controls frame changes and requires a combination tape or record sound unit and projector

If a tape-recorded narration is to be prepared, refer to earlier suggestions relating to the selection and duties of personnel, recording facilities and equipment, and recording and tape-editing procedures (pages 129–134). Inexpensive duplicate disk recordings may be made as necessary, from the master tape. Sources for this service are given on page 241.

PREPARING TO USE YOUR FILMSTRIP

With the completion of the filmstrip and of your preparations for using it, consider the advisability of developing an instruction guide as described on pages 57-58. Consider also correlating the filmstrip with other materials for use in an instructional program.

Remember that the success of your filmstrip will depend not only on its content and quality, but also on the manner in which you introduce and show it to an audience. As you prepare for your first showing, if your materials are designed for group use, follow the suggestions on page 60.

Now review what you have learned about producing filmstrips:

1. Does your camera permit the preparation of a single-frame or a double-frame filmstrip?
2. For what reasons is it not advisable to make a filmstrip by direct filming?
3. What are three special considerations when planning a filmstrip?
4. What does "cropping" mean as it refers to slides for use in a filmstrip?
5. Which method of filmstrip preparation would you select to use? What steps in production does this entail?

21. Tape Recordings

Class Listening

Group Use

Individual Study

Tape recordings may be used by themselves to convey information, teach a skill, or affect an attitude; or they may be used in conjunction with visual materials. The latter uses are described with specific audiovisual materials in other chapters of this book. This chapter considers tape recordings, by themselves, for instructional purposes.

PLANNING A RECORDING

If recordings are simply oral duplications of reading matter or contain information that could be read more readily and probably more quickly, then recordings have little to offer as carefully designed, thoughtful, and exciting instructional materials. But if recordings are for small-group and independent study, as part of instructional packages, in which students participate actively, then such recordings can be thought provoking, making positive, creative contributions to instruction. In such cases planning becomes essential.

Planning a tape recording (or series of recordings) requires the same care as does the planning of other audiovisual materials, and should follow this sequence:[1]

---

[1] Refer to the work of S. N. Postlethwait, Purdue University, West Lafayette, Indiana, for use of the tape recorder as a guide for independent study. *See* S. N. Postlethwait, "Teaching Tools and Techniques: An Audio-Tutorial Approach to Teaching," *Pacific Speech,* vol. 1, no. 4, May 1967, pages 57-62.

- Establish objectives (page 23)
- Consider audience characteristics (page 24)
- Develop the content outline (page 28)
- Correlate with other media and learning experiences
- Prepare the script (page 42)
- Write the worksheet (page 57)

Instructional recordings designed for small-group or individual use must be self-teaching, without direct supervision by the teacher. Therefore a worksheet or other materials for the student should be furnished for use with the recording. The worksheet provides directions for using the recording and has places for responses to questions, for solutions to problems, and for activities initiated on the tape.

The tape portions of the lesson should be structured to contain the following:

- A motivational portion that introduces the lesson, its purposes, and any special preparation required (unless these are provided in the worksheet)
- Explicit oral directions that relate the worksheet and other available materials to the recording
- The teaching portion of the recording, usually recorded in a normal speaking voice
- Instructions for participation work
- Pauses of sufficient length (or instructions to turn off the recorder) to allow for completion of responses or performance of activities

• Indications of correct responses for immediate feedback
• Summary and/or instructions leading to other materials or activities

PREPARING A RECORDING

In some ways preparing recordings as instructional resources by themselves are easier than combining recordings with visual materials. In addition to the recording itself, the latter require attention to synchronization and pacing with the visuals.

The procedures for making recordings are presented in Chapter 17. Follow those steps that are important in your situation, especially with regard to:

• Recording facilities and equipment
• Selection of magnetic tape
• Recording procedure
• Tape editing and splicing
• Preserving and duplicating the recording

Also, consider the possible value in using a time-compressed-speech technique (page 134) for rapid scanning and reviewing of recordings.

Now, apply what you have read about planning and preparing tape recordings:

1. If recordings are planned as part of an instructional package, with what other materials or experiences might you correlate a recording?
2. What planning steps will you follow in developing a recording for group or individual use?
3. Of the procedures described in Chapter 17, which ones will you study for help in making the recording?
4. How will you make duplicates of your recording for use?

22. Overhead Transparencies

Large Groups   **Average-Size Classes**   **Small Groups**

Transparencies are large slides for use with an overhead projector from the front of a lighted room. They project a large, brilliant picture.

Transparencies can visually present concepts, processes, facts, outlines, and summaries to small groups, to average-size classes, and to large groups.

A series of transparencies is like any other audiovisual materials in requiring systematic planning and preparation. Before you set about making your actual transparencies, therefore, always consider this planning check list:

- What *objectives* will your transparencies serve? (page 23)
- What factors are important to consider about the *audience* which will see the transparencies? (page 24)
- Have you prepared an *outline* of the content to be included? (page 28)
- Are transparencies the best medium to accomplish your purposes and to convey the content? (page 34) Might they even be combined with other media for greater effectiveness? (page 34)
- Have you *organized the content* and made *sketches* to show what is to be included in each transparency? (page 40)

161

FEATURES OF OVERHEAD PROJECTION

[See Appendix A for film correlated with this topic.]

When showing visual materials with an overhead projector, you can make your presentation effective by using these techniques:

- You can show pictures and diagrams, using a pointer on the transparency to direct attention to a detail. The silhouette of your pointer will show on the screen.

- You can use felt pen or a special pencil to add details or mark points on the transparency during projection.

- You can move overlay sheets so as to rearrange elements of a diagram or a problem.

- You can control the rate of presenting information by covering a transparency with paper or cardboard and then exposing the data as you are ready to discuss each point.

- You can superimpose additional transparent sheets as overlays on a base transparency so that you separate processes and complex ideas into elements and progressively present them.

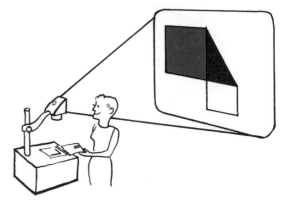

- You can simulate motion on parts of a transparency by using the effects of polarized light on special plastic with a polaroid spinner. (See "Polarizing the Projectual," *Visucom,* published by Tecnifax Corp., Holyoke, Mass., vol. 1, no. 3, pages 11-14; vol. 1, no. 4, pages 5-6; vol. 1, no. 5, pages 5-6.)

• You can show three-dimensional objects from the stage of the projector—in silhouette if the object is opaque, or in color if an object is made of a transparent color plastic.

• You can duplicate inexpensively on paper the material to be presented as transparencies. Distributing copies to the class or audience may relieve them of the mechanics of copying complex diagrams and outlines.

• You can simultaneously project other visual materials (slides or motion pictures) which illustrate or apply the generalizations shown on a transparency.

Evidence from research studies reported in chapter 3 indicates the value of student participation during learning. Develop some transparencies that involve the learner by requiring the completion of parts, replies to questions, or solutions to problems. Or, provide students with paper copies of the content of transparencies and instructions for activities relating to your presentation.

DIMENSIONS OF THE WORKING AREA

The area of the stage (the horizontal glass surface) of most overhead projectors is $10'' \times 10''$. The entire square can be used for the transparency, but it is better to avoid the extreme edges. Also, since a square is less attractive for most purposes than a rectangle, it is well to work within a rectangle having a height-to-width ratio of about 4:5. Thus a convenient transparency size, made on $8\frac{1}{2}'' \times 11''$ film, is $7\frac{1}{2}'' \times 9\frac{1}{2}''$. This is normally projected with the $9\frac{1}{2}''$ dimension horizontal because it is difficult to view some parts of vertically oriented transparencies in rooms with low ceilings or in those with suspended lighting fixtures.

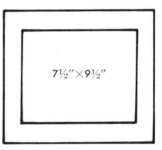

You can buy cardboard or plastic frames with the opening cut in them, or you can make your own from 6- to 10-ply cardboard. An outline of the open area of a frame is printed inside the back cover of this book.

Whatever the size of the mask opening you plan to use, prepare all art work, pictures, and lettering to fit within this opening or to have its proportion if size changes are to be made by photographic or other enlargement or reduction.

NECESSARY SKILLS

Design and art work

Limit the content of a transparency to the presentation of a single concept or a limited topic. Do not try to cover too many points in a single transparency. A complex transparency may be confusing to the viewer and thus lose its effectiveness. Design a series of transparencies rather than a crowded single transparency.

As you plan diagrams and outlines, or to add captions and labels to your materials, consider the applications of:

• Planning the design and artwork (page 91)
• Illustrating and coloring techniques (pages 95–98)

- Legibility standards for lettering projected materials (pages 99–100)
- Lettering materials and aids (pages 101–108)
- Preparing the lettering

If you select diagrams and printed materials from books or magazines to convert to transparency form, be alert to certain limitations:

- The format will probably be vertical rather than horizontal as recommended above.
- The quantity of information included in printed materials may be more than can properly be presented in a single transparency.
- Materials printed in a book, to be read and studied close-up at the reader's own pacing, may be too dense and thus not suitable for projection and group use.
- Finally, realize the limitations due to copyright and the need to request permission for certain uses (page 47).

Therefore, at first glance some printed materials may look suitable for use, but may in actuality be too small, too detailed, and even illegible as transparencies.

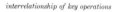

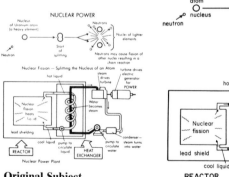

Original Subject

Redesigned for Transparency

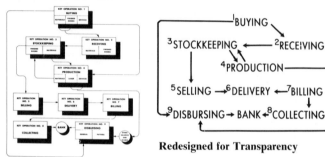

Original Subject

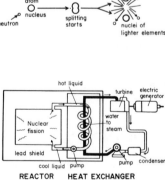

Divided into Parts for Series of Transparencies

Adding color

[See Appendix A for film correlated with this topic.]

The addition of color to parts or areas of a black-line transparency will clarify details or give emphasis to the content of a diagram. Use color purposefully.

Color must be transparent and can be applied in various ways:

- Use sharp-tipped felt pens directly on a transparency to write and draw lines (see page 97).
- Use broad-tipped felt pens to color areas on a transparency. Color may be applied as a solid area, although overlapping strokes build up layers of color and these irregularities become visible. Felt pens can also be used to color by applying parallel lines, as in hatching, or by making dots, as in stippling.
- Use diazo films (page 169), which are available in a number of colors. They give even, rich coloring effect.
- Use transparent color adhesives, available in a wide range of colors and black-and-white shading patterns. Color adhesives can be applied to areas of any shape and a number of colors can be used on a single transparency sheet. Add the color to the *underside* of a transparency. Follow the instructions on page 98 for using color adhesives.

Making overlays

[See Appendix A for film correlated with this topic.]

One of the most effective features of overhead projection is the *overlay technique*. As indicated on page 162, problems, processes, and other forms of information can be divided into logical elements, prepared separately as transparency sheets, and then shown progressively for effective communication.

In preparing a transparency in overlay form, first make a sketch of the total content. Decide which elements should be the *base* (projected first) and which elements, from the original sketch, will comprise each overlay. Make separate *masters* for the base and for each overlay. Then prepare a transparency from each master, using one or more of the techniques described in the following pages.

When mounting the final transparent sheets, attach the base to the underside of the cardboard frame and the overlays to its face on the appropriate sides (see page 184 for details in mounting).

To insure proper alignment of all layers of the final transparency carefully *register* the master drawings to the original sketch and also each piece of film to its master when printing. Do this by placing a guide mark (+) in each of two corners (outside the projected area) on the master exactly over the marks on the original sketch; or preferably, use punched paper and film aligned on a register board (page 91).

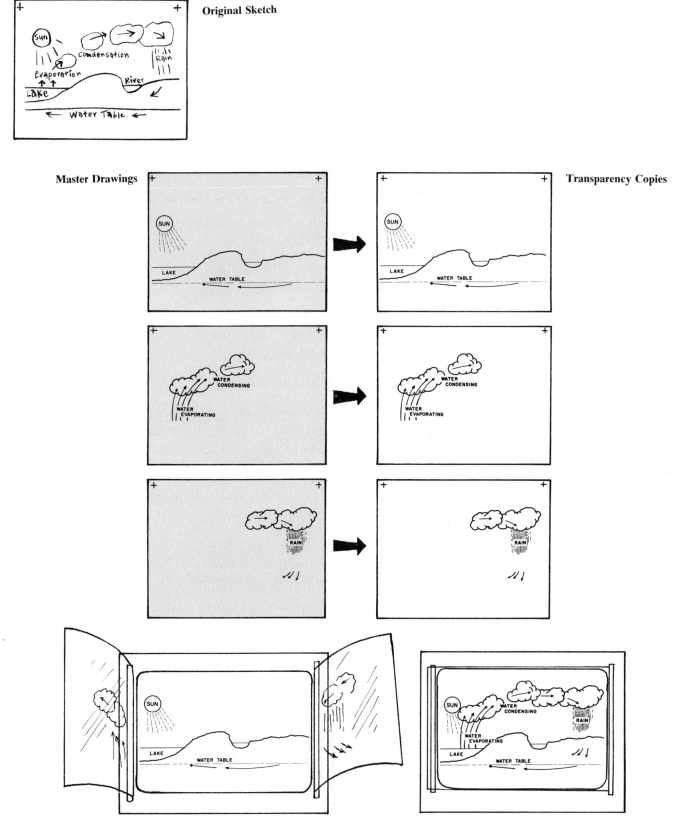

Original Sketch

Master Drawings

Transparency Copies

Mounted Transparency

Now, review what you have learned about planning transparencies:

1. Of all the features of overhead projection, which ones seem of most value to you?
2. Should you plan transparencies to be viewed horizontally or vertically, or does it matter? Reasons?
3. What are the inside dimensions of a standard transparency mount?
4. How might you plan one or more transparencies that require student participation during their use?
5. For what reasons might it *not* be advisable to use available printed pages as transparencies?
6. For what reasons might you use coloring on a transparency?
7. What should be the minimum letter size used on transparencies?
8. What lettering aids might you use in preparing transparencies?
9. To insure proper alignment, when preparing to make overlays, what procedure is followed?

PREPARING TRANSPARENCIES

Many processes have been developed for preparing transparencies. They range from very simple hand lettering or drawing to methods requiring special equipment and particular skills. Of these, the most practical and proven techniques are considered here. The methods are grouped as follows:

Making transparencies directly on acetate
  on clear acetate with felt pens
  on clear acetate with tapes and dry-transfer letters
  on frosted (matte) acetate
Making transparencies as reproductions of prepared diagrams
  with the spirit duplicator
  on diazo film
Making transparencies as reproductions of printed illustrations—with no size change
  on heat-sensitive film
  on diffusion-transfer (photocopy) film
  on electrostatic film
  as a picture transfer on pressure-sealing acetate
  as a picture transfer on heat-sealing acetate
Making transparencies as reproductions of printed illustrations—with size change
  high-contrast subjects
  halftone and continuous-tone subjects

Which method or methods to use? First, consider those most appropriate to your purposes, the subject matter, and the planned use for the transparencies. Your final decision should be based upon accessibility of equipment and materials, on your skills and available time, and certainly not of least importance, on your standards for quality.

Finally, ask yourself these questions as you start your preparation:

• Is the layout of the subject simple and clear?
• Have you checked the accuracy of content details?
• Will this be a single-sheet transparency or should you consider using overlays to separate elements of the subject—or might masking and uncovering of parts be effective?
• Will you plan to write some information on the finished transparency in addition to what is presented? (It is often more effective and attention-getting to add details or key points to an outline or diagram as the transparency is used or to involve the audience with activities relating to the transparency during use.)
• Is color important to the subject and treatment? If so, how should it be prepared?
• Is it satisfactory to do the lettering freehand or should you consider using a lettering aid like a boldface typewriter, dry-transfer letters, Wricoprint, or a Leroy set? (see pages 101-107) Remember to make lettering large enough for easy viewing—¼″ to ⅜″ minimum size.[1]
• Will duplicates of the transparency be needed for other users?
• Will paper copies of the content of the transparency, or related information, be needed for distribution to the audience before or after seeing the transparency?

MAKING TRANSPARENCIES DIRECTLY ON ACETATE

With these simple techniques transparencies are prepared quickly. They are not durable. For repeated use, neater and more permanent methods are advisable. But use these techniques for trying out your visuals; then, if necessary, make revisions before redoing them in permanent form.

On paper, outline the boundaries of the opening in the mount that you will use. Still on paper, make a sketch or position an illustration for tracing. Then, using the appropriate tools below, put your drawing or tracing on acetate. Complete the transparency as directed later in this section.

On clear acetate with felt pens

[See Appendix A for film correlated with this topic.]

Materials and tools: clear acetate sheets (.005″-.010″ thick preferred); a cardboard mount; fine-tipped and broad-tipped felt pens in colors.

See page 102 for a discussion of types and characteristics of felt pens. As indicated on page 97 under Coloring, the fine-tipped felt pens are designed for drawing lines and writing, while the broad-tipped ones are useful for coloring areas. All felt pens produce transparent colors and are therefore suitable for transparency preparation. The permanent-type inks require

[1] Sarah Adams and others, "Readable Letter Size and Visibility for Overhead Projection Transparencies," *AV Communication Review*, vol. 13, no. 4, Winter 1965, pp. 412-417.

a plastic cleaner or other solvent (such as lighter fluid) for removal. Marks made with water-base felt pens can be removed with a water-dampened cloth.

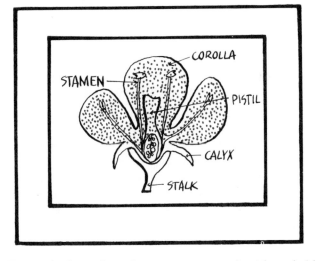

To protect the surface of a transparency made with washable inks, cover it with a clear sheet of acetate.

Some inks tend to run slightly; therefore use pens lightly. Also, colors may not take to the acetate evenly; therefore consider using a stippling method (small dots of ink) to color large areas.

On clear acetate with tapes and dry-transfer letters

[See Appendix A for film correlated with this topic.]

Materials and tools: clear acetate sheets; a grid or graph paper; rolls of transparent-color tapes or patterns; sheets of transparent-color dry-transfer letters.

Charts, graphs, and similar diagrams can be prepared quickly using tapes and dry-transfer letters. The tapes are available in various widths, colors, and black-and-white patterns. The letters and numerals are the dry-transfer sheets described on page 101, but with two differences—the colors are transparent and no wax is visible around a letter after it is transferred to the acetate.

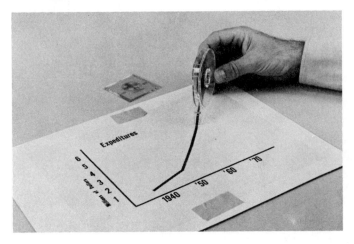

Use a grid sheet or graph paper under the acetate as a guide for placement and alignment of tapes and letters. When cutting strips of tape to length on the acetate, avoid making cut marks on the acetate—they will project as dark lines.

On frosted (matte) acetate

Materials and tools: frosted or matte acetate (.010″ thick and having a fine tooth); cardboard mount; black and transparent drawing inks; felt-tipped pens, or transparent-color pencils; lettering aids; clear plastic spray.

1. With the frosted side of the acetate up, trace the original sketch, using black or colored inks.
2. Apply color to the desired areas with pencils, felt pens, or inks.
3. Evenly and carefully coat the *frosted* side with plastic spray.
4. After the spray coat is dry, mount the transparency for use.

1

2

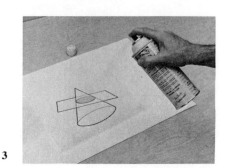

3

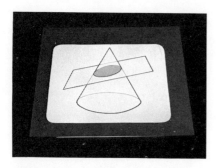

4

The difficult part of this process is in applying the plastic spray. It transparentizes the surface to permit brighter projection and also protects the drawing. Use the spray carefully to flood the surface lightly and evenly. Too much spray will cause certain coloring agents to run, while too little spray gives a spattered appearance.

In addition to these materials for direct preparation of transparencies on acetate, the following may also be used:

- A clear acetate that can be written or typed upon, resulting in a sharp, etched image that is opaque when projected (called "Type-on" film).
- A unit made up of clear acetate backed with a carbon-coated sheet (like a spirit master). Writing and typing directly on the acetate will transfer opaque carbon markings to its underside, resulting in a transparency. The acetate sheet, with its carbon markings, can also be used as a master on the spirit duplicator to make paper copies.

Now, review what you have learned about transparencies made directly on acetate:

1. Are all felt-pen colors suitable for use on acetate?
2. How can you remove the markings of a permanent felt pen?
3. Do felt pens cover areas evenly?
4. How would you protect from smearing a transparency that has been made with water-base felt pens?
5. What is special about the dry-transfer letters used on transparencies?

6. What is the warning offered when using a blade to cut color tapes on a sheet of acetate?
7. What writing materials are easy to use on frosted acetate that are *not* suitable for use on clear acetate?
8. What is the proper way for using the plastic spray?

MAKING TRANSPARENCIES AS REPRODUCTIONS OF PREPARED DIAGRAMS

To make transparencies as reproductions requires the preparation of one or more master drawings on appropriate paper and then the duplication of these drawings on transparent material. The spirit-duplicator and diazo methods are described immediately hereafter. In addition to these, the methods of copying on heat-sensitive film and on photocopy film, described in the next section, are suitable for making transparencies from original diagrams.

With the spirit duplicator

[See Appendix A for film correlated with this topic.]

Just as in making paper copies from a master with the spirit duplicator, a sheet of frosted (matte) acetate can be run through the machine. The acetate will pick up color carbon from the master, resulting in a translucent-type transparency.

Materials, equipment, and tools: sheets of frosted (matte) acetate, 8½″ × 11″, having a fine tooth; cardboard mount; spirit duplicating masters (with colored carbons); duplicating paper; a spirit duplicating machine; ball-point pen and lettering aids; clear plastic spray.

1. Prepare the duplicating master in the same way used for making paper copies; use colored carbons as may be appropriate.
2. Attach the master to the drum of the duplicating machine, cause fluid to flow to the wick, and adjust pressure.
3. Feed some paper through the machine and when a good image is being transferred send through a sheet of acetate (matte side up).

1

2

3

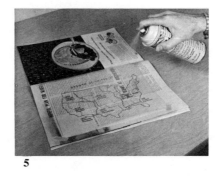

4   5   6

4. The acetate will pick up the image from the master just as did the paper.
5. Allow the image to dry. Then carefully coat the frosted side with clear plastic spray to transparentize and to protect the image. (See the warning about spray use in the previous process.)
6. After the spray coat is dry, mount the transparency for use.

There may be some difficulty in feeding the frosted acetate sheet through the spirit duplicator. The smooth surface of the acetate can cause slippage against the feed rollers. Experience has shown that you can push the acetate sheet into the machine, up against the drum, and it will then catch easier than if you depend on the feed rollers for transport. Also, owing to the attraction of static electricity charges after it passes through the machine, the acetate may stay on the drum, over the master, rather than move straight to the take-up tray. If it clings, carefully remove the acetate sheet from over the master so as not to smear the image.

For the last two processes described, frosted acetate was required. Select a fine grade of material. Some frosted acetates will not transmit sufficient light to make good transparencies. *Drafton,* a product of the Ozalid Division, General Aniline and Film Corporation, is an example of a suitable grade of frosted acetate for transparency preparation.

On diazo film

[See Appendix A for film correlated with this topic.]

Diazo films have been designed especially for the preparation of brilliantly colored transparencies. The term "diazo" refers to the organic chemicals, *diazo salts,* that along with *color couplers,* are coated on acetate. If the coating on the film is exposed to ultraviolet light, it is chemically changed so that no image will appear. But if the coating is *not exposed* to ultraviolet light and is *developed* in an alkaline medium, like fumes of commercial ammonia (ammonium hydroxide), the diazo salts combine with the color coupler in the film to form a colored image. By using various color couplers during manufacture, any one of about ten colors can be coated on acetate.

When film, or a section of a sheet of film, is first exposed to ultraviolet light and then developed in ammonia, color appears only in those sections *not* affected by the ultraviolet light. Thus

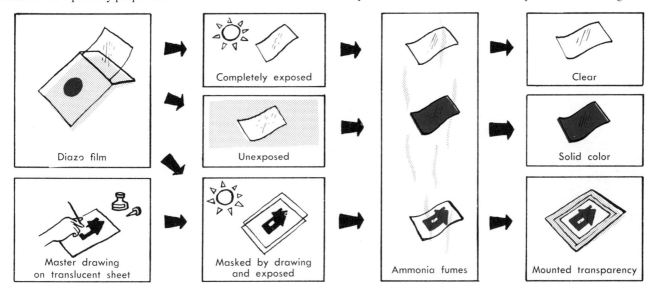

Diazo film | Completely exposed | Clear

Unexposed | Solid color

Master drawing on translucent sheet | Masked by drawing and exposed | Ammonia fumes | Mounted transparency

exposure to ultraviolet light *prevents* the color coupler uniting with the diazo salts to form a visible color.

Four simple experiments can be performed to aid in understanding the principle of the diazo process as explained above:

1. Take a sheet or piece of diazo film from its storage box and immediately place it in a jar of ammonia vapor.
2. Expose a sheet of diazo film to sunlight (3 to 5 minutes) or to another ultraviolet-light source and then develop it in the ammonia jar.
3. Cover a sheet of diazo film partially with opaque paper, expose as in experiment 2, and develop in ammonia.
4. Prepare an *opaque* line drawing on a sheet of tracing (translucent) paper; place it in contact with a sheet of diazo film; proceed to expose the two (light source—drawing—diazo film, in that order) and then develop.

Now, explain why the color appears on the film or does not appear for each experiment.

To prepare a diazo transparency, therefore, put lettering or drawing on a translucent sheet and expose it in contact with the diazo film to ultraviolet light; then develop the film in ammonia vapor. The opaque marks on the master diagram prevent the ultraviolet light from affecting the film next to them, hence color appears in these areas when the film is developed in the ammonia.

Materials, equipment, and tools: translucent tracing paper; cardboard mount; diazo film of selected color; black drawing ink; pen and lettering aids; diazo reproduction unit—ultraviolet-light printer and ammonia-vapor developer.

1. From a sketch, prepare a master drawing on translucent paper using black inks or other materials that make opaque marks.
2. Cover the drawing with a sheet of diazo film.
3. Place the drawing and film in the ultraviolet light printer. (Note the correct order: light below, drawing, film on top).
4. Close the cover and set the timer for proper exposure time.
5. After the exposure time has elapsed, transfer the exposed sheet of film to the container of ammonia vapor.
6. In a short time the image will appear. Keep the film in the ammonia until the color appears fully. (Overdevelopment is not possible.)

1

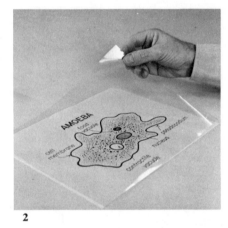

2

3

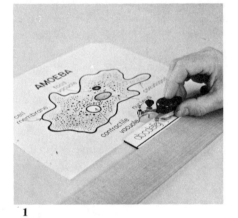

4

5

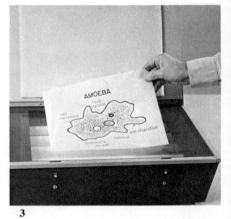

6

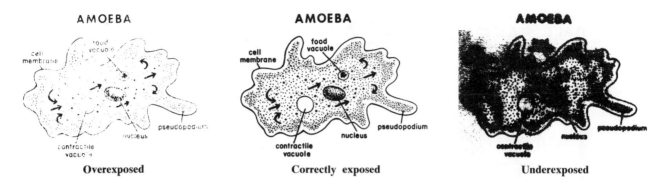

| Overexposed | Correctly exposed | Underexposed |

The transparency image may be too *light* or *faint* for projection; if so, print it again with a new sheet of film, *reducing* the exposure time. A *faint* diazo transparency has been *overexposed*.

If, on the contrary, the transparency shows some *unwanted tones* in the background, print it again with a new sheet of film, *increasing* the exposure time. A *muddy* diazo transparency with unwanted background has been *underexposed*.

In practical use, a number of different brands of diazo reproduction equipment (including ultraviolet-light printer and ammonia-vapor developer) are available. With each, the principle of diazo reproduction is the same.

**Visual Aid Printer
(VariTyper Corp.)**

**Mercury
(Keuffel & Esser Co.)**

**Ozamatic
(General Aniline and Film Corp.)**

**Protoprinter
(Tecnifax Corp.)**

Of key importance to the success of the diazo process is the paper used in making the master. Ultraviolet light must pass through the paper in those areas that are *not* to result in color on the film, while opaque marks are *necessary* on the master to block the ultraviolet light from reaching the film in order for color to appear. Thus for the master a transparent film or translucent paper is essential. Tracing paper, commonly used for engineering and drafting work, is highly translucent and is recommended. Select a grade with a fine fiber texture and use the same kind for *all* masters. If you change your master paper you may also change the correct exposure and thus waste film until the correct exposure is redetermined.

Another factor for success in the diazo process is the quality of the opaque marks made on the tracing paper. Black India ink makes good opaque lines. Pencils and typewriter ribbons are often not suitable.

The diazo process requires attention to a number of details and permits use of a number of effective techniques both in preparing the master and in modifying the transparency. Among these are:

- Exposure time in the printer is critical, but development time is not. Film must be developed long enough to obtain maximum color and can be removed from the ammonia any time thereafter.
- As many transparencies as are needed may be made from the one master drawing.
- For distribution to an audience, copies of the master drawing can also be made by the diazo process on inexpensive diazo paper.
- If areas of a transparency are to be in solid color, attach construction or other opaque paper in proper place on the translucent master. It will entirely block the ultraviolet light and result in a rich, even colored area.
- If more than a single color is needed on one sheet of diazo film, areas can be colored by applying one or more pieces of color adhesive material. See page 98.
- A heat-process transparency (next process) can be used as the master for color diazo work.
- Diazo films do not have a long shelf life. Keep unopened packages under refrigeration until ready for use. Allow the film to reach room temperature before use.

Cut the error out of the paper or acetate master.

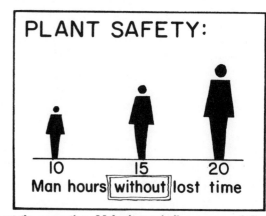

Insert the correction. Make it on similar paper and fix it in place with the tape. Do not overlap the edges of the paper.

- If an ink spot or other imperfection must be removed from the translucent master, the paper can be cut and the spot removed. The resulting hole in the paper has no effect on exposure or on the final transparency.
- Minor mistakes on the master may be corrected before the diazo film is exposed. Use a translucent tape (Scotch No. 810) that will not block ultraviolet light.
- On one brand of diazo film (Multicolor by VariTyper Corporation), more than a single color can be produced on a sheet of film. In this method, after exposure of the master and film to ultraviolet light, various color couplers are applied to areas of the image on the film to form any of five colors. In addition, both sides of the film are coated, permitting not only the coloring of intersecting lines and words, but the combining of two colors to form a third (a blue on one side and yellow on the other will produce a green area). The company also makes diazo-coated cardstock that is excellent for preparing slide, filmstrip, and motion-picture titles in colors.

Now, review what you have learned about transparencies as reproductions of diagrams:

1. Can you use color carbons, other than purple, when preparing a spirit master for a transparency?
2. Which side of the frosted acetate is upward when run through the spirit duplicator?
3. What technique can be used to insure that the acetate will pass through the duplicator?
4. Why is the spirit transparency sprayed after preparation?
5. Explain in your own words the principle of the diazo process.
6. What material is used as a master in the diazo process?
7. How would you prepare a master requiring a solid color to cover a large area?
8. What is the order in which materials are placed in the ultraviolet-light printer?

9. Which is critical for time—ultraviolet exposure or ammonia development?
10. If the lines on a diazo transparency are very weak, does this condition indicate *over-* or *under*exposure. Would you expose for a *shorter* or *longer* time?

MAKING TRANSPARENCIES AS REPRODUCTIONS OF PRINTED ILLUSTRATIONS—WITH NO SIZE CHANGE

Of the five methods described under this heading, the first three may be used either with printed line drawings or with original drawings prepared in black ink on white paper. The two described thereafter can be used with illustrations printed on clay-coated paper. Whatever method is being considered, keep in mind the following:

- Permission may be necessary to reproduce copyrighted materials. (page 47)
- Legibility standards for projected materials should be observed when printed items are considered, as most materials printed on paper are for close-up study and are not directly suitable for overhead projection. (page 99)

On heat-sensitive film

[See Appendix A for film correlated with this topic.]

This is a rapid process. It is completely dry and transparencies are ready for immediate use. Heat from an infrared-light source passes through the copy film to the original. The words and lines on the original must be prepared with "heat absorbing material" such as carbon-base ink or a soft lead pencil. These markings absorb heat and the resulting increase in temperature affects the film, forming an image on it within a few seconds.

Several brands of thermal copy machines are available. In each, the principle of thermal reproduction is the same. Most carry the original and film on a belt or between rollers around the infrared-light source. In one type (the Masterfax) the original and film lie flat and the infrared-light tube moves under them (page 120).

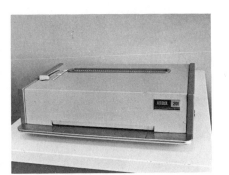

Master Transparency Maker (A. B. Dick Co.)   Secretary (3M Co.)   Masterfax (Ditto Co.) (For use, see page 120)

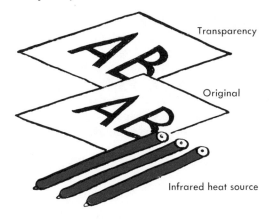

Transparency

Original

Infrared heat source

2. Place the projection film (with the notch in the upper right corner) on the original material.
3. With the film on top, feed the two into the machine.
4. When the two emerge, separate the film from the original.

2

The film to make basic transparencies in these machines is of three types:

• One step: heat-process film placed in direct contact with the master drawing (3M Co. product)
• One step: ordinary acetate and a sheet of special carbon paper are placed in contact with the master drawing.
• Two step: the master is charged; then the charged master and the film are placed in contact (Parlab product—see below)

Materials, equipment, and tools: printed or original material on paper; a cardboard mount; heat-sensitive projection film; copy machine.

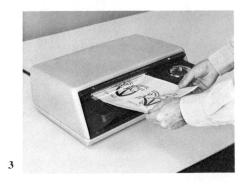

3

1. Set the control dial as directed (usually at the white indicator). Turn on the machine if necessary.

1

4

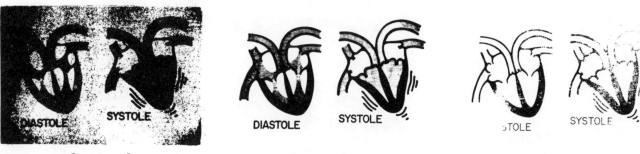

Overexposed   Correctly exposed   Underexposed

The transparency image may be *too light* or *too faint* for satisfactory projection; if so, print it again with a fresh sheet of film, *increasing* the exposure time (that is, with the machine running at *slower* speed). A *faint* heat-transfer transparency has been *underexposed*.

If, on the contrary, the transparency is *too dense,* or if there is *unwanted background tone,* print the transparency again with a fresh sheet of film, shortening the exposure time (that is, with the machine running at *faster* speed). An *overdense* heat-transfer transparency has been *overexposed*.

The thermal process requires attention to a number of details and permits the use of a number of effective techniques:

- There is no special requirement for paper on which original printing or master diagrams are prepared.
- Original materials for thermal reproduction should be prepared with black India ink, soft lead pencil, or large-size typewriter having a carbon-paper or well-inked cloth ribbon. Black printing inks are satisfactory, but inks of other colors, regular ball point pens and spirit duplicated copies (purple) are not suitable for thermal reproduction.
- If using India ink, make sure the ink is completely dry before the master is run in the copy machine.
- If you are uncertain about correct exposure or about the reproduction quality of a diagram, use test strips of the thermal film before exposing a whole sheet. Cut 4 to 6 vertical strips from one piece of film, being sure to clip a corner of each for proper placement on the diagram.
- In addition to black-image film, various colored-image, tinted (color background for black image), and negative films (black background with clear or colored image) are available.
- One manufacturer (Parlab) markets a thermal film which permits the addition of any number of eight colors to an etched image on the film resulting after exposure to heat. With the proper film, by this process, acceptable reproductions of photographs and negative transparencies may be prepared. For the standard process use the Parlab materials as follows:

a. Set the thermal copy machine at a setting used for buff-colored Thermo-fax paper.

b. Place a charging sheet over the original (gray side of charging sheet *down*) and pass the two through the machine *twice*.

c. Place Parlab film on top of the charged original and pass the two through the machine with the control set as above.

d. Discard the charging sheet and lay the film face down (image reversed) on paper larger than the film. Stain the image by swabbing with Wipe-on color using cotton, tissue, or other applicator. Use as many different colors over different areas as desired.

e. Remove any color on the acetate, outside of an image area, with a water-dampened cloth or the scratch-protective Scuff-Coat Lacquer.

- Add color to areas on a transparency with felt pens (page 97) or use color adhesive material (page 98).
- A thermal transparency, because of its opaque image, can serve as a master for the previously described diazo process.

On diffusion-transfer (photocopy) film

[This once widely-used method is being superseded by dry-process methods. Since the existing equipment will remain in use for some time, the process is explained here.]

The diffusion-transfer process is useful for reproducing pages from books, magazines, and other bound references, as well as from single sheets. It is a contact photographic process which takes place in subdued room light. A sheet of negative paper, held against the original page or sheet, is exposed to light which is transmitted through this negative to reach the original. The lighter areas of the original reflect light back to the negative sheet, while the printing or other marks on the original page absorb the light. This is *reflex exposure*.

Then the negative, placed in contact with a sheet of film positive, is developed in a single chemical solution. The image from the exposed negative transfers to the positive. After 10 to 30 seconds the two sheets are peeled apart carefully.

Several brands of photocopy machines are available. With the exception of the models from the 3M Company, the principle of diffusion-transfer reproduction is similar. Like the others, the 3M machines require a two-step process, but development is dry, requiring heat instead of a chemical solution.

Book Copier (Copease Corp.)

Model 120 (A. B. Dick Co.)

209 Copier (3M Co.)

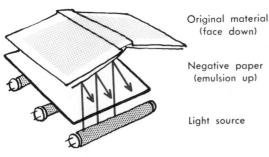

Original material
(face down)

Negative paper
(emulsion up)

Light source

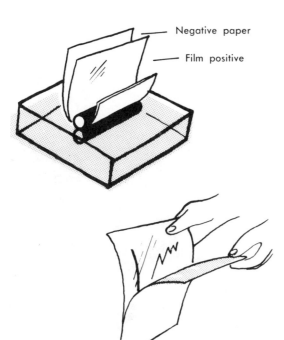

Negative paper

Film positive

Materials, equipment, and tools: original or printed material to be copied; diffusion-transfer negative paper; diffusion-transfer film positive; developing solution; cardboard mount; diffusion-transfer (photocopy) printing and developing units.

1. In the copy machine place a sheet of photocopy negative paper (sensitive side up) against the sheet or page to be copied.
2. Adjust and clamp the cover so that even pressure is exerted.
3. Set the timer for the recommended exposure and click on the switch.

1

2

3

4   5   6

4. After the exposure is completed, remove the negative sheet, placing against it a sheet of film positive (use either side).
5. Feed the two sheets through adjacent slits in the developing unit.
6. As the negative and film emerge from the developer the image will be visible.

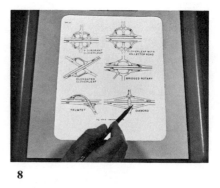

7   8

7. After 10 to 30 seconds, separate the film from the negative.
8. Hang the transparency to dry and then mount it for use.

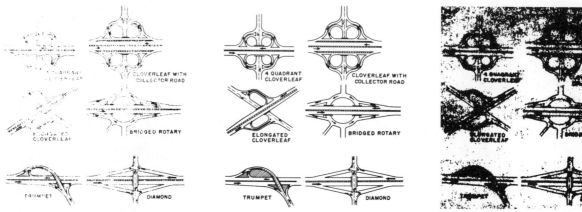

From Overexposed Negative   **From Correctly Exposed Negative**   **From Underexposed Negative**

The transparency image may be too *light* or *faint* for projection; if so, repeat the entire photocopy process using another negative sheet and film positive and *reducing* the exposure time slightly (one second makes a big difference). A *faint* diffusion-transfer transparency has been made from an *overexposed* negative.

If, on the contrary, the transparency shows some *unwanted tones* in the background, repeat the entire photocopying process using another negative sheet and positive film and *increasing* the exposure time. A *muddy* diffusion-transfer transparency with unwanted background tone has been made from an *underexposed negative*.

All printed pages (in any color or combinations), even though not reproducible by the thermal process, are reproducible onto paper or film by the photocopy method. A paper copy can be made and will serve as a master for a heat-process transparency or for making a thermal spirit master for duplication (page 124).

You can make an original by pasting up materials (page 121), then make a photocopy on paper or film. All paste-up marks will disappear.

On electrostatic film

The latest reproduction method—the *electrostatic process*—makes use of electrical charges. In this method specially coated electrically charged and light-sensitive film (or paper) is used. The original sheet or page is exposed to light which is reflected from the white parts, but not from the printed or drawn image, to the electrostatic film. Where the light strikes the paper the coating is discharged. The remaining charged areas (where the image will be) then collect a charged *toner* (a fine black powder) which, upon deposit, results in a visible, opaque image.

With appropriate film, most office-type electrostatic-copy machines can be used to prepare transparencies. For a further description of the process and pictures of equipment see page 126.

As a picture transfer on pressure-sealing acetate

[See Appendix A for film correlated with this topic.]

In this process the inks of printed pictures (color or black-and-white, *on clay-coated paper*) adhere to specially prepared acetate to make a transparency of the picture. The picture and the acetate are sealed together with heat and/or pressure, then submerged in water to dissolve the clay coating and soak the paper free from the inks. The inks remain on the acetate. A plastic coating applied after the acetate is dry transparentizes and protects the picture side.

A similar method that employs equipment is explained next after this.

Materials and tools: picture printed on clay-coated paper; sheet of Con-tact brand *clear* adhesive-backed shelf paper (available from hardware and houseware stores); wooden roller (used in craft work); tray of water; wad of cotton; clear plastic spray; cardboard mount.

1. Test the selected picture for clay coating by rubbing a moistened finger over a white area of the page, outside the picture. A white deposit on the finger indicates the presence of clay.

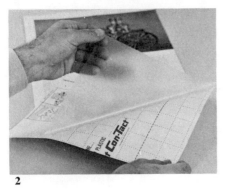

2

3

4

2. Separate the adhesive-backed acetate from its backing sheet.
3. Carefully adhere the acetate to the *face* of the picture.
4. Use a roller or other tool to apply pressure over the entire surface. Roll or rub in all directions.

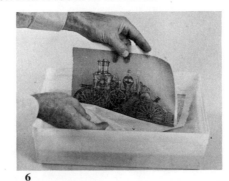

5

6

7

5. Submerge the adhered picture and acetate in a pan of cool water.
6. After 2 or 3 minutes separate the paper from the acetate. The inks of the picture and some clay adhere to the acetate.
7. With wet cotton, rub the image side (ink side) of the acetate to remove the clay. Be sure to loosen all the clay. Then rinse the transparency in clear water.

8

9

10

8. Blot the transparency between sheets of paper toweling or hang it to dry.
9. When the transparency is dry, coat the picture side with plastic spray to transparentize and protect the image. See suggestions on page 168 for correct use of the spray.
10. When the spray coating has dried, mount the transparency for use.

A pressure-roller laminating machine can be used to seal the picture to adhesive-backed laminating film.

Translifter (National Adhesive Co.)

Suggestions for avoiding problems when making a picture transfer include:

- Select bright pictures with sharp color contrasts for best-looking results.
- Keep the surface of the picture to be used as clean as possible because dirt, dust, and oil from fingers can prevent the ink from adhering to the film.
- Do not trim the picture before starting. Allow excess paper around the picture for film overlap.
- Cut the acetate so none will extend beyond the edge of the paper. If the film laps beyond the page it will stick to the table.
- Applying pressure to the acetate and picture is important to insure a good seal. Use a roller on both sides and in all directions. If a roller is not available, any blunt tool, like the back of a comb wrapped in a handkerchief, can be used.
- If a transparency does not fit the standard cardboard frame, cut a piece of cardboard with the necessary opening.
- Among the magazines from which successful picture transfers have been made are *Better Homes and Gardens, Cosmopolitan, Life, Look, National Geographic, Newsweek, Saturday Evening Post, Sports Illustrated, Sunset, Time,* and *U.S. News and World Report.*

As a picture transfer on heat-sealing acetate

[See Appendix A for film correlated with this topic.]

This method is in principle the same as the proceeding pressure-sealing one. In this one, heat is used and a dry-mount press is required to provide the heat and pressure. Use either Seal brand Transpara-film or Seal-lamin laminating film (page 118). The latter is much thinner, but less expensive.

Materials and equipment: picture printed on clay-coated paper; Seal film; pair of glossy metal plates; piece of flannel; tray of water; wad of cotton; plastic spray; cardboard mount; dry-mount press; timer.

1. Set the dry-mount press at 270°F.
2. Test the picture for clay (as in the preceding process).
3. Insert the metal plates in the dry-mount press and preheat the flannel between the plates to drive out moisture.

1

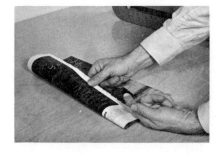

2

3

4   5   6

4. Dry the picture in the press on the flannel between the metal plates.

5. Remove the metal plates, flannel, and picture from the press and set the top metal plate to one side. The flannel should remain on the shiny side of the bottom metal plate, the picture face-up on the flannel. Cover the picture with a sheet of film, coated side down.

6. On top of the film set the other metal plate, shiny side down, and place the complete sandwich in the press. Have two pieces of thick cardboard on the base to increase the pressure.

7   9

7. Shut the press and apply heat for 2 minutes.

8. Follow steps 5 through 10 of the previous process on page 178.

9. The resulting transparency.

Note the suggestions on page 179 for avoiding problems when making a picture transfer. In addition to those listed, for this process allow the picture and film to curl naturally when removed from the dry-mount press. They will straighten out when cooled or in water.

The flat-bed thermal unit, the Masterfax (page 120), exerts great pressure as well as heat and also can be used with laminating film to prepare picture-transfer transparencies. Follow the same procedure as described for laminating on page 118.

Now, review what you have learned about making transparencies as reproductions of printed illustrations:

1. What is the main thing to check when preparing or selecting a diagram to be made into a heat-process transparency?

2. Is the kind of paper for the master important in the heat process?

3. If lines on a heat-process transparency are very weak and thin, is the film *over-* or *underexposed?* The next time, must you *slow down* or *speed up* the machine?

4. How might small areas be colored on a heat-process transparency?

5. Which process might be used to reproduce a printed diagram having three colors?

6. Explain why the photocopy process is a "two-step photography" process?

7. What is the first step in preparing to make a picture transfer from a picture?

8. How is pressure applied in both picture-transfer methods described?

9. Why must all the clay be removed from the transferred picture?

10. What is the difference in the use of the dry-mount press for a picture transfer and regular dry mounting?

MAKING TRANSPARENCIES AS REPRODUCTIONS OF PRINTED ILLUSTRATIONS—WITH SIZE CHANGE

To change the size of an illustration requires a camera and application of photographic methods. The following two techniques are basic ways of using photography to prepare overhead transparencies. Both use the same easy-to-handle film, but require different developers.

Before proceeding, review the following:

- Legibility standards for projected materials when printed items are considered for reproduction (page 99)
- Permission to reproduce copyrighted materials (page 47)
- Use of your camera, especially with reference to:
  sheet-film cameras, if available (page 66)
  camera settings (page 67)
  correct exposure (page 74)
  close-up and copy work (page 82)
- Processing film (page 86)
- Making prints (page 90)

Two processes are used: one for *high-contrast* subjects, the other for *halftone* subjects. Here are examples of the two kinds:

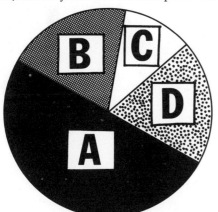

High Contrast: Lines, dots, or solid areas, with the paper between these unprinted.

Halftone: printed picture consisting of uniformly spaced dots, which blend together and convey shades of gray. The dots in this picture can be separated by the eye only under high magnification.

High-contrast film is used to make the transparencies, both for high-contrast and halftone subjects. High-contrast film is preferable to common orthochromatic sheet films for transparencies because it is easier to work with, has a clear base for projection, can produce more saturation in gray shades, and dries quicker by reason of being thinner.

High-contrast subjects

[See Appendix A for film correlated with this topic.]

Use this process to prepare transparencies from line prints and other high-contrast subjects.

Materials, equipment, and tools: subject for reproduction; high-contrast cut film or 35mm Eastman Kodalith; appropriate film developer, stop bath, fix; cardboard mount; press or view camera or 35mm single-lens reflex camera; camera accessories; film holders; copy stand; lights; darkroom facilities for film developing, printing, and enlarging under red safelights.

The high-contrast process has four steps:

1. Film the subject, using high-contrast film.

2. Process the film to a negative under a darkroom red safelight, using a recommended high-contrast developer.

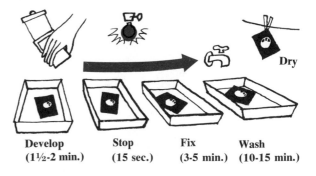

Develop (1½-2 min.)	Stop (15 sec.)	Fix (3-5 min.)	Wash (10-15 min.)

3. Opaque the negative to eliminate clear spots, paste-up marks, or unwanted printed areas.

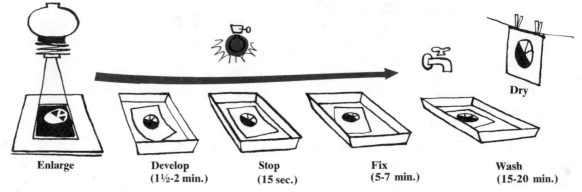

Enlarge   **Develop** (1½-2 min.)   **Stop** (15 sec.)   **Fix** (5-7 min.)   **Wash** (15-20 min.)   **Dry**

4. Enlarge the negative onto an 8″×10″ or larger sheet of the same high-contrast film and process the film in the same chemicals as in step 2.
5. Dry and mount the transparency for use.

Other suggestions:

• Prepare a large (8″×10″ or greater) high-contrast negative and *reverse it,* after development, to a positive transparency. Doing this requires using an etch bath and then permits coloring the positive image with transparent dyes. For a detailed explanation of this process see *Making Black and White Transparencies for Overhead Projection,* pamphlet S-7, Eastman Kodak Co., and "Reversing Negative Photographic Images," *Visucom,* Tecnifax Corp., Holyoke, Mass., vol. 1, no. 3, pages 4-6.

• Use high-contrast transparencies as masters for reproduction by the diazo process to make additional transparencies in color. (See page 169).

• Separate a subject into its components for preparing overlays by making a number of negatives of the subject equal to the number of overlays needed. Block out all but necessary areas on each negative by opaquing. Print each one, in the enlarger, onto a separate sheet of high-contrast film.

• Prepare a negative rather than a positive transparency by contact printing the original camera negative onto a piece of high-contrast film and then using this positive in the enlarger to make a negative transparency. Color clear areas of the final transparency with felt-pen colors. Or, if a copy camera 8″×10″ or larger is used, the negative prepared with it can be used directly as a transparency.

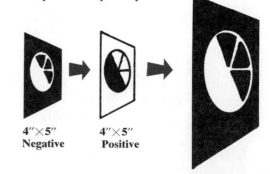

4″×5″ **Negative**   4″×5″ **Positive**

Enlarged Negative Transparency

• If a number of transparencies are to be prepared at one time, consider using the *photo stabilization* method with the appropriate high-contrast film and a rapid processor unit (page 89).

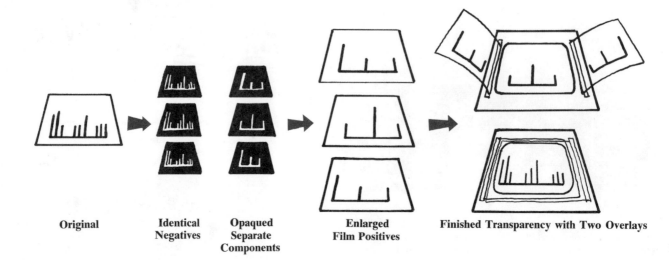

Original   **Identical Negatives**   **Opaqued Separate Components**   **Enlarged Film Positives**   **Finished Transparency with Two Overlays**

• Add color to areas on a transparency with colored adhesives. Apply it to the base (shiny) side of the transparency. (See page 98)

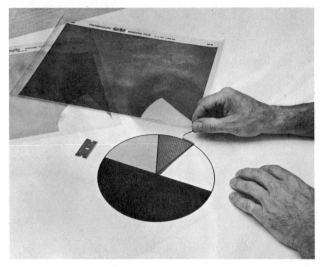

• Add special stressed plastic to areas of a transparency and use it in conjunction with a rotating polarizing disk (page 162) to create simulated motion or other unusual effects—an on-and-off blinking motion, an effect of turbulence, a swirling effect, a rotating effect, a flow effect, and a radiation effect. The plastic material is most easily applied to negative transparencies for which careful cutting is not important. See sources for this material and special equipment on page 240.

Halftone and continuous-tone subjects

In this category of subjects are halftone illustrations printed in books and magazines, photographs, and original works of art which contain shades of gray varying from white to black. Be sure to recognize the difference between such subjects and high-contrast subjects, which consist only of black marks on white paper.

A Halftone (or Continuous-Tone) Subject

Most transparency-making techniques previously described, except for the picture-transfer methods, start with masters that result in high-contrast transparencies (black or colored lines on a clear background). The quality of continuous-tone transparencies made by these methods is generally fair to poor. The results of the method described here are highly acceptable.

Although high-contrast film is used primarily for reproducing line subjects, it can be adapted to prepare continuous-tone transparencies from negatives of halftone and continuous-tone subjects. It is necessary to change the developer used in the first processing step from the normally used high-contrast developer to a regular photographic paper developer (Dektol or equivalent), diluted 1 part to 12 parts of water.

Materials and equipment: halftone or continuous-tone subject for reproduction; regular continuous-tone black-and-white film (see page 72), film developer, high-contrast sheet film, paper developer, stop bath, fixer, cardboard mount; camera and darkroom accessories.

1. Prepare a negative of the subject using regular black-and-white film

2. Process the film as recommended (page 86).

3. Enlarge the negative onto a sheet of high-contrast film. Make tests, as correct exposure time will be less than when enlarging a regular high-contrast negative or enlarging onto photo paper.

4. Process the film under a red safelight in *paper developer* (diluted 1:12 with water). Development proceeds rapidly and should be completed in 1½ minutes. Completion is indicated by the appearance of the full image on the base side of the film, but judge quality only under white light. A rich, dense image is the best for projection. The use of stop bath, fixer, and wash are the same as in the regular high-contrast process.

Transparency of Continuous-Tone Subject

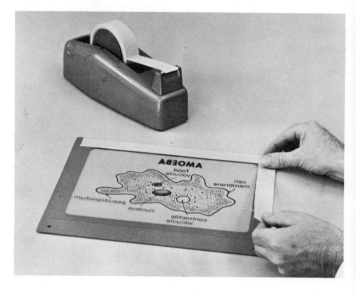

Now, review what you have learned about photographic methods to prepare transparencies:

1. What film is used in this process? Is the same film used for making the transparency, whether of a high-contrast or continuous-tone subject?
2. Can you differentiate between a high-contrast and a continuous-tone or halftone subject for a transparency?
3. What is meant by *opaquing* the negative?
4. In what ways does the enlarging process differ from that of making the negative?
5. In what ways does the preparation of a continuous-tone transparency differ from the preparation of a high-contrast one?
6. How can you use the photographic process to make a transparency involving overlays?

COMPLETING AND FILING TRANSPARENCIES

Mounting

[See Appendix A for film correlated with this topic.]

Mounting adds durability and ease to the handling of a transparency, but it is not always necessary to mount transparencies in cardboard frames. Transparencies to be used only once can be left unmounted as the cost of frames and the time to attach them may not be justified. Some people prefer to keep transparencies unmounted for ease of filing in notebooks, but the standard-size cardboard or plastic frame easily fits into letter-size filing cabinets. If overlays are to be used, mounting is essential.

Tape a single-sheet transparency to the *underside* of the frame. Use masking or plastic tape rather than cellophane tape for binding.

If the transparency consists of a base and overlays, tape the base to the underside of the mount as usual, and the overlays to the face. Be sure the overlays register with the base and with each other (page 164). Then fasten each overlay with a tape or plastic hinge along one edge of the cardboard frame.

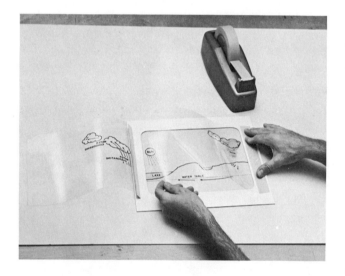

Overlays for successive or cumulative use can be mounted on the left or right sides of the cardboard frame, also if necessary on the bottom and top (the top edge should be the last one used). Trim any excess acetate from the edges of overlays so opposite or adjacent ones fit easily into place.

After mounting overlays, fold and attach small tabs of masking tape or adhesive-back labels on the loose upper corner of each overlay. Number them to indicate the order of use. These tabs are easy to grasp when overlays are to be set in place over the base transparency.

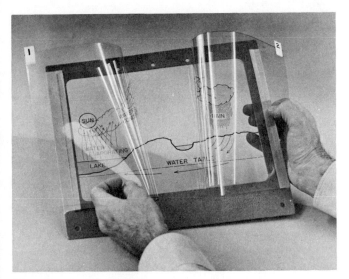

Transparency with Overlays

Masking

[See Appendix A for film correlated with this topic.]

To control a presentation and focus attention on specific elements of a transparency, use a paper or cardboard mask as was mentioned on page 162. The mask may be a separate unit, mounted to move vertically or horizontally, or may be a hinged opaque overlay. (For additional suggestions see "The Art of Masking," *Visucom,* Tecnifax Corp., Holyoke, Mass., vol. 1, no. 3, pages 2-3.)

Exposing Areas under a Sliding Cover

Exposing Areas under Hinged Masks

Adding notes

Write brief notes along the margin of the cardboard mount for reference during projection.

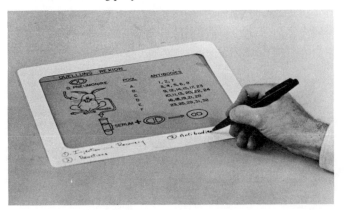

Filing

If your transparencies are in mounts 10″×12″ or smaller, they will fit in the drawer of a standard filing cabinet. File them under appropriate subject, unit, or topic headings.

PREPARING TO USE YOUR TRANSPARENCIES

Remember that the success of your transparencies will depend not only on their content and quality, but also on the manner in which you use them before an audience. Follow the suggestions on page 60 as you prepare to use your transparencies.

Now, review what you have learned about completing and filing transparencies:

1. Do you correctly mount a single-sheet transparency on the underside or the face of the cardboard frame?
2. How is a transparency with overlays mounted?
3. What are two ways of masking transparencies?
4. What filing system for transparencies might you use?

SUMMARY OF METHODS FOR PREPARING TRANSPARENCIES

	Method	Equipment	Cost of materials (approximate)	Time for preparation	Evaluation
Directly on acetate	1. With felt pens (page 166)	none	3¢ to 6¢	short to moderate	Suitable for quick preparation and temporary use; lack professional appearance.
	2. With tapes and letters (page 167)	none	10¢ to 15¢	short to moderate	Limited applications but useful for charts and graphs.
	3. On frosted (matte) acetate (page 167)	none	15¢	moderate	Frosted surface permits easy use of a variety of drawing and coloring agents, results in pleasing effects; requires careful use of spray; quality fair-good.
As reproductions of prepared diagrams	1. With spirit duplicator (page 168)	duplicator	20¢	moderate	Good way to make simple transparencies in color; requires both care and practice when passing acetate through machine and when spraying; also easy to make paper copies for distribution.
	2. On diazo film (page 169)	diazo printer and developer	25¢	moderate	Excellent method for preparing color transparencies; requires translucent originals; a variety of applications of the process are possible.
As reproductions of illustrations—with no size change	1. On heat-sensitive film (page 172)	thermo-fax machine; infrared-light copy machine	20¢ to 40¢	very brief	Good method for rapid preparation of one-color transparencies from single sheets; additional colors with Parlab film.
	2. On diffusion-transfer (photocopy) film (page 174)	photocopy printer and developer	23¢	short	Good method for transferring all kinds of printing from single sheets or bound volumes to film; requires drying film before use; provides copies on paper for further duplication.
	3. On electrostatic film (page 177)	electrostatic copy machine	25¢	brief	Requires an expensive machine, not always available, and a special film; quality not as good as other methods.
	4. As picture transfer on pressure-sealing acetate (page 177)	none	10¢	short	Converts any magazine picture printed on clay-coated paper to a transparency; a simple process to apply; results are very effective if suitable original pictures are available.
	5. As picture transfer on heat-sealing acetate (page 179)	dry-mount press	25¢	moderate	Similar to above process, but takes a few minutes longer; equipment often available in school or graphic production center.
As reproductions of illustrations—with size change	1. On high-contrast film (high-contrast copy) (page 181)	camera and darkroom	30¢	long	Most complex process in terms of skills, equipment, facilities, and time; but essential when original materials must be changed in size; results in high-quality transparencies.
	2. On high-contrast film (continuous-tone copy) (page 183)	camera and darkroom	30¢	long	Similar to above process; extends the use of high-contrast materials to preparing transparencies from color and gray tone subjects.

23. Motion Pictures

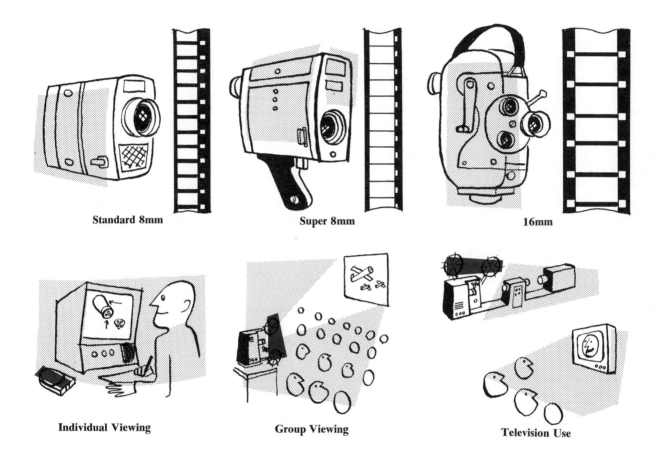

Standard 8mm **Super 8mm** **16mm**

Individual Viewing **Group Viewing** **Television Use**

Motion pictures for instructional use may be prepared as 8mm or 16mm films with subtitles or with sound.

A motion picture may present information that involves motion, describes processes, and shows relationships in order to convey knowledge, teach a skill, or affect an attitude through individual study, through group viewing, or by means of television.

For many purposes motion pictures continue to be the most effective and efficient medium of communications of all audiovisual materials. This advantage holds not only for treating subjects that require motion, but also for the ease of presenting sequences of still pictures (known as *filmographs*), with or without narration, or even combinations of still and motion, as required by the treatment. For some individuals these latter uses may seem to violate the basic premise that *subject motion is required in a motion picture*. But, as will be explained later in this chapter, this premise is not necessarily true.

With the development of cartridge-load projectors (silent and sound), the potential uses of motion pictures, especially for independent or self-instructional learning, are greatly enhanced. No longer need motion pictures be thought of as 10- to 30-minute-long complete treatments of total topics. Now fresh approaches to motion-picture planning and production can be made. For many purposes brief films, or *film clips,* often called *single-concept* films, may be prepared to illustrate a discrete skill or to present information on a limited aspect of a topic. Such films, generally in the 8mm size, may be from a few seconds to a few minutes in duration—just long enough to serve the objective and without formal introduction or summary. Also, directions for viewer participation can be incorporated in such films—as in programed instruction requiring responses to questions or actual performance.

Furthermore, in producing these brief films liberties can be taken with many of the formal "rules" of motion-picture photography without loss of communication effectiveness. But you should become aware of the standard procedures first. See page 212 for further discussion of some of these factors to be considered when making 8mm single-concept films.

So today, film-making should be viewed in a broader perspective than solely as the traditional *motion* picture that rapidly presents an explanation and illustrations on a total topic. This broader approach requires consideration of these factors and techniques:

- Visualizing static subjects and using still as well as moving subjects on motion-picture film.
- Flexibility in film length; sufficient length ranging from a few seconds to many minutes, to serve the objectives and to treat the subject.
- Incorporating programing techniques in the film that require the viewer to participate through response or performance.
- Using simple filming techniques that take liberties with traditional film-making procedures.
- Relating the film to other materials as part of a package for instruction.

But before you can consider departing from the rules you must be acquainted with the rules. This chapter presents the most important accepted techniques of film production for treating educational or instructional subjects. You should also review the evidence summarized from research on design elements in motion pictures. Much of the information presented in chapter 3 bears directly on film production.

Before any filming, planning is necessary—whether a brief single-concept film or a full-length production is to be made. The success of any film depends in great part on the care in planning. Consider this planning check list:

- Have you expressed *your ideas* clearly and limited the topic? (page 23)
- Have you stated the *objectives* to be served by your motion picture? (page 23)
- Have you considered the *audience* which will use the film and its characteristics? (page 24)
- Have you prepared a *content outline?* (page 38)
- Have you considered whether a motion picture is the *best* medium for accomplishing the purposes and handling the content? (page 34)

- Will your film be a *complete production* or will it be brief and treat a *single concept?* (page 187)
- Have you written a *film treatment* to help organize the story? (page 40)
- Have you sketched a *storyboard* to assist with your visualization of the content? (page 40)
- Have you prepared a *scene-by-scene script* as a guide for your filming? (page 42)
- Have you considered the *specifications* necessary for your motion picture? (page 43)
- Have you, if necessary, selected other people to assist with the preparation of your film? (page 26)

Following careful planning, the preparation of a motion picture involves a number of production steps:

1. Filming scenes, utilizing a variety of techniques.
2. Processing film.
3. Editing.
4. Preparing titles and/or adding sound.
5. Preparing to use the film.

The information in Part Three, Chapters 15 and 16 on photography and on graphic techniques is basic to the successful preparation of a motion picture. As necessary, refer to the page references indicated with the following topics.

BACKGROUND INFORMATION

Your motion-picture camera

[See Appendix A for film correlated with this topic.]

Get to know your camera. Doing this takes time. Sit down for an evening with your unloaded camera. Study the instructional booklet and try all the controls. Such experimentation is very useful.

Make certain that you can locate these external parts on your camera: lens, viewfinder, speed selector, footage counter, winding handle, release button. In its operation, each one serves an important purpose.

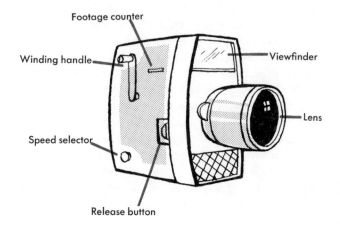

Footage counter

Winding handle

Viewfinder

Lens

Speed selector

Release button

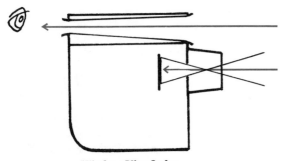

Window Viewfinder

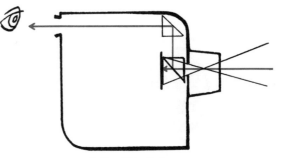

Reflex Viewfinder

- The *lens* (the single most important and often most expensive part of the camera) focuses light rays on the film.
- The *viewfinder* lets you see what will be included in the scene—either directly through the lens as *a reflex viewfinder* to give the same picture as that transmitted by the lens, or through its own window, resulting in a picture slightly different from that transmitted by the lens. This difference may be important when filming subjects at extremely close range. For a discussion of close-up techniques and the problem of parallax, see page 82.
- The *speed selector* indicates the speed with which the film will move through the camera, expressed as *pictures* or *frames per second*. (Common settings are for 8, 16 or 18, 24, 32, 48, and 64 frames per second.)
- The *footage counter* indicates either the amount of film exposed or that still remaining unexposed in the camera (commonly a maximum of 25 feet for Standard 8mm, 50 feet for Super 8mm, and 100 feet for 16mm).
- The *winding handle* permits you to tighten the camera spring in order to run film through the camera (most cameras operate on electric motors, either from batteries or house current).
- The *release button* starts film through the camera and exposes the individual frames of film.

Within your camera are these operating parts: supply spool, sprocket wheels, film gate, aperture, pull-down claw, take-up spool.

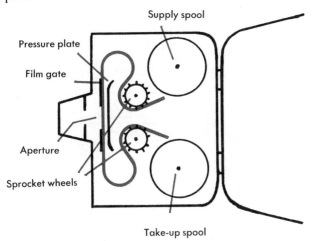

Supply spool

Pressure plate

Film gate

Aperture

Sprocket wheels

Take-up spool

1. The *supply spool* releases film by rotating clockwise.
2. The film passes around one side of a toothed *sprocket wheel* (not included on many newer cameras) and forms a loop before entering the *film gate* (channel).
3. Within the gate the film passes behind the rectangular opening, the *aperture*. Alongside the aperture the *pull-down claw* (see below) engages film sprocket holes, advancing the film one frame at a time, then disengaging and moving upward to pull down the next picture area.

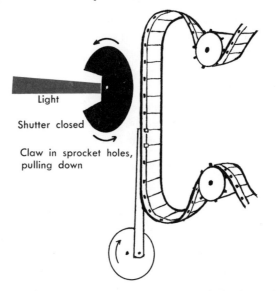

Light

Shutter closed

Claw in sprocket holes, pulling down

4. While the claw mechanism moves upward, the film is at rest behind the aperture, and light, passing into the camera through the lens and the open part of the shutter, reaches the film. See next page.
5. The movements of the pull-down claw and the shutter are carefully timed so that the opaque area of the shutter blade covers the aperture while the film is being advanced. Therefore light reaches the film only for a brief part of a second while the film is standing still and the shutter is open. For cameras operating at *sound speed* this cycle takes place 24 times a second and the exposure time, as based on the movement of the open area of the shutter, is about 1/50 second; at *silent speed* the cycle takes place 16 or 18 times per second and the exposure is approximately 1/30 second.

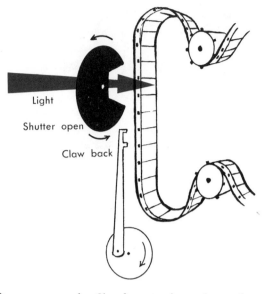

6. After exposure the film forms a lower loop, then passes around one side of a *sprocket wheel* and on to the *take-up spool*, which also rotates in a clockwise direction.

Even though your camera requires a magazine containing film rather than a spool of film, all the operational sequences described above apply.

The lenses on the camera

Although your camera may be equipped with a single lens, additional ones add to the versatility of your filming. Each lens takes in a certain "field of view" and a variety of lenses permits flexibility in selecting fields. Lenses are classed with respect to field of view as *wide-angle, normal,* and *telephoto.*

A single lens of the *zoom type* may include all three, permitting a smooth change of the field within a single scene.

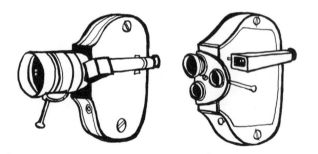

Camera with Zoom Lens and Camera with Three Separate Lenses on a Turret

The classification of lenses is based on the focal length of each lens—the distance from the lens to the film in the camera when a subject located at a distance (infinity) is in focus. The focal length is measured generally in millimeters (25 millimeters equals 1 inch).

Field with Wide-Angle Lens

Field with Normal Lens

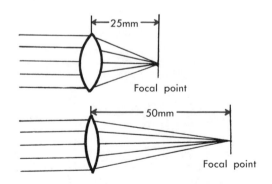

Field with Telephoto Lens

For example:

	Wide angle	*Normal*	*Telephoto*
For 8mm cameras	10mm	13mm	25mm (or greater)
For 16mm cameras	15mm	25mm	50mm (or greater)

Zoom lenses have variable focal lengths from wide angle to telephoto. An 8mm camera's zoom lens may range in focal length from 10mm to 40mm, while one for a 16mm camera may be from 20mm to 80mm.

Focusing scale
(distance)

Lens opening
(f/ number)

As with still-camera lenses, motion-picture lenses (except for fixed-focus lenses) require *two* settings—$f/$ number and distance (shutter speed is determined by the frames-per-second setting). Understand what each of these settings means and how they are properly used (pages 67–70). Also apply the *depth-of-field* principle to relations between $f/$ numbers and distance settings (pages 70–71). This principle is particularly important in motion-picture photography when close-up scenes are filmed. With short camera-to-subject distances the depth of field is reduced greatly, especially for lenses of longer focal length. Notice the reduction in depth of field for the closer distances with the three common 16mm lenses, and from one lens to the other at the same distances in the following table.

Lens (focal length)	Distance setting (feet)	Field at selected lens setting		
		$f/2$	$f/4$	$f/8$
16mm	4	3′3″ to 5′2″	2′10″ to 6′10″	2′2″ to 26′2″
	10	6′4″ to 24′0″	4′10″ to ∞	3′2″ to ∞
	25	10′10″ to ∞	7′1″ to ∞	4′0″ to ∞
25mm	4	3′7″ to 4′5″	3′4″ to 4′11″	2′11″ to 6′5″
	10	8′0″ to 13′8″	6′9″ to 19′6″	5′1″ to ∞
	25	16′6″ to 161′	12′1″ to ∞	7′7″ to ∞
75mm	4	3′11″ to 4′1″	3′10″ to 4′2″	3′9″ to 4′3″
	10	9′9″ to 10′3″	9′6″ to 10′7″	9′0″ to 11′2″
	25	23′5″ to 26′10″	22′0″ to 28′10″	19′8″ to 35′0″

As an example, for a 25mm lens set at $f/2$ and focused at 10 feet, the depth of field is 5 feet 8 inches, but when the same lens is focused at 4 feet the depth is only 10 inches. To increase the latter depth of field, bringing a whole scene into focus (which requires at least 1 foot of depth), it is necessary to increase the light level and film at a lens setting of $f/4$ (which permits a depth of field of 1′7″ at 4 feet). The other alternative is to move the camera back and increase the distance to the subject, which, as the table shows, also increases the depth of field.

Use the depth-of-field scale on your lens in the above way to select distances and $f/$ numbers insuring sufficient depth of field (or lesser depth if necessary) in your scenes. If your lens does not include such a scale, refer to a good motion-picture handbook such as the one from which the table was taken.[1]

In operation, motion-picture cameras are more complex than are still cameras, since they require additional settings and special precautions. Develop the habit of checking all settings and adjustments before each scene is filmed. Possibly a reminder, such as the *SAFER* formula, will help you.[2]

S peed of camera (16 or 18, 24, or other number of frames per second)
A perture of lens ($f/$ setting)
F ocus (distance setting)
E xpose the scene
R ewind the spring

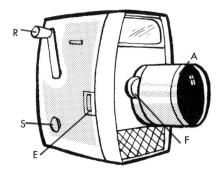

Accessories

You may find need for:

• A photographic light meter to determine exposure accurately (page 74)
• A tripod to steady the camera
• Photoflood lights to light indoor scenes (page 78)

Film

Review the general characteristics of film on page 72.

Select a film balanced for the light conditions under which it will be used. For example:

Light source	Film	Exposure index (ASA)
Daylight	Kodachrome II, Daylight	25
Photoflood	Kodachrome II, Type A	40

For fluorescent lights, no example of film type can be suggested, since the many types of fluorescent tubes affect color film differently. For general purposes, unless true color is criti-

---

[1] *The American Cinematographers Handbook,* Jackson J. Rose, American Society of Cinematographers, North Orange Drive, Hollywood, California.

[2] Adapted from *Better Movies in Color,* publication AD-4, Eastman Kodak Company.

cal, assume that fluorescent light is similar to daylight, especially in rooms having windows that admit a great amount of daylight.

Some characteristics of various 16mm films are shown in a table. This table gives significant but not complete information, and lists representative films but not all films. For further information on all films, see the film information sheets packaged with each roll; for information on Kodak films see also *Kodak 16mm Movie Films: Data and Selection,* pamphlet D-22, Eastman Kodak Company.

The data about films, as indicated in the accompanying chart, are correct as of the time of writing; but changes and new developments can be anticipated. Carefully check the data sheet packaged with your film for the latest assigned exposure index and other details.

For 8mm cameras, only color reversal films normally are available. Special orders are required for black-and-white film.

For 16mm cameras, the choice of film is somewhat broader. Your decision is made with reference to:

• Light conditions
• Black-and-white or color
• Reversal or negative
• Single or double perforations (sprocket holes)

Black-and-white or color? Consider whether color is an important feature of the subject or whether black-and-white film would be satisfactory. Recall the reports in Chapter 3 that color does not contribute significantly to learning over black-and-white unless color is an important feature of the subject. Color film is more expensive, and it requires higher light levels while filming.

Reversal film or negative film? Reversal films, both black-and-white and color, are used commonly when one or only a few copies of the final film are required. During processing the image is reversed from a negative, resulting in positive pictures (page 87). Negative films have advantages when being exposed, but require positive prints before they are useful. Their use should be considered when many copies of the final film are to be made, although some film laboratories recommend that reversal film be used at all times.

Single or double perforations (sprocket holes)? The perforations or sprocket holes in 16mm film may run along one side or both sides. Film with one row of sprocket holes should be used whenever it is anticipated that magnetic striping for sound may be added to the original reversal film.

For best results, motion-picture film should be processed by a professional film laboratory. Some laboratories handle color as well as black-and-white, while others specialize in only one kind. For a list of processing laboratories see pages 241-242. If you plan to do extensive filming, contact two or three laboratories in your area and check their services and prices.

Motion pictures from videotape? The majority of television facilities include videotape recorders. Subjects for motion pictures, as well as for television programs, can be recorded on

TYPICAL 16MM FILMS

Film	Type	Exposure Index (ASA)		Use
		Daylight*	Photoflood*	
Black and white:				
Plus X	Negative	80	64	Exterior or interior scenes
	Reversal	50	40	under good light
Tri X	Negative	320	250	Subjects under low light
	Reversal	200	160	
Color reversal:				
Anscochrome	Daylight	100	50 (80B)	Subjects under moderate
	Tungsten	64 (85B)	100	light
Ektachrome ER	Daylight	160	32 (78A)	Subjects under low light
	Type B	80 (85B)	125	
Commercial Ektachrome	Tungsten (3200 K)	16 (85)	25	Subjects under good light; low-contrast film designed for reproduction, not projection
Kodachrome II	Daylight	25	12 (80B)	Subjects under good light; film designed for projection, not reproduction
	Type A	25 (85)	40	

* Numbers in parentheses are filters recommended for converting film to use with other than recommended light sources. Note how the exposure index drops.

videotape and immediately viewed to determine whether a scene will be suitable. Many film producers use this videotape technique as a "dry run" prior to actual motion-picture filming.

But there is increasing use of videotape as the filming medium, using two or more television cameras. The television director literally "edits the film as it is shot" by calling for a *long shot* with one television camera, then a *close-up* with a second camera, matching the action between the two scenes exactly. A poorly performed scene can be erased and repeated without waste of tape. Synchronous sound or narration is recorded on the tape along with the picture. Certain film laboratories (page 241) can then convert the electronic images of sound and picture from the videotape to 16mm film. From a good-quality videotape recording, the resulting film quality is very acceptable, although some loss in definition must be expected. This procedure can take place in either black-and-white or color. Much time and cost for materials can be saved when using videotape to produce a motion picture.

Exposure

Exposure for motion pictures is determined by methods similar to those used in still photography (pages 74–77). But realize that the still photographer has the advantages of being able to have partial corrections for wrong exposure made when printing. Some correction can be made with motion pictures when duplicates are made from the original footage. But when filming, if you are not sure of exposure, film a scene more than once, varying the lens setting.

Lighting

As in still photography, fast black-and-white films often require no supplementary lighting. But when lights are necessary, apply the basic photoflood lighting pattern—key, fill, back, and accent lights, explained on pages 78–79. Then balance the lights and determine the exposure carefully.

Now, apply what you have learned about motion-picture cameras, lenses, and film:

1. What settings must be made on your camera and what operational controls does it have?
2. What is the threading path for loading film in your camera, or does the camera use a magazine? Do the film spools turn clockwise or counterclockwise?
3. Do you have a reflex or window viewfinder? Which one is preferred? Why?
4. Explain why *still* pictures are taken even though film *moves* through the camera?
5. What is/are the focal length(s) of your camera lenses?
6. What are some advantages of having lenses of different focal lengths, as against a zoom lens that covers a range of focal lengths?

7. What does *depth of field* mean?
8. Do you have *more* or *less* depth of field, at the same distance setting, with your lens set at $f/8$ as compared to $f/4$?
9. If you use a 75mm lens set at 10 feet and you wish to have a depth of field of at least 2 feet, what $f/$ number must be used? Does this require *more* or *less* light on the subject than if only 1-foot depth of field is required?
10. What 16mm color film might you select for use if a number of prints are to be made from the final film?
11. How might videotape be used in motion-picture production?

TECHNIQUES OF MOTION-PICTURE PHOTOGRAPHY

Planning a motion picture is similar to planning other audiovisual materials. But a major difference becomes apparent when you load your camera and start filming. This difference lies in the word *motion*. Movement is basic to successful motion pictures, whether it is in the subject, caused by camera movement when filming still subjects, or created by editing. Motion gives a film its interest, its pacing, and its strongest feature—its sense of continuity or logical progression.

The mere fact that someone or something moves in a scene is not enough to supply this motion. The *ideas* of the film must move along their planned development, make progress. The audience must be given the sense of this kind of motion, even when the projector is throwing such stationary things as a mountain or a building on the screen.

Motion in film may be accomplished by action within a scene, by change of camera angles, by camera movement, by varying the length of scenes, by movement created as you edit and arrange scenes, or by combinations of these elements.

Bear in mind this factor of motion as you consider the following filming techniques—it will determine, to a great extent, the effectiveness of your film.

Shots, scenes, takes, and sequences

A motion picture is made up of many scenes, filmed from different camera angles and put together into sequences to carry the message of the film.

The terms *shot* and *scene* will be used in this section interchangeably. Each time you start film moving past your camera lens and then stop it, you have recorded a scene or a shot. You may film a scene from the script two or more times, calling each one a separate *take* of the particular scene. A *sequence* is a series of related scenes depicting one idea. It corresponds to a paragraph in writing.

When filming, start the camera just before the action begins (the proper directions are, "Camera start" . . . "Action start") and keep shooting for a few seconds after the action ends. In this way you not only make sure of getting the complete action, but have some additional footage for overlap and splicing.

A scene may run from 2 seconds to as long as 30 seconds; average scene length is 7 seconds. There is no set rule on scene length; the required action and necessary narration must determine effective length. A scene with much detail and activity may require a longer viewing time than does a static scene of only general interest. So keep scenes long enough to convey your ideas and present the necessary information, but not so long as to drag and become monotonous.

TYPES OF CAMERA SHOTS

[See Appendix A for film correlated with this topic.]

The appearance of a motion-picture scene can be judged only when viewed through the camera lens. How the camera sees the subject is important, not how the scene appears to the director, to a person in the scene, or to others. Keep this in mind as you apply the following principles.

Basic shots

Three types of scenes make up the fundamental sequence in motion-picture photography:

- The *long shot* (L)—a general view of the setting and the subject. It provides an orientation for the viewer, by establishing all elements in the scene, and if important, shows size proportions relating to the subject.
- The *medium shot* (MS)—a closer view of the subject, eliminating unnecessary background and other details.
- The *close-up* (CU)—a concentration on the subject, or on a part of it, excluding everything else from view.

When the subject is the same, three successive shots assume a relation to each other.

LS, MS, and CU do not mean any specific distances. A long shot of a building may be taken from a distance of hundreds of yards, whereas a long shot of a small child may be taken from only a few yards' distance. You may be close-up to a building when you are across the street but you may need to get within a few feet of the small child to take a close-up.

Although the subject does limit the kinds of shots that are called for in the script, two cameramen covering the same subject may film the three scenes differently, each imparting his own interpretation and emphasis. To say that one version is right and the other wrong would most likely depend on personal preference. See facing page.

Long Shot

Medium Shot

Close-up

Long Shot

Medium Shot

Close-up

LS, Cameraman A

LS, Cameraman B

MS, Cameraman A

MS, Cameraman B

CU, Cameraman A

CU, Cameraman B

At the two ends of the LS-MS-CU sequence you can introduce *extremes* if they are important to your story.

Extreme Long Shot (ELS)

Extreme Close-up (ECU)

Although LS-MS-CU is a fundamental sequence, it is not to be rigidly followed in successive topics. Sequences need variety; without variations, your film may become monotonous and lose its pacing, its motion. For straightforward explanation the LS-MS-CU sequence may be satisfactory. For a slower pace, gradually increasing interest, LS-MS-MCU-CU may be used. For suspense or drama consider CU-CU-CU-LS.

Note the differences in two four-shot sequences. See next page.

LS   MS   MCU   CU

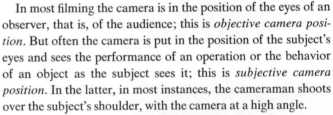

MS   CU   LS   MS

Angle and position shots

Variety, emphasis, and dramatic effect can be accomplished through the use of *camera angles*. The normal camera position is at about normal eye level for a person standing. A camera in a higher position, looking down on the subject, makes a *high-angle shot* that gives the illusion of reducing the size of the subject and slowing its motion. A camera in a lower than normal position, looking up at a subject, makes a *low-angle shot* that seems to exaggerate height and to speed up movement.

High-Angle Shot

Low-Angle Shot

Also, high- and low-angle shots can be used to eliminate undesirable background or foreground details.

In most filming the camera is in the position of the eyes of an observer, that is, of the audience; this is *objective camera position*. But often the camera is put in the position of the subject's eyes and sees the performance of an operation or the behavior of an object as the subject sees it; this is *subjective camera position*. In the latter, in most instances, the cameraman shoots over the subject's shoulder, with the camera at a high angle.

Objective Scene

Subjective Scene

Moving-camera shots

Camera movement itself, during filming, adds to the variety of possible shots. These possibilities include *panning*, *tilting*, and *zooming*.

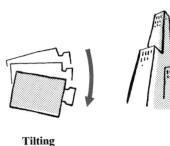
Tilting

Panning

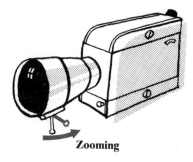
Zooming

These techniques are generally too much used, are often unnecessary, and are frequently poorly done. If a subject in a scene moves, the camera might logically follow him. This is a good use of camera movement. Or, if a scene is too broad to be caught by the motionless camera, a *pan* (panorama) may show its size and scope. Or you may pan or tilt if it is important to connect two subjects by relating them visually. But do not pan across nonmoving subjects which can be handled satisfactorily by a longer still shot or by two separate scenes.

Closely related to pans and tilts is the use of a zoom lens—*zooming* (a smooth change of field during a single scene; page 190). Here the same cautions apply about over-use. A series of straight cuts (MS to CU) is often more effective. Save the zoom shot until you feel a real need and one that makes an important contribution to the continuity of your film.

When panning, tilting, or zooming, apply these practices:

- Attach your camera to a tripod and adjust the head for smooth movement (a long handle on the tripod is desirable for good control).

- Always start a moving shot with the camera held still for a few seconds and end the shot in the same way.
- When shooting a moving subject try to "lead" the subject in the frame slightly. (page 80)
- Always rehearse the shot a few times before exposing film.

Cautions as you plan your shots

[See Appendix A for film correlated with this topic.]

When a sequence becomes long and you include a number of related close-ups, frequently *re-establish* the general subject for the viewer with an LS or MS so he does not lose his orientation to the subject. An establishing shot (LS or MS) also is important when moving to a new activity before close-up detail is shown.

If the viewer has to figure for himself where the camera has suddenly shifted or why an unexplained change has occurred in the action, then you have done something wrong. Always plan your scenes to keep the viewer oriented.

MS (Establishing)

CU

CU

CU

LS (Re-establishing)

When you treat one subject in a number of related scenes (as in the LS-MS-CU sequence), change the angle between the camera and the subject for adjacent scenes (but not over 180°), or change the vertical camera position. If you do not, as you move directly in or back, you create the effect known as *pumping-in* or *pumping-out,* which is quite jarring to the viewer. The differing impacts of good and faulty techniques in this respect can be appreciated fully only if the scenes are viewed in motion; but note the changes of angle in previous sequences and in the brief sequence of wire-welding scenes.

MS, Subject Directly before the Camera

MS, Subject Directly before the Camera

CU, Camera Moved Straight in

CU, Camera Moved in and 45° to Left

In summary, there is a variety of filming shots at your disposal:

- Basic shots—long shot, medium shot, close-up
- Extremes—extreme long shot, extreme close-up
- High-angle and low-angle shots
- Objective and subjective camera positions
- Pan, tilt, and zoom shots

And, remember to:

- Use a variety of shots purposefully; they contribute to good motion-picture technique.
- Use establishing and re-establishing shots to keep your audience oriented to the subject.
- Change angle between shots of the same subject; the change is important to smooth flow of action.
- Shoot scenes slightly longer than actually needed; the extra frames will be helpful when editing.

For each scene, the camera angle and the selected basic shot (LS, MS, or CU) determine the *viewpoint* and the *area* to be covered. Thus, as you choose camera position and lens you must answer two questions: What is the best *viewpoint* for effectively showing the action? How much *area* should be included in the scene?

To help in visualizing the content of key scenes and the placement of the camera with respect to the subject, consider making simple sketches to show the subject position and the area to be covered by the camera. Two examples are shown. These sketches will aid other people (including members of the production crew) to understand what you have in mind. (These sketches do not serve the same purposes as did the general pictures made for the storyboard during planning—page 40.

Scene 10   MS Child reading

Scene 22   CU (High Angle) Inserting Drill

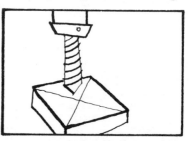

Visualization Sketches in a Shooting Script

Now, apply what you have learned about types of camera shots:

1. Give an example of how you might use the terms *shot, scene, take,* and *sequence.*
2. Relate the following scenes (from the same sequence) to these terms—LS, CU, MS, high-angle, low-angle.
3. In what order would you arrange the six scenes shown to make a sequence?
4. What is meant by the term "pumping-in"? How do you avoid it?

PROVIDING CONTINUITY

Selecting the best camera positions, the proper lens, and the correct exposure under the best light conditions may result in good scenes, but these do not guarantee a good motion picture. Only when one scene leads logically and easily to the next one do you have the binding ingredient of smooth *continuity*. Continuity is based on thorough planning and an awareness of a number of factors that must be taken care of during filming.

Matching action

As you film scenes within the same sequence, the subject normally moves. Shoot adjacent and related scenes in such a way that a continuation of the movement is evident from one scene to the next. Such continuation *matches the action* between scenes.

Medium Shot

Close-up

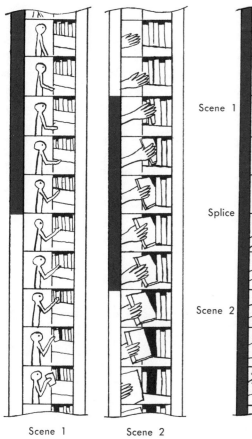

Scene 1   Scene 2

Scene 1

Splice

Scene 2

In order to insure a smooth flow from the MS to the CU, match the action at the end of the first scene to the beginning of the second one. Accomplish this matching by having some of the action at the end of the MS repeated at the beginning of the CU.

Then, when editing, from this overlap of action select appropriate frames at which the two scenes should be joined. This transition is most easily accepted by the viewer if the scenes are joined at a point of change—in direction of movement, when something is picked up or shifted, or similar change—rather than in the middle of a smooth movement where the natural flow of action may be disturbed.

In this way "action is matched" and a smooth flow results. As you plan matching shots remember to:

- Change angle slightly between adjacent shots (recall the improper practice of pumping-in or pumping-out; page 198).
- Match the tempo of movement from a medium shot to a close-up. Since action in a close-up should be somewhat slower than normal or it will appear highly accelerated and disturbing to the viewer, the movement in the previous medium shot should be slowed down.
- Notice where parts of the subject or objects within the first scene are placed, which hand is used and its position, or how the action moves. Be sure they are the same for the second and any closely following scenes. Be particularly observant if scenes are filmed out of the script order.

It is not always essential to match action unless details in adjacent scenes are easily recognizable to the viewer. A long shot of general activity (for example, a playground scene) does not have to match a medium shot of a group at play, but when the camera turns from this group to an individual the action should be matched.

For some purposes action can best be matched by using more than one camera, one taking longer shots and the other taking close-ups, the two shooting scenes simultaneously while the action is continuous.

Shooting Close-up   **Shooting Long Shot**

This *multicamera technique* speeds up filming and insures accurate matching of action, even though it may require the use of more film than when shooting with only one camera. Waste can be minimized by starting the second camera on signal just before the first one stops in order to provide the overlap. Multi-camera filming is particularly useful when documenting events like athletic meets, meetings, carnivals, demonstrations, and news events. Assign camera teams to work together and coordinate their filming to cover related activities at the same time from positions that will *cut* (edit) smoothly together.

Screen direction

Another kind of matching action is required when a subject moves across the frame. If he moves from left to right, make sure the action is the same in the next scene.

When action leaves the frame on one side, it must enter the next scene from the *opposite* side of the frame for proper continuity.

If directions must change between two scenes, try to show the change in the first scene by having the subject make a turn. If a turn is not possible, include a brief in-between scene of the action coming straight toward the camera. Then a new direction in the following scene seems plausible to the viewer.

Be careful when filming parades, races, and similar activities with more than one camera unless someone is assigned to show the action changing direction (going around turns, or moving directly toward or away from the camera). If you do not do this and cameras are located on opposite sides of the activity one will show action from left to right and another from right to left. The audience will receive the impression that the moving subject has turned around and is returning to the starting point—and no one will ever get to the finish line!

Protection shots

Careful though you may be, there are times when things go wrong with your planning or filming. Possibly you did not quite match the action between scenes; the left hand instead of the right one was used in the close-up, the screen direction between two scenes changes, or you create a *jump* by momentarily stopping the camera during a scene and then starting it again while the action is continuing. Often such situations are not discovered until the editing, and then you may be in trouble. Therefore by all means protect yourself from possible embarrassment and poor practice.

Protection is afforded by shooting *cut-in* and *cut-away* shots, even though these shots are not indicated in the script. A *cut-in* is a close-up (or extreme close-up) of some part of the scene being filmed. It also is called an *insert*. Examples of common cut-ins are faces, hands, feet, parts of objects, and other items known to be in the scene. See facing page.

A *cut-away* is opposite to a cut-in in that it is a shot of another subject or separate action taking place at the same time as is the main action. This other subject or action is not in the scene (hence *away*) but is related in some way to the main action. Examples of cut-aways are people or objects that complement the main action; faces of people watching or reacting to the main action are commonly used. See facing page.

Either cut-ins or cut-aways serve to distract the viewer's attention momentarily and thus permit acceptance of the next scene even though the action may not match the preceding one accurately. By using cut-ins and cut-aways in this way, two scenes may be given continuity even though they would be illogical in direct succession.

Cut-in Shot

Cut-away Shot (Reaction Shot)

Keep these points in mind as you shoot cut-ins and cut-aways:

- Always shoot a number of them, as you may not know until editing when you may have need for one or more. Complete the unused ends of film rolls with such brief scenes.
- Make them long enough: a minimum of 5 or 6 seconds, although you may only use 2 or 3 seconds.
- Make them logical, in keeping with the appropriate sequences (watch expressions and backgrounds so they will be consistent with the main action).

Transitions

[See Appendix A for film correlated with this topic.]

One of the strengths of motion-picture photography is being able to take viewers from one place to another or to show action taking place at different times—all this presented in adjacent scenes within a very short period of actual screen time, and accepted quite realistically by the audience. How is this acceptance accomplished? It is achieved through the use of *transitional devices,* which bridge space and time.

The simplest method for achieving smooth pictorial transitions is by use of printed titles or directions placed between scenes. See next page.

Also, cut-ins and cut-aways can give the impression of time passing and may reduce a long scene to its essentials without the audience realizing that time has been compressed. An example of this may be showing the start of an activity, then a cut-in, then the completion of the activity, with the insert scene 2 to 3 seconds in length. See next page.

Exiting from a scene and subsequent entrance at another location creates an acceptable transition in time as well as in space. (Always film the scene for a few seconds after the subject has left the scene to insure an acceptable period of time for the subject to appear in the next scene at a different location.)

A *montage* is a series of short scenes connected by cuts, dissolves, or possibly wipes (see below), used to quickly condense time or distance or to show a series of related activities and places. The audience accepts this rapid series of scenes as if the complete operation or various places had been seen in their entirety.

Transition Scene (Title)   Transition Scene (Cut-in)   Transition Scene

Optical transitions are common ways of expressing time and space changes. But research evidence in Chapter 3 does not indicate that optical effects significantly contribute to learning. Opticals are sometimes created in the camera, but more commonly are added by a film laboratory when copies are made from the original film.

A *fade-out* and *fade-in* serve to separate major sequences in a film. They consist of the gradual darkening of a scene to complete blackness (fade-out) followed by the gradual lightening (fade-in) of the first scene of the next sequence. Fades are also used at the beginning of a film (fade-in) and at the end (fade-out). Use fades sparingly, as too many may produce a disturbing effect which disrupts the flow of the film.

A *dissolve* commonly indicates lapse in time or a change in location between adjacent scenes. It blends one scene into another by showing the fade-out of the first scene and the *superimposed* fade-in of the next scene. A dissolve is sometimes used to soften the change from one scene to another that would other-

wise be abrupt or jarring, due possibly to poor planning or incorrect selection of camera angles in adjacent scenes. A *jump-cut* is an example of a mismatch in adjacent scenes, like sudden change in body position resulting in a jerk or sudden jump between scenes.

A *wipe* is an optical effect in which a new scene seems to push the previous scene off the screen. The wiping motion may be vertical, horizontal, or angular. This effect is infrequently used but may be important for situations that are closely related, like the start of an experiment followed immediately by the result. A group of scenes connected by wipes may give the impression of looking across a row or a series of objects.

Fades and dissolves can be created in many cameras. If yours has a variable shutter, move it smoothly from its open to its fully closed position (taking about 2 seconds) for a fade-out. Reverse the procedure for a fade-in. To dissolve, make a fade-out, then wind the film back (with the lens covered) 48 frames and make a 2-second fade-in. Fades less satisfactory, but often ac-

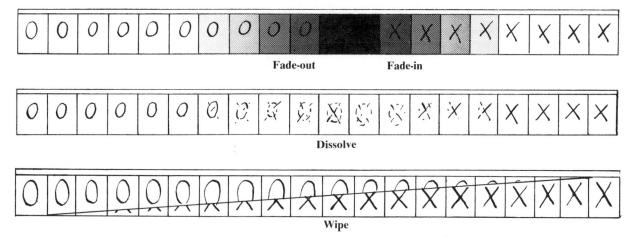

Fade-out   Fade-in

Dissolve

Wipe

ceptable, are made by closing down the lens diaphragm to the smallest opening (fade-out) and then opening it to the proper setting (fade-in).

If optical effects for your film are to be made at a film laboratory, be sure to provide sufficient footage for the fades and dissolves. Most laboratories require at least 48 frames of film at the ends of scenes for fade or dissolve overlap. Most major laboratories have instructions on preparing films for printing. Contact one or more film laboratories listed on pages 241-242 for their requirements and services.

Now, apply what you have learned about providing continuity in motion pictures:

1. Give an example in which you would have continuity from one scene to the next by using matched action and screen direction.
2. What protection shot might you use in filming a sequence showing a woman sewing a lengthy seam?
3. What transition device would you use in each of these situations:
   a. a board being painted and then used after it has dried.
   b. a man leaving home and arriving at his office.
   c. a scoreboard showing the score after the first inning and then at the end of the game.
4. How might you make a fade-out and fade-in with your camera? Can you also make a dissolve?

OTHER CONSIDERATIONS

Composition

As with still photography, composition is a matter of personal aesthetics. Note the general suggestions for good composition on pages 80-81. For a detailed consideration of composition applied specifically to motion pictures, see Chapter 5 of *The Five C's of Cinematography* by Joseph Mascelli.

The proportion of the motion-picture frame should always be kept in mind when selecting subjects and composing scenes.

Since the frame has the proportions of 3:4 (page 92), preference should be given to subjects with horizontal rather than vertical configurations.

Special care must be taken in composing scenes involving motion. Always lead a moving subject with more area in the direction of motion and carefully rehearse anticipated movement so that proper framing or camera motion can be planned.

When a person handles an object or performs an operation, the camera should be situated for the best view, although it may appear unnatural from the subject's viewpoint. Exaggeration and simplification are acceptable in information or in skill films in order to convey a correct understanding or impression.

Scheduling and record keeping

Follow the suggestions on pages 46-48 for preparing a shooting schedule, making arrangements for filming, checking facilities, and keeping a record (a log sheet) of filming. To facilitate editing, identify each scene and its takes by *slating* just before the scene begins. To slate a scene, write the scene number and the take number boldly on a sheet of paper (a small blackboard is often used) and hold it in front of the camera at a readable distance. Film a few frames of it; then proceed with the actual scene.

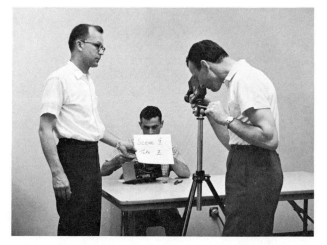

Be mindful of the need for obtaining permission from those appearing in scenes or from owners of copyrighted materials used. For a sample release form, see page 49.

Special filming techniques

[See Appendix A for film correlated with this topic.]

To record action that normally takes place *too rapidly* for ease of study, use a *slow-motion* technique. Set the camera speed to *exceed* the projection rate—a speed of 32, 48, or 64 frames per second instead of 16 or 24 frames per second. When the film is projected at normal speed, a slow-down effect results because the action on the screen takes a longer period of time than the action took before the camera. Remember to compensate for change in exposure when using faster camera speeds; refer to your camera instruction booklet or to a motion-picture handbook (such as the *American Cinematographer Manual*).

To record action that normally takes place *too slowly* for ease of study, use a *time-lapse* technique. By setting camera speeds *slower* than the projection rate and then projecting the film at normal speed, action is visually compressed or speeded up. The slowest setting on most cameras is 8 frames per second. Below this, individual frames must be exposed one at a time;

this procedure is called *single framing*. Your camera may be equipped with a special control which permits single framing. In this way you can record subjects having a very slow movement (like the opening of a flower bud or the formation and movement of clouds) by exposing individual frames at a predeter-

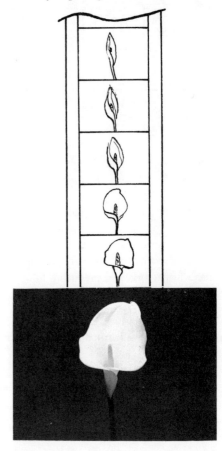

mined rate, for instance 1 per second or 1 per minute or 1 per hour. Find out how long the action to be filmed normally takes. Then decide how much film time you want to use and determine how often a picture should be taken. Here is a problem:

Purpose: To film a color reaction change in a test tube
Normal time for reaction to take place: 8 hours (480 minutes)
Film time to be used: 10 seconds at 24 frames per second (240 frames)

$$\frac{480 \text{ minutes}}{240 \text{ frames}} = 2 \text{ minutes per frame}$$

This means that for a period of 8 hours a frame should be exposed every 2 minutes.

Result: 8-hour change is shown in 10 seconds

Motor-driven commercial equipment is available for such automatic-timed single-framing. See the references on page 236 for further details and techniques on time-lapse photography.

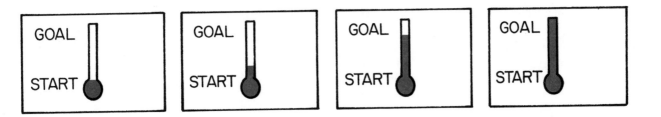

To visualize action that cannot readily be photographed, use *animation* techniques. Animation resembles time-lapse in that single-framing is used to film sequences and the method to determine movement per frame is similar. But here the sequence consists of successive drawings, slight movement of three-dimensional figures and objects, or progressively developed parts of a diagram. Stages in a process may be shown by preparing a series of drawings, each of which adds a small detail to the previous one, and then filming each drawing on one or a few frames. This is a *pop-on* method of animation. In the reverse method, called *wipe-off* animation, small segments of a completed diagram are progressively removed as individual frames are exposed. In this case, when the film is turned end-for-end and viewed (possible only with 16mm double-perforated film), the diagram appears to develop from nothing and grow to completion. There are many variations to the process of film animation, some simple and others very complex and time-consuming. For a complete discussion of animation, see the references on page 236.

Titles and illustrations

Titles should serve the purposes noted on page 54. Often they are prepared as editing nears completion when the need for special subtitles, captions, or labels becomes evident. Preparing them at this time helps to insure their being properly placed and effectively worded.

The same techniques described for preparing titles and illustrations for slides on page 144 can be used for making motion-picture titles. Review these procedures:

1. Word each title so it is brief but communicative.
2. Select materials or aids for appropriate lettering. As you select lettering sizes, be sure to consider the legibility standards for projected materials described on page 99.
3. Prepare the lettering and artwork (pages 91–97), keeping in mind the correct 3:4 proportions of the film area, using simple design features (page 92), and selecting appropriate backgrounds (page 109). If your motion-picture camera is not equipped with reflex viewing (page 188), prepare titles and illustrations large enough to be filmed at a distance that will overcome the parallax problem (page 82).
4. Then attach each prepared title and illustration to a wall or easel and photograph it with your camera on a tripod (page 84), or use a copy or titling stand.

Special titles or captions can be *overlayed* on a prepared background. Black and colored lettering only can be superimposed over flat pictures (pages 109–110). White letters, in addition to this, can also be *overprinted* on a filmed background (pages 109–110). This latter method is often used for adding subtitles and captions to scenes. Film the background scene (slightly underexposed) and wind the film back to the start of the scene (with the lens capped). Then expose the white-lettered title (printed on black). This double-exposing prints the white title over the background scene. Most film laboratories can overprint titles for you if you supply them with footage of the background scene and footage of the titles prepared from black printing on white cardboard and photographed on 16mm high-contrast positive film.

Film length for titles should be sufficient for you to read through the title twice. It may be shortened somewhat when editing, but film with this timing as a guide. A fade-in is commonly used with the main title and a fade-out at the end. Dissolves are appropriate between adjacent titles.

Now, apply what you have learned about some special filming techniques:

1. You wish to show the form of a diver by slowing down his action on the diving board. What camera setting is changed and what is the possible new setting?
2. Describe an application you might make of *time-lapse* or simple *animation* techniques?
3. How often would a frame be exposed if you wished to show the changes in clouds across the sky from 10 A.M to 4 P.M. and covering 20 seconds of film shot at silent speed (18 frames per second)?

FILM LABORATORY SERVICES

A list of commercial film laboratories is included in the Appendixes on pages 241–242. Contact one or more of them concerning their specific services, requirements, and prices.

As rolls of film are exposed you can send them to a film laboratory for processing. Seeing the footage shortly after it has been shot gives you a continual check on your exposure, on your filming techniques, and on the proper operation of your camera. On the other hand, some film-makers hold all exposed film until shooting is completed so that it all may be processed at one time to eliminate inconsistencies that arise from variations in developing.

Most commercial film laboratories offer a variety of services in addition to the processing of film. One of the most worthwhile is the preparation of a duplicate or a *workprint* from the original footage for use in editing. Handling the original film will blemish it with scratches and dirt; worse, a wrong cut or a tear during projection would be disastrous. The original film is irreplaceable. But if you have a black-and-white workprint made (at a cost of 5¢ to 6¢ a foot) from the original, you need not handle it until the time comes to *conform* it to the edited workprint.

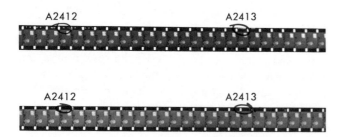

After the workprint is made, matching numbers, called *edge numbers,* are applied at each foot interval both to the original and to the workprint. These numbers make locating scenes easy when conforming the original film to the edited workprint. Certain films, like 16mm Commercial Ektachrome, include edge numbers which print through to the workprint film, thus eliminating the need for additional number printing.

Then, if copies of the motion picture are to be ordered, it is customary for the film laboratory to prepare an *answer print* in which exposure corrections and optical effects (fades and dissolves) are included. Reduction printing of 16mm film to 8mm size may be done at this time also. Once an answer print is accepted, duplicate or *release prints* are made.

FILM EDITING

[See Appendix A for film correlated with this topic.]

The selection of visuals for the script, the choice of camera angles when filming, and finally the editing make up the main creative aspects of a motion-picture production. Film editing is the process of selecting, arranging, and shortening (cutting) scenes to remove superfluous footage so that the final result satisfies the objectives you established originally.

When all film has been returned from processing, editing starts. The script and the camera log sheet are essential guides for your editing. When editing you must do three things:

• Eliminate unusable film—bad exposures, blurred or out-of-focus shots, light flares, blank film, incomplete takes, poor action.
• Organize scenes in order of the script.
• Rearrange and cut scenes for the best continuity.

Tools and equipment for editing include:

A projector	A scene-filing box
A viewer	A splicer
A pair of rewinds	Film cement
Spare reels	A film scraper
A pair of scissors	A pair of cotton gloves
A grease pencil	

Always do your editing on a clean table and keep the area neat. This requirement is especially important if you edit *original* film (the film from the camera). Be sure the film channel of the viewer and the film gate of the projector are kept clean. Wear a pair of thin cotton gloves to help protect the film from collecting dirt.

The stages of editing, as described are:

1. String-out
2. Rough cut
3. Fine cut

First editing stage—string-out

Using the viewer, cut all scenes apart. Roll each one separately, identifying it with a piece of masking tape marked with the scene (and take) number. A small reel, from which one side has been removed, makes scene-rolling easy.

During this process eliminate all unusable footage and slate marks. Splice all scenes (and multiple takes of scenes) together in proper order. The entire film should now be on one reel. In a *carefully cleaned* projector, view the footage, making notes which will help you to select the best takes and roughly where to cut scenes for best action.

For studying details of scene content and specific movement, use a viewer; but for timing action and observing continuity, project the film at normal speed.

Second editing stage—rough cut

Return to the rewinds and the viewer. Eliminate all but the best take for each scene. Mark the points for cutting on the film

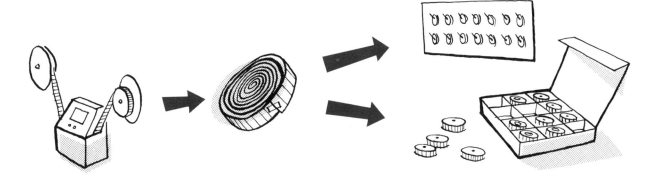

base with a grease pencil. Then start removing unnecessary footage from the beginnings and ends of scenes. *Be careful not to shorten scenes too much at this stage.* Keep in mind all film techniques—LS-MS-CU relationships, establishing scenes, the use of cut-ins and cut-aways, screen direction, matching action, transitions, and the like.

As you accumulate *out-takes* (good footage, but not to be used in the film), roll and mark them with scene numbers just in case you have need for them later.

As the film takes definite form, review the script and particularly the narration. Revise it as necessary, keeping in mind the suggestions for writing narration on pages 50–51. Then read narration as the film is projected at proper speed. You will find that about 4 words cover one foot of 16mm film at sound speed. Observe the continuity. If scenes do not fit, rearrange them. If necessary, plan further filming to replace inappropriate scenes or to fill previously unrealized needs.

With the editing nearing completion it may be advisable to show the film and to read the narration to other interested and qualified persons or to a potential audience group. See the suggestions on page 51 for developing a questionnaire to gather reactions and suggestions which may help you to improve your film.

Final editing stage—fine cut

Working with both the film and the narration, gradually refine the two until they match and flow smoothly. This requires shortening scenes, splicing at matched-action frames between related scenes, and polishing the narration by eliminating words and by rephrasing. This final editing stage is a slow one that requires projection and reading, checking for pacing, marking the film places to cut, rechecking on the viewer, cutting and splicing, and then projecting again. But once completed, your efforts will result in a smoothly flowing film in which narration is closely correlated with the picture—a key element in successful sound motion-picture production.

Editing in the camera

For some purposes, such as to conserve film and to avoid having to make splices, you may attempt to film all scenes in normal sequence and of proper length. The result, with luck, is a complete film ready for use. This procedure is termed *editing in the camera*. It is similar to making a filmstrip by shooting frames in sequence with a 35mm camera.

In order to edit in the camera, each of the following is important:

- You are certain of the sequence of scenes to be filmed.
- You can control all action to be filmed and know how long each scene will be. Rehearsals are important.
- Titles and illustrations are prepared and ready for filming. You must have the titles set up so you can turn the camera to them for filming in proper order and then go back to the next action scene.
- Exposure and other camera settings will be correct for each scene.

Editing unscripted films

Possibly all or part of your film was shot using a newsreel or documentary approach—with little preplanning or script preparation (see page 200 for a discussion of this method). If so, editing follows the same procedure outlined here, but requires a pre-editing step.

As you examine the footage for the first time (using a film viewer), write a brief description of each scene (type of shot, content, special remarks as to quality or action, and other information) on a separate, numbered 3″×5″ card. Then cut apart each scene, roll it, tape it, and give it the same number as the corresponding card. Now study the cards and re-arrange them into a script. String together the scenes according to the order of the cards and proceed with the editing procedure as already explained.

Suggestions when editing

- Avoid interruptions; try to complete a whole sequence during one work period.
- Keep your audience in mind, anticipating its lack of familiarity with the subject and the need for continuity of action which you might overlook as a consequence of your own knowledge of the subject.

- Do not let your personal familiarity with a scene or action lead you to cut it too short.
- Avoid joining scenes where wide variations of exposure or color exist.

Splicing film

[See Appendix A for film correlated with this topic.]

You may have occasion to splice film at almost any time during the course of editing. There are two methods for splicing motion-picture film.

One method uses prepared, adhesive-backed, clear plastic tape and a simple splicing unit. This method results in a *butt* splice—the two film ends *touch* one another. The procedure is:

1. Align the cut ends of the film on the pins in the splicing unit.
2. Trim the ends so they match exactly. Use the cutter blade in the top of the splicer.
3. Place a piece of splicing tape over the pins and the joined ends of film. Pull off the protective paper on one side.
4. Pull off the protective paper on the other side.
5. Rub the tape to insure good adherence.
6. Flip the film over and reset on the pins.
7. Repeat steps 3 and 4 with another piece of splicing tape.
8. Again rub the tape to insure good adherence.
9. Examine the finished splice.

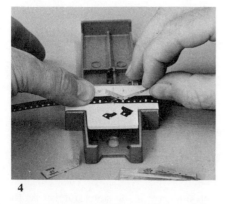

1

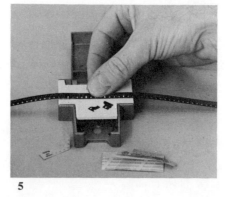

2

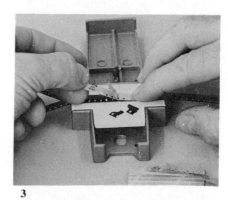

3

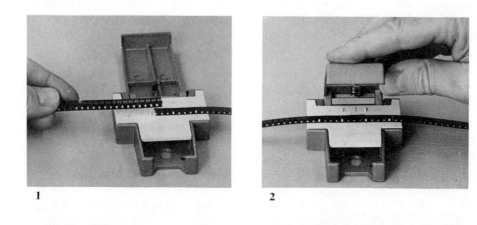

4

5

6

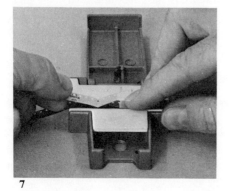

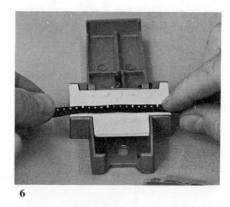

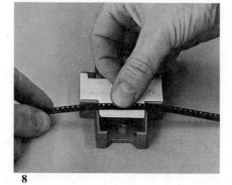

7

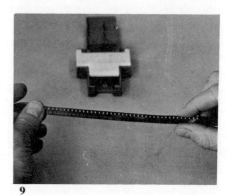

8

9

The second method for splicing motion-picture film uses film cement. The film cement is a fast drying solvent, capable of fusing the film base (cellulose acetate) of each end of film to the other. This is an *overlap* splice. To permit this, it is first necessary to remove the photographic emulsion that covers the base so the two pieces of film have base-to-base contact.

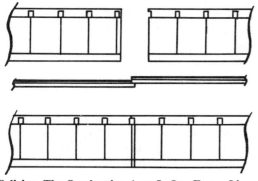

Splicing. The Overlapping Area Is One Frame Line

These items are necessary when splicing with cement—cotton gloves, a splicer, a scraper (here an emery board), a bottle of film cement.

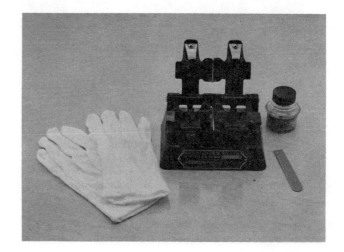

1. Set one piece of film on the sprocket pins at the right side of the splicer with the emulsion (dull) side up.
2. Lower the cutter bar and trim the film evenly. Then put the right section of the splicer up out of the way, with the film still in place.
3. Set the second piece of film, emulsion up, in the left side of the splicer.
4. Lower and secure the left upper section to hold the film in place.
5. Scrape the emulsion from the edge of the film exposed on the left. Work carefully but remove *all* the emulsion, down to the clear film base.
6. Remove any deposits or dust from the scraped film.
7. Apply a small amount of film cement to the exposed film base.
8. Quickly lower the right upper section and secure the clamp.
9. After 20 seconds raise both upper sections and remove the spliced film carefully.

1

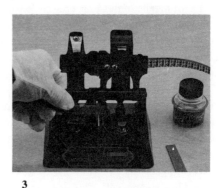

2

3

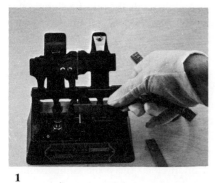

4

5

6

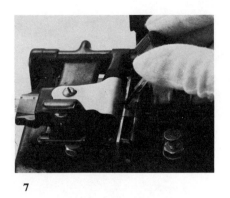

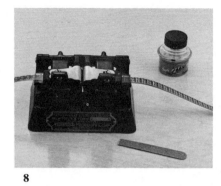

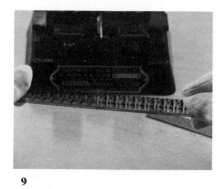

7   8   9

By following this procedure you should be able to make consistently good splices. If your splices do not hold, the reason may be one or more of several:

- Using old, thick film cement
- Not removing all the emulsion when scraping
- Excessive scraping that weakens the film base
- Removing spliced film from the splicer before the cement has set
- Poor adjustment of the splicer—faulty alignment of the sprocket pins or of the clamp which puts pressure on the splice

Preparing film for the laboratory

If a workprint has been made from the original footage for editing purposes the original must be matched (conformed) to the workprint before laboratory services can be requested. *To conform* means to put in proper order the original footage that matches the footage in the workprint. This is accomplished by matching up the *edge numbers* printed on the original to the edge numbers of the workprint footage. Upon completion the original footage will exactly match the edited workprint.

Many times it is necessary to put the conformed original footage into *A and B rolls* for the laboratory. This is generally done when optical effects (fades or dissolves), overprint titles and labels, or other special laboratory services will be requested. This method is also used to avoid having any splice marks appear in the resulting prints. Alternate scenes are placed in the same roll. Thus scenes 1, 3, 5, 7, . . . become roll A and scenes 2, 4, 6, 8, . . . are roll B. Adjacent scenes in the same roll are separated by lengths of black leader. The amount of leader used is determined by the length of the scene at the same place in the other roll. Only when scenes require double exposure (dissolves or overprint titles, for example) is black leader not used. The final A and B rolls will be of exactly the same length. The film laboratory will print each roll on the same film stock to make a negative or print.

ADDING SOUND

When editing is completed, titles are in place, and the narration is in final form, you are ready to put sound on the film. There are various ways of correlating sound with picture. See Chapter 17 for recording procedures.

Live commentary

If proper equipment is not available for putting sound on the film you can plan to read the narration as the film is projected. To be most effective, use a public-address system to give depth to your voice (talking into a microphone attached to the amplifier of the projector will feed your voice through the speaker). Sound effects and background music may be added on cue from disk recordings or from a tape.

The shortcomings of this live-commentary method are obvious—the need for close co-ordination and timing by the narrator and by those operating the equipment; the involvement of a number of persons in addition to the projectionist; and the need to set up extra equipment every time the film is shown. But this method is suitable for limited uses of your film.

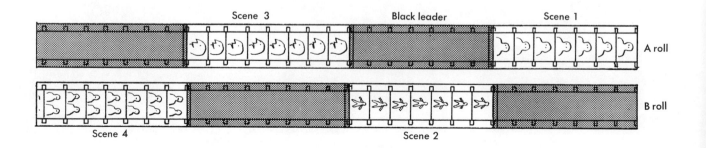

Magnetic sound

One of the simplest ways of adding sound to a film is to use a tape recorder. Record the narration as the edited film is projected for the purpose, and thereafter play the recording as the film is projected before audiences. Unfortunately the sound may not stay in synchronization with the picture because of variations in the motor speed controlling the tape movement or because of tape stretch. Control units have been made which connect a recorder directly to the projector, thus guaranteeing their operation at the same speed.

It is better to use a magnetic sound projector, which includes a recorder. Using this equipment gives you the flexibility of synchronized sound recording (on a magnetic stripe that is on the film itself), immediate playback, erasing and re-recording as necessary. Models in both 8mm and 16mm are available. See page 213. After editing is completed, send the film to a film laboratory for magnetic or *sound-striping* at 2¢ to 5¢ per foot. It will be returned ready for the addition of sound.

Magnetic Sound Track

Record at the same speed as the film was taken (unless special effects were used). Normal sound speed, 24 frames per second, gives better sound quality than does 16 frames per second. The latter is suitable if only voice is to be recorded. Refer to pages 129–134 for suggestions concerning the selection and duties of recording personnel, recording facilities, and the recording procedure.

Splices on an original film may cause irregularities in the sound or, more seriously, splices may break at any time. Therefore consider having at least one print made from the original film. A sound-striped print will insure a better-quality recording and by having it you are protected since you can store the original film in a safe, dry, and cool place. If a number of prints are needed, the magnetic sound track can be converted to *optical sound* on additional prints and then used with a sound motion-picture projector.

Optical Sound Track

Lip synchronization

There may be times when it is desirable to record the speech of those appearing in the film (as during interviews, discussions, or dramatic sequences). To do this requires a *sound-on-film* motion-picture camera (which records the sound magnetically or optically on the film in the camera as it is being shot). Or, instead, separate magnetic recording equipment that can be synchronized with the camera can be used. This procedure requires lip synchronization and is an ambitious undertaking for those without experience in *lip sync* recording work. Also, editing becomes more complex as both sound and picture must be handled simultaneously and additional editing equipment is required. 8mm magnetic sound-on-film cameras offer some simplification for this complex process, but quality, as yet, is limited. For further information about preparing and editing films requiring lip synchronization, see the references on page 236.

Moviola for Editing Sound Film

Now, apply what you have learned about film laboratory services, film editing, and adding sound to film:

1. What is the advantage of having a *workprint* made?
2. With which process is the term *edge number* related—printing, editing, conforming, splicing?
3. Which type of film splicing do you use or prefer to use? What are its advantages or disadvantages?
4. Explain these terms—*string-out, rough cut,* and *fine cut.*
5. How does the process of editing an *unscripted* film differ from that of editing a film *in the camera?*
6. What method of adding sound to film would you most likely use? What are its procedures?

SUMMARY OF 16MM-MOTION-PICTURE PRODUCTION STEPS

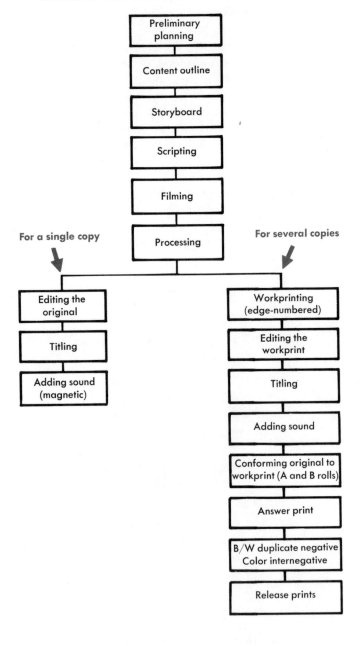

For a single copy — For several copies

RATIONALE FOR 8MM FILMS

[See Appendix A for film correlated with this topic.]

As was discussed at the beginning of this chapter, concepts of educational-film production are changing. This is due primarily to new developments in 8mm projectors, easily adaptable to new educational needs; and the realization that brief films can serve specific operational objectives (page 187) as part of an instructional package or sequence.

Simple-to-operate 8mm silent and sound projectors make it possible for individuals to study films by themselves, either as complete treatments of topics or as parts of a programed sequence. Now more people are encouraged to make brief films to serve specific instructional objectives.

While the information already presented in this chapter on motion-picture production techniques is fundamental, there are some changes in emphasis when making an 8mm film for other than regular class or group use. This section will consider these factors.

Before proceeding it is necessary to explain that a film intended for use as an 8mm motion picture can originate on either 8mm or 16mm film stock. Copies of the 16mm would be made into the 8mm size by optical-reduction printing. Therefore, the recommendations that follow apply when the final, using medium is to be 8mm, regardless whether 8mm or 16mm film is shot in the camera.

8mm film stock

There are two types of 8mm film stock—Standard 8 and Super 8. Standard 8 film has been considered an amateur film until recently. With the development of the Technicolor 8mm silent cartridge projector and the Fairchild 8mm magnetic sound cartridge projector, 8mm films started to find applications in business and industry. Eventually the potential values of 8mm films for education were realized. (See the references by Forsdale on page 237.)

A number of film laboratories built or acquired printers to reduce 16mm film to 8mm prints in satisfactory quality. Then with the introduction of Super 8 film the acceptance of 8mm films for instruction took a big step forward. Eventually Super 8 will dominate the 8mm field, but at present, both types of film, cameras, and projectors are used.

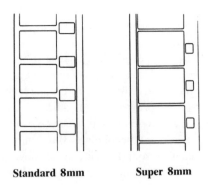

Standard 8mm   **Super 8mm**

As compared to Standard 8, Super 8 film has certain advantages—an exact 16mm aspect ratio (4:3) which makes reduction from 16mm to 8mm accurate for covering the entire picture area, which Standard 8 does not permit; an adequate area for a sound track alongside the picture area; and about a 50-percent larger picture area. The latter is permitted by a reduction in the size of the sprocket holes, their placement closer to the film edge, and a reduction in the width of the frame line. The sprocket holes are also spaced slightly farther apart, thus increasing the height of the picture area. In comparison to Standard 8, Super 8 film is 10% longer for the same running time. (This latter point is what increases the film and printing costs of Super 8 about 10% over that of Standard 8.)

Because of the larger picture area, the increase in quality of present-day projection lenses, and the increased light output of projection lamps for Super 8 projectors, the projected image from Super 8 film is appreciably sharper and brighter than is the image from comparable Standard 8 films. The projected-image quality of Super 8 film approaches that from 16mm films (about the same as 16mm projected images approach those of 35mm). This means that Super 8 can be used satisfactorily for class viewing, while Standard 8 should be restricted to small-group and individual viewing.

8mm projectors

Projectors for 8mm film are of four types:

- silent film, reel-to-reel (meaning that film moves through the projector from *feed reel* to *take-up reel*)
- silent film, cartridge load
- sound film, reel-to-reel
- sound film, cartridge load

The silent-film projectors operate at 16 or 18 frames per second. There are many reel-to-reel units, but one designed especially for educational use is the Eastman Kodak Ektagraphic 8 projector. Although a plastic cartridge for film is available, it is not required and the projector is essentially reel-to-reel. An important feature of this unit is the ease of instantly rewinding film onto the feed reel at any time, during or at the end of projection. Up to 200 feet of Super 8 film can be used with this projector.

Eastman Silent Reel-to-Reel Projector

The only widely distributed 8mm silent cartridge projector is made by the Technicolor corporation. The cartridge can hold up to a maximum of 60 feet of 8mm film (running time 5 minutes for Standard 8 and 11 percent less, 4½ minutes, for Super 8 film). Much shorter lengths can be used (a minimum of 20 feet is recommended). Special service is required for loading

the cartridges. This can be done through a photo dealer, or a unit can be purchased if a large number of cartridges are to be loaded locally.[1]

Technicolor Silent Cartridge Projector

8mm sound projectors, besides being either reel or cartridge types, can be for either magnetic or optical sound. Optical sound, employed on the 10- and 30-minute long cartridges for the Technicolor Super 8 sound projector, will find its widest use with commercially produced films. Magnetic sound, handled by the Eastman Kodak reel-to-reel units, can be added locally (page 211). Magnetic sound requires the use of a magnetic-sound-recording projector for recording at either 18 or 24 frames per second.

Technicolor Optical-Sound Cartridge Projector

Eastman Magnetic-Sound Playback-Only Projector

[1] For fast cartridge service a school or business concern can send film directly to the Technicolor Corporation, Cartridge Branch, 3402 W. Osborn Road, Phoenix, Arizona 85017.

Eastman Magnetic-Sound Recorder and Playback Projector

Finally, 8mm projectors, for group and individual viewing, can be either for front reflected projection or for rear-screen, transmitted projection, the latter under ordinary room illumination.

Front Projection

Rear-Screen Projection

There is no difficulty of principle in designing a projector to permit stopping a motion picture to show single frames of the film as still pictures. Since being able to do this has advantages for learning, equipment will shortly become available. Such equipment, offering the user more resources, will challenge him to employ them to best advantage.

Production considerations

Much of the evidence gathered from research concerning the design and use of motion pictures can find more extensive applications in the 8mm single-concept medium than has been applied in 16mm-film production. The 8mm approach narrows the variables (audience, objectives, content, and so forth) so the practical situation becomes closer to the conditions under which the experimental procedures may have taken place. Again, review the research reports in Chapter 3 and determine how they may be applied in your 8mm film-production activities in terms of the following suggestions:

- *Emphasis:* On simplicity of content treatment, action, composition, and detail.
- *Content:* Treating a single idea, concept, or limited topic concisely. This requires careful planning and a willingness to continually examine and evaluate development. The 8mm films that correlate with this chapter, and with other chapters of this book, are examples of the single-concept treatment. See
- *Length:* Sufficient to do the job without including lengthy titles, credits, introduction, summary, and irrelevant material.
- *Filming techniques:* Often simplified, such as longer scenes of how-to-do-it activity filmed from one position; emphasis on close-up details; subjective camera angles from the learner's point of view. Other techniques such as matching action, screen direction, accounting for passage of time, and so forth, should be considered, but may be dispensed with in some filming situations.
- *Pacing:* Owing to close-up filming the action should be at a slightly slower pace than that found in other films, but not so slow as to drag and lose attention-holding power. It is recommended that a film be viewed more than once by the learner, if necessary for comprehension.
- *Scene content:* Limiting items in a scene to those that directly contribute to or are required by the action. All distracting background elements and movements should be eliminated.
- *Accompanying narration:* A minimum use of voice to cue and interpret action as shown. Sound must be related directly to visual activity.
- *Accompanying titles:* Topic headings and instructions, briefly worded, should be included in silent films (and probably in sound films for reinforcement) as separate scenes rather than as *overprints* on action scenes. The latter use tends to distract attention from the visual action. Overprint labels and arrows should be used as necessary.
- *Correlated materials:* Review outlines, details not covered in a film, related activities, participation questions, problems, and activities, should all be available in printed or other form to accompany the film. If a film is part of a programed sequence, directions must be clear concerning the film's use at the proper place in the sequence along with lead-in and lead-out materials.

Silent-film production requires more careful attention to visual detail than may be adequate in the production of a sound film. In the latter, directing attention and making explanations and interpretations can be the responsibility of the sound track. But in a silent film only the picture (and accompanying titles) can communicate. Therefore extreme care must be used to insure that a scene conveys its intent accurately and easily.

Making a silent film is a challenging form of production and can be very effective if it is done carefully. The required concentration of the viewer on a message carried through the single most perceptive sense—sight—can be a stimulating way of learning. Keep in mind the factors enumerated above and supplement them with others derived from studying available 8mm silent films and from your own experiences.

Production procedures

If a motion picture is to be made directly on 8mm film certain cautions should be recognized:

- Splices can be troublesome if the film is cartridged and used in a Technicolor unit. Splices close together may catch on each other or on parts of the cartridge, stopping the film and resulting in damage. Therefore try to eliminate splices by *editing the film in the camera* as explained on page 207.
- One way of overcoming the problem of splices is to have a print made from the original film. This will be splice-free. The commonly used 8mm film is Kodachrome II (for Standard 8 or Super 8). This film is meant for projection and not for duplication. Duplicate prints from Kodachrome tend to be grainy and therefore not as sharp as the original; true colors are lost and the contrast between light and dark areas becomes greater (light-color areas become whiter and dark-color areas become blacker). Thus the appearance of a duplicate may be disappointing as compared with the original film.
- If prints must be made from original 8mm film, the film should be handled and projected as little as possible. Scratches and embedded dirt will appear on prints as obvious dark lines and marks.

If it can be anticipated that duplicate 8mm prints of good quality may be needed, it is recommended that filming be done on 16mm film and then reduced to either Standard 8 or Super 8. The film to use is Commercial Ektachrome (page 192), which is a film of low contrast and designed for duplication. It is not available through regular photo dealers, but must be obtained from a store carrying professional or commercial film items. Once the film is processed and edited (with or without a workprint as explained on page 206), certain film laboratories can prepare 8mm prints in one of three ways:

- *Direct optical reduction of original 16mm film to 8mm print:* This method gives the sharpest print as nothing comes between the original and the final print. Costs are high and the process is not advisable if a quantity of prints are needed.

There is always the possibility of damage to the original which is used to make every print.

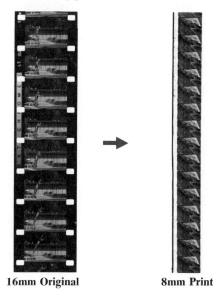

16mm Original   **8mm Print**

- *Preparation of a 16mm color internegative from the original 16mm film and then optical reduction from internegative to 8mm positive prints:* While this is a costly method for a few prints, the relative costs drop considerably as numbers of prints above about eight are made. The quality is good, although there is some loss in sharpness as the final 8mm print is now *two* generations (steps) away from the original. This method is commonly used for making Super 8 prints and in large-volume printing the internegative is optically reduced onto 35mm positive film stock to make 3 or 4 side-by-side 8mm prints.

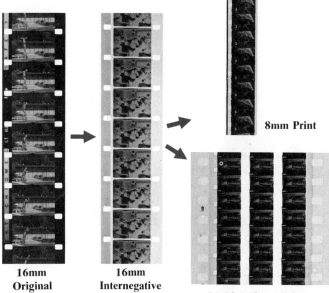

16mm Original   **16mm Internegative**   **8mm Print**

Multiple 8mm Prints on 35mm Film

• *Preparation of a double-8mm color internegative (consisting of two optically reduced 8mm negatives side by side on 16mm film) from the original 16mm film and then contact printing from the internegative to make 8mm prints in pairs.* The cost for this service is slightly less than that of the previously described printing method. This technique is used solely for making Standard 8 prints. Experience has shown that the quality of 8mm prints made by this method is generally not as satisfactory as that of prints made by the other methods described above.

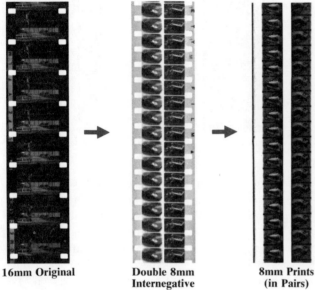

16mm Original   **Double 8mm**   **8mm Prints**
                    Internegative   **(in Pairs)**

PREPARING TO USE YOUR FILM

With the completion of the film and of your preparations for using it, consider the advisability of developing an instruction guide as described on page 57.

Remember that the success of your motion picture will depend not only on its content and on the quality of your production, but also on the manner in which you introduce and project it for the audience. As you prepare for the first showing, follow the suggestions on page 60.

Now, review what you have learned about producing 8mm films:

1. What are the advantages of Super 8 over Standard 8 film?
2. For what instructional purpose might you prepare an 8mm film for use with these type projectors:
   a. a silent cartridge projector
   b. a magnetic-sound reel-to-reel projector
3. What are some factors in film production to keep in mind as you plan and prepare an 8mm silent film? Which of these directly relates to the findings of research?
4. What are some disadvantages in duplicating a film made in 8 millimeter?
5. Which laboratory process for making 8mm prints from 16mm original footage results in the best quality? What are its drawbacks?

24. Television and Display Materials

Graphics

Photographs

Transparencies

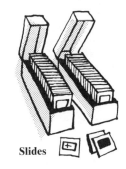

Slides

Motion Pictures

Displays

Visual materials for television and display may include graphics, photographs, slides, transparencies, motion pictures, and items on felt, hook-and-loop, and magnetic boards.

The methods described in this book for making visual materials apply when preparing them for television use. In addition, keep in mind special requirements of the television medium as you plan and prepare them.

SPECIAL REQUIREMENTS FOR TELEVISION

Format and proportions

The television format is 3 units high and 4 units wide. Therefore, whenever possible, arrange subjects with this orientation. Use proportions relating to this ratio (6:8, 9:12, . . .) when preparing graphic materials and plan photographic materials to fit the ratio closely.

Carefully consider content within the format size. Provide for loss of one-sixth the marginal area *on each side* and keep important parts of the visual within the middle two-thirds portion. This restriction is necessary because of variations in the adjustment of television receivers.

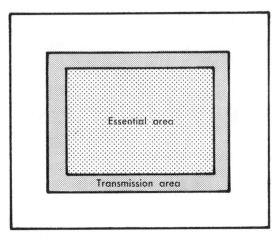

Detail and size

One important feature of television is its use of the *close-up*—being able to center attention on the object or visual and bring it, greatly magnified, to the viewer. Therefore:

- Keep materials simple, bold, and free from unnecessary detail.
- Use suitable, clear-cut lettering.
- Adhere to recognized legibility stands for ease of reading—minimum letter size of 1/25 the height of the area (page 99).
- Limit outlines and other lists to 4 or 5 lines, each containing no more than 3 to 5 words.

CAPITALIZATION PROCESS
1. Estimate adjusted gross income
2. Estimate expenses
3. Compute net income
4. Determine recapture rate
5. Compute property valuation

Contrast and colors

Colored materials that are put before the television camera appear on the black-and-white television receiver screen as shades of gray. Thus a green line on a red background may disappear because the green and the red are equivalent to the same shade of gray, that is, have the same gray value.

The range of shades of gray reproduced by black-and-white television is limited. Only five or six shades can be clearly recognized. Avoid black symbols or drawings on white background or any materials with such extreme contrast (unless for special purposes). Lower contrast, as between shades of gray and black, is preferable.

Check the gray value of colors to be used for preparing visuals by holding *these* colors before the television camera. Only by this method can you make sure what effect they will exhibit in use. The same color, on two different surfaces or under two different lighting conditions, may be picked up as different shades of gray; contrasting colors may match and fail to contrast when television has grayed them. For rough planning *only*, you may assume that colors will group themselves as shades of gray according to the lists shown in the diagram.

PREPARING MATERIALS

Before making any visuals always consider this planning check list:

- Has careful planning for the program taken place? (pages 23–30)
- Have the visuals been developed as an integral part of the planning?
- Are the selected visuals the most suitable ones in terms of—
    —the purpose of the program?
    —the ideas to be communicated?
    —the most effective visual medium to use?
    —the time and expense for preparation?

The inevitable problem with television production work is TIME—generally not enough time for careful and detailed preparation of materials. Therefore, select and develop techniques which not only will help you to prepare your visuals rapidly, but also will result in attractive and effective instructional materials.

Graphic materials

Charts, diagrams, outlines, summaries, and titles may be presented "on the set" (that is, displayed before the television camera directly) so that the television instructor himself, or an assistant, can indicate features of the visual and control the rate of use.

1. Prepare a rough pencil sketch of the visual and show layout

BLACK	brown	red	light blue	light gray	WHITE
	dark green	medium blue	orange	tan	
	dark blue	medium green		pastels	

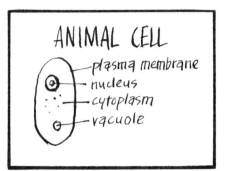

and proportions for all elements (8½″×11″ paper will approximate the 3:4 ratio).

2. Select a convenient size of cardboard for working and for storage. Use 14-ply television illustration board or a dull-finish gray board ("middle gray"). Stay within a 9″×12″ working area on 14″×17″ cardboard, or 6″×8″ area on 11″×14″ board to insure plenty of extra margin.

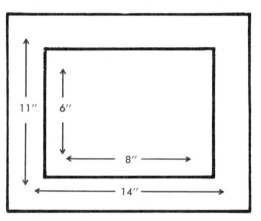

3. Select suitable lettering aids (pages 101–108) and practice the necessary lettering. Note the suggestions for preparing lettering on pages 99–100. Apply recommended legibility standards for lettered materials (page 99).

4. Sketch the visual on cardboard, using a simple illustrative technique (pages 95–97). Then locate the areas for lettering.

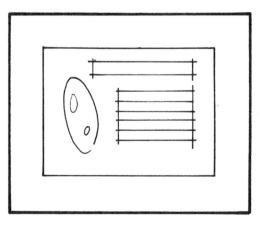

5. Do the lettering; then complete the diagram with pen and ink, felt pen, crayon, or gray pencils. Erase all guide lines. (Retouch colors, that match cardboard colors, for correcting mistakes, are available from art-supply stores.)

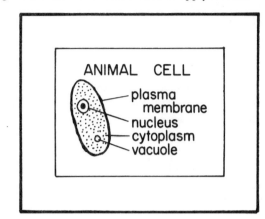

Photographs

Enlargements from camera negatives have the same "on-the-set" uses as graphic materials.

1. Record activities on film (pages 137–141) or photographically copy materials (pages 82–85). If captions and labels on materials are too small, block them out if they are unnecessary, or reletter them on slips of paper and lay the slips in place before photographing. *Remember,* written permission is necessary for using copyrighted materials over television (see the release form on page 49). Then develop the film.

2. Print the negative, being sure that the important parts of the picture are kept within the selected working area (for the 9″×12″ area use 11″×14″ enlarging papers; for 6″×8″ use 8″×10″ paper). The printing paper should be of *matte type* (an "A" or "C" surface is acceptable) to avoid light reflections during use on the set. Maintain a low contrast level in photographs by avoiding deep shadow areas or bril-

liant white areas. When printing negatives that will produce large white areas, "flash" the paper before use to gray the white areas (exposure to the darkroom white light for 1 to 4 seconds is satisfactory).

3. Mount photographs on 14-ply gray cardboard backing using the dry mount method (page 112).

2″×2″ slides

2″×2″ slides are inexpensive visuals for television. They usually are shown from a remotely controlled projector directly into a preset television camera, thus requiring no on-the-set handling. Slides may also be projected from behind and onto a translucent screen, as part of the set. This method permits the instructor to control the slide projector himself, and to indicate features directly on the projected image.

Make slides as records of activities, as copies of printed materials, and for titles. For slide-making techniques, see pages 142–152.

Keep the following points in mind as you plan, prepare, and select slides for use on television:

• The projected area must conform to the wider-than-high television format, 3 units high by 4 units wide.
• The slide image must provide for loss at the sides and top in consequence two conditions: first, the difference in proportion between the television 3:4 format and the slide 2:3 format cuts off some of the image at the sides; second, one-sixth of the television camera's image may be lost at top, bottom, and each side of the receiver image, as was explained on page 218.
• Many slides will have been made in color. Remember the gray-scale limitations on televising color
• A slightly overcast day for outdoor filming and a low contrast ratio for indoor filming are preferable.
• For fast preparation of black-and-white slides use Polaroid transparency film or direct-positive film (page 157).

• For superimposing titles use 35mm high-contrast film to prepare negative title slides (page 144).
• For adding labels when copying printed materials, see suggestions on page 219.
• If desirable, when slides are completed, mount them between glass and then number them according to the program script (page 148).
• If comments are to accompany a series of slides, tape record the instructor's narration to insure consistency and pacing.

Filmstrips

Only rarely are filmstrips prepared for television use. Projectors which handle filmstrips are not normally a part of television equipment. It is more common to prepare slides, or to cut frames from a filmstrip (preferably the double-frame size—page 154), and mount them as slides for handling in a remotely controlled projector.

Overhead transparencies

There are many worthwhile television uses for overhead transparencies. They may be placed over a light box to be viewed by an overhead television camera, or projected onto a rear screen for regular camera pick-up. (The rear-screen method for displaying visuals is described on page 223.) The feature of a large, bright image, of being able to write on the transparency as it is projected, and the techniques of progressive disclosure, adding overlays to a base transparency, and simulating motion, all merit consideration (page 162).

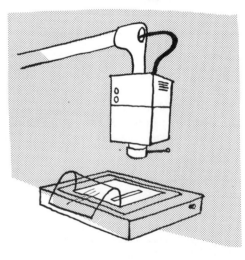

The preparation of transparencies outlined on pages 166–184 can be applied to materials for television. Photographic high-contrast transparencies (pages 180–183) with clear white areas and sharp black lines and letters are most suitable. Continuous-tone black-and-white transparencies (page 183), when projected, serve as suitable backgrounds for studio sets as well as for illustrations of subject matter.

Motion pictures

Motion pictures are especially compatible with television. The mechanical equipment is adapted to handle the film and the picture-story techniques of motion pictures and television are much alike. Complete films or short film subjects (*film clips*) may bring to the audience personalities otherwise unavailable and also activities, examples, and processes, either too varied, too complex, or too distant, to telecast from the studio.

Film projection, like slide projection, is remotely controlled, generally by the program director.

- Keep in mind the special requirements of television—low picture contrast, the one-sixth marginal loss of picture area when projected, and the value of close-up scenes.
- Keep long shots to a minimum because of the small size of the television screen as related to a motion-picture screen and the inability of television to resolve a great amount of detail.
- Use 16mm film at normal sound speed of 24 frames per second. (Some educational television stations are adapting equipment for using 8mm film.)
- Apply the basic planning and production techniques on pages 186–206.
- Consider using *multiple cameras* for speed in shooting film materials (page 199).
- Add sound to film through use of magnetic striping (page 211), or more commonly, let the television instructor narrate the film as it is projected. Synchronous sound may be recorded when filming if proper equipment and experienced personnel are available.

VIDEOTAPE RECORDING

In the last few years the cost and complexity of videotape recorders have been reduced appreciably. Such equipment is now within the price reach of all school television facilities. Therefore selected portions or complete television presentations can be recorded on videotape and played back at any convenient time.

The usual requirements of television, as noted in this section, apply when materials are to be recorded on videotape. Also, a common practice is to convert the original videotape recording

to 16mm motion picture film for continual use and distribution. As indicated on page 193, in motion-picture production, a videotape recording may be used to preview the action before actual filming takes place. See the list on page 241 for laboratories that can convert videotape recordings to film.

DISPLAYING MATERIALS

The way in which visuals are used in a television program controls some aspects of their preparation. The controlling qualities involve answers to questions like these:

- Is it necessary for the instructor to handle the materials?
- How can the use of the visuals best be co-ordinated, paced, and given variety?
- Will it be best to develop an idea sequentially or can the whole visual be shown at one time?

These questions must be in mind as the planning and preparation of the visuals take place. To make the decisions, you need to become familiar with the methods commonly used for displaying materials.

For a long time teachers have used felt and flannel boards to display materials that present information and develop concepts. Recent developments, such as magnetic and other surfaces, extend the effectiveness of such display boards by providing increased flexibility. Whether these display surfaces are to be used in a classroom or in a television studio, the following information is basic.

Display easels

A set of visuals may be placed on a table easel or floor stand, and their use controlled by the instructor or an assistant, in the studio or in the classroom.

Flannel (felt) boards

This display surface frequently is used to develop concepts or processes by the progressive addition of prepared parts. The board itself is made of plywood, masonite, or wallboard covered with high-grade flannel or felt. It is set on an easel for use. Pastel or light colors are advisable for the cloth covering. Prepare lettered materials and diagrams in black ink on gray cardboard (unless different colors are important to register shades for separation). Back the cardboard with strips of felt or sandpaper. This textured or rough backing will adhere to the flannel or felt surface.

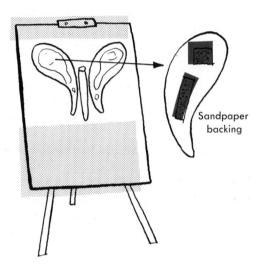

Sandpaper backing

Hook-and-loop boards

A new type of presentation board, the *hook-and-loop board,* safeguards against the possible slippage of flannel-covered surfaces. The surface material consists of a cloth containing countless tiny nylon loops, while display materials are backed with small strips of tape having numerous nylon hooks.

Use a strong adhesive such as white glue or an epoxy cement to attach the tape to the back of objects. In use, the nylon loops intertwine with the nylon hooks, joining the two surfaces securely. The strength of this union is sufficient to hold not only paper and cardboard objects, but also heavy three-dimensional items.

Magnetic chalkboards

The magnetic chalkboard is even more flexibly useful and permits more versatility than the flannel board or the hook-and-loop board, since the television instructor can draw or write on the board in addition to positioning prepared materials. The magnetized materials hold their position and can be moved at will. The painted writing surface does not interfere with magnetic attraction.

Magnets

The magnetic board consists of sheet steel or fine-mesh steel screen covered by a writing surface. Small magnets are cemented or taped to the backs of objects or graphic materials. Magnets may be of metal or of magnetized rubber strips with adhesive backing.

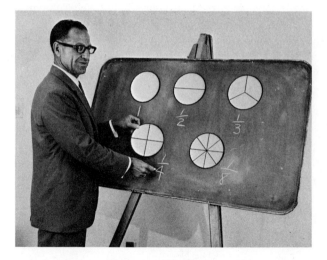

Portable magnetic chalkboards are available commercially. Flexible metallic-surfaced materials can be obtained and are easily framed for use. Also, a home-made magnetic chalkboard can be made from a galvanized-steel oil drip pan sold in auto supply stores. To give the drip pan a chalkboard surface, vinegar and chalkboard spray paint (carried by major paint suppliers) are needed. Follow these instructions to prepare the chalk surface over the galvanized metal:

1. Pour some vinegar on the pan and, with a cloth, spread it over the surface for 15 minutes. This will clean and "cure" the galvanized surface.
2. Rinse off the vinegar with water.
3. After the surface is dry spray it with chalkboard paint. At least two coats are recommended. Sand the first coat lightly with extra fine sandpaper before applying the second coat.
4. Before use, thoroughly chalk the surface by working it over with the side of a large piece of soft chalk. This will insure smooth writing and easy erasure of chalk marks.

Film chain

Slides and motion pictures generally are handled on what is called the *film chain* of the television system. Each projector is aimed (or the projection beam is reflected) into a special television camera. Projection is controlled by the program director or by his assistant according to the script, or by verbal instructions from the instructor.

Slide Projection for Television

Rear-screen projection

Slides, transparencies for the overhead projector, and even filmstrips may be displayed from the rear onto a translucent screen. Such a screen is made from a sheet of high-quality tracing paper held between pieces of glass, or from commercial rear-screen material (source on page 234). Careful studio lighting is necessary in order to protect against reflections and dimming of the image on the screen. A television studio camera picks up the projected picture from the front side of the screen. Either of two methods may be used:

• Place the projector directly behind the screen (depending on the screen size and on the lens, a distance of 8 to 12 feet may be required). By using a remote-control accessory, the instructor himself may control slide changes, but an assistant must show overhead transparencies on cue. Slides and transparencies must either be projected backwards so they read correctly on the front of the screen; or the image must be reversed by attaching a 90° prism to the front of the projection lens, thus permitting the use of materials in their correct position. In either case the instructor stands beside the projected image where the television camera can pick him up as he points to the projected picture or comments on it.

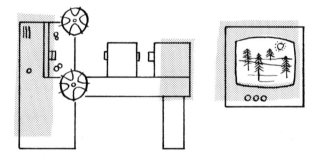

Motion-Picture Projection for Television

• Place the overhead projector beside the rear screen, where the television instructor can operate it, and project the image onto a mirror behind the screen and thus onto the rear of the screen. (For best reflection, a front-surface mirror should be used; a wide-angle projecting lens is necessary.) The instructor can point to features on the transparencies while facing the television camera. Slides can also be projected via a mirror in this fashion, but the instructor refers to the screen. The mirror method permits using a shallower studio.

Now, apply what you have learned about preparing visual materials for television and display:

1. What three categories of special requirements must be considered when planning materials for television.
2. How should photographs and slides be prepared for television use?
3. On what bases do you decide whether materials should be used in the studio or via projection on the film or slide chain?
4. How might you adapt equipment in order to use overhead transparencies on television?
5. What are some advantages of hook-and-loop material over flannel or felt?
6. What is an advantage of the magnetic chalkboard over the other two display boards?
7. How might you proceed to prepare your own magnetic chalkboard?

APPENDIXES

A. *Correlated 8mm Films*

B. *Answers to Review Questions*

C. *Books, Films, Pamphlets, and Periodicals*

D. *Sources for Equipment and Materials*

E. *Services*

F. *Glossary*

Correlated 8mm Films

Below is a list of 8mm silent films for use with the Technicolor Instant Movie Projector that correlate with topics and explanations in this book.

The films are available from McGraw-Hill Book Co., Inc., Text-Film Division, 330 W. 42 Street, New York, N.Y. 10036. Write to the distributor for further information and prices.

Photography

Camera Settings
Composition
Determining Exposure
Film Characteristics
Lighting Scenes
Close-up and Copywork
Making Titles
Processing Black-and-White Film
Opaquing and Spotting Prints
Printing Black-and-White Negatives
    a. Contact Printing
    b. Enlarging

Graphics

Bulletin Board Design
Coloring and Shading Films
Lettering: Prepared Letters
Lettering: Felt Pen Skills
Lettering: Felt Pen Applications
Lettering: Wrico Signmaker
Lettering: Wricoprint
Lettering: Leroy (small)
Lettering: Leroy (large)
Mounting: Rubber Cement (Permanent)
Mounting: Dry Mount (Press)
Mounting: Dry Mount (Hand Iron)
Mounting: Cut-out Picture
Mounting: Two-Page Picture
Mounting: Overcoming Problems
Mounting: Cloth Backing
    a. Roll
    b. Fold—part 1
    c. Fold—part 2
Mounting: Laminating

Preparing Spirit Masters (by Hand)
Preparing Spirit Masters (Thermal Machine)
Operating the Spirit Duplicator

Recording

Operating the Tape Recorder
Operating the Record Player
Combination Uses of Audio Equipment
Splicing Magnetic Tape

Overhead Transparencies

Features of Transparencies
Making Overlays
Coloring Transparencies
Felt Pens on Acetate
Using Tapes and Transfer Letters
With the Spirit Duplicator
Principle of Diazo Process
Diazo Process
Heat Process (Thermo-fax)
Heat Process (Masterfax)
Picture Transfer (Seal Process)
    a. Part 1
    b. Part 2
Picture Transfer (Shelf Paper)
High-Contrast Film Process
Mounting and Masking

Motion Pictures

Motion-Picture Shots
The Motion-Picture Camera
Building Sequences
Developing Continuity
Making Transitions
Special Filming Techniques
Editing in the Camera
Multicamera Uses
Shooting Unscripted Films
Editing Film
Splicing Film
Special Techniques for 8mm Film Production

In addition to the above production films, the following 8mm silent cartridged films on audiovisual equipment operation are available:

Still Picture Projectors

2″ × 2″ Kodak Carousel
2″ × 2″ Viewlex
35mm Viewlex Filmstrip
35mm Bell and Howell Filmstrip
Opaque Projector
Overhead Projector

Motion Picture Projectors

Motion Picture Projection Practice (2 parts)
RCA—Junior and 25016 Models (3 parts)

RCA—1600 Model (manual)
RCA—1600 Model (automatic)
Graflex—Model 815 (2 parts)
Kodak Pageant—Model AV-126-TR (2 parts)
Kalart/Victor—Model 70-15 (3 parts)
Kalart/Victor—Series 75
Bell and Howell—Model 399 (3 parts)
Bell and Howell—Model 542 (2 parts)
Bell and Howell—Model 552 Autoload
Splicing Motion-Picture Film

Audio Equipment

Tape Recorder
Record Player
Splicing Magnetic Tape
Combination Uses of Audio Equipment

Appendix B.

Answers to Review Questions

Each following answer is handled in one of three ways:

1. The question is answered directly.
2. Reference is made to the page on which the topic of the question is discussed.
3. The answer is based on the decision of the reader according to his use of equipment and processes.

CHAPTER 15. PHOTOGRAPHY

Camera types (page 67)

1. 35mm camera.
2. Sheet-film camera.
3. Box camera (or automatic-setting camera).
4. Polaroid camera.
5. Twin-lens reflex camera.
6. Automatic-setting camera.

Camera settings (page 72)

1. Twice as much.
2. Page 69.
3. $f/22$ and 1/30 second.
4. 3⅓' to 5'.
5. Greater.

Film (page 74)

1. Type of light source (sunlight, photoflood, or other).
2. Kodacolor or Ektacolor negative film.
3. You can use a higher $f/$ number or a shorter exposure time with the 100 film.

Exposure (page 77)

1. Film speed, $f/$ stop, shutter speed; $f/$ stop and shutter speed; film speed.
2. Film speed and light-level indication.
3. $f/$ stop and shutter speed.
4. $f/32$ and ⅛ second.
5. Incident-light meter.

Lighting (page 79)

1. Small areas.
2. $f/16$.
3. Page 78.
4. Incident meter reading of key light, measured at the scene, is

twice that of the fill light. Yes, this is an acceptable ratio.
5. Page 79.
6. Page 78.

Picture composition (page 81)

Generally, No. 4 is preferable because of the careful framing.

Close-up and copy work (page 86)

1. Box, 35mm with window viewfinder, twin-lens reflex, Polaroid, automatic-setting, and motion-picture with window viewfinder.
2. No. Calculation is necessary if a bellows is used.
3. Larger number (that is smaller opening). Slower. Tripod essential.

Processing film and making prints (page 90)

1. Page 87.
2. Page 82.
3. Page 90.
4. —
5. Page 89.
6. Page 88.

CHAPTER 16. GRAPHICS

Planning art work (page 95)

1. Page 91.
2. Page 92.
3. Pages 93-95.

Illustrating (page 97)

1. Page 95.
2. Page 95.

Coloring and shading (page 98)

1. Spray paints are quicker to use and provide a more even covering, but time is required for masking and protecting areas not to be sprayed with a color.
2. It is too hard to separate the color sheet from the backing sheet unless a "lip" remains for insertion of a blade. If a piece is cut to exact size it is very difficult to line it up exactly over area to be covered. Cutting it larger allows some margin when placement is made.
3. Air brushing

Legibility standards (page **100**)

1. So they can be read easily by audience at an anticipated maximum distance.
2. Legibility decreases as quantity of information increases.
3. Page 99.
4. One inch.
5. About .15″ tall.
6. Larger.
7. Larger.

Lettering for titles (page **108**)

1. Page 102.
2. Page 101.
3. Page 102.
4. Wricoprint or Leroy.
5. Signmaker: stencil guide, guide holder, and brush pen. Wricoprint: lettering guide, lettering pad, and pen. The major difference is in filling the pens.
6. 1½ inches; ¼ inch; ¼ inch.
7. See pages 104 and 105.
8. Both are held vertically.
9. Page 106.
10. —

Mounting and protecting surfaces (page **120**)

1. Coat only one surface and put two surfaces together for temporary mounting. Coat both surfaces and allowing them to dry for permanent mounting.
2. You can see guide marks through it; it does not adhere to rubber cement.
3. A heat-sensitive adhesive is coated on both side of tissue paper.
4. So both picture and tissue can be accurately trimmed together.
5. Page 112.
6. —
7. The edges of the picture to be joined are trimmed *before* the dry-mount tissue is tacked to the back; tacking the second piece of the picture is done with the picture face-up.
8. For cardboard or cloth, size is the deciding factor. Choose rolling or folding on the basis of convenience of use.
9. So there is no exposed adhesive that might stick to the working surface or to the dry-mount press.
10. The dry-mount press is set at 270° and extra pressure is necessary, so a sheet of cardboard or masonite is used in the press.

CHAPTER 17. RECORDING SOUND

1. —
2. Page 131.
3. Page 132.
4. Page 132.
5. Page 132.
6. Page 132.

CHAPTER 18. PHOTOGRAPHIC PRINT SERIES

1. Page 137
2. —
3. Page 86.
4. Selecting the negatives for enlargement printing.
5. Page 89.
6. Page 140.

CHAPTER 19. SLIDE SERIES

1. —

2. Page 143.
3. Page 144.
4. Page 145.
5. Page 147.
6. Mount them in glass; page 148.
7. —

CHAPTER 20. FILMSTRIPS

1. —
2. Page 155.
3. Page 154.
4. Deciding what areas of the edge of a slide to eliminate when copying.
5. —

CHAPTER 21. TAPE RECORDINGS

1. —
2. Page 159.
3. —
4. —

CHAPTER 22. OVERHEAD TRANSPARENCIES

Planning transparencies (page **166**)

1. —
2. Horizontally, because in low-ceiling rooms the lower portions of a vertical transparency cannot easily be seen by the audience.
3. 7½″×9½″.
4. Page 163.
5. Page 164.
6. Page 164.
7. ¼″ to ⅜″ (see page 99).
8. Dry-transfer, Wricoprint, Leroy (most preferred).
9. Page 164.

Direct preparation on acetate (page **168**)

1. Yes.
2. Use a solvent, like lighter fluid.
3. No.
4. Cover with a sheet of acetate.
5. They project in color and there is no wax deposit around the letters.
6. Page 167.
7. Page 167.
8. Page 168.

Reproductions of diagrams (page **172**)

1. Yes.
2. Page 168.
3. Page 169.
4. To protect the image and make the acetate more transparent.
5. Page 169.
6. Page 171.
7. Use opaque paper on tracing paper for that area.
8. Page 170.
9. Ultraviolet exposure.
10. Overexposure. A shorter time.

Reproductions of printed illustrations (page **180**)

1. The material used to make the image on the paper.
2. No.
3. Underexposed. Slow down the machine.
4. With felt pen or colored adhesive.

5. Diffusion transfer (photocopy).
6. Page 174.
7. Check the picture for clay coating.
8. First with a roller; second with dry-mount press.
9. Any remaining clay will appear as dark areas on the final transparency as the clay is opaque to light.
10. The temperature is set at 270°, extra pressure in the press is necessary, and metal plates and felt are needed.

Photographic methods (page 184)

1. High contrast. Yes.
2. Page 181.
3. Brushing on a water-soluble carbon material to cover spots and areas so no light will pass during enlarging.
4. The enlarger is used instead of the camera. A larger sheet of film is used. Washing time should be longer.
5. The developer is different and processing times may vary.
6. Page 182.

Completing and filing (page 185)

1. On the underside.
2. Page 184.
3. Page 185.
4. —

CHAPTER 23. MOTION PICTURES

Motion-picture cameras, lenses, and film (page 193)

1. —
2. —
3. Page 189.
4. Page 189.
5. —
6. Flexibility in selecting fields of view from various camera positions; different lenses give different perspective effects.
7. The distance within a scene that is in focus, from a point closest to the camera to the farthest.
8. More.
9. Use $f/8$; more.
10. Commercial Ektachrome.
11. Page 192.

Camera shots (page 198)

1. —
2. (1) MCU, low angle; (2) MS; (3) MCU; (4) LS; (5) CU High angle; (6) MS.
3. —
4. Page 198.

Providing continuity (page 203)

1. —
2. —
3. —
4. Page 202.

Special filming techniques (page 205)

1. Frames per second. Use 48 or 64 f.p.s.
2. —
3. 1 minute per frame.

Film laboratory services, film editing, and adding sound (page 211)

1. Using the workprint protects the original film from handling, scratches, and dirt during editing.
2. Conforming.
3. —
4. *String-out:* putting all scenes filmed in proper order. *Rough cut:* shortening scenes to approximate length and eliminating multiple takes and unnecessary scenes. *Fine cut:* tightly editing the film into final form.
5. Unscripted film will have many more scenes than needed, some not useable; scene length will vary greatly, and many decisions about the character of the film will be determined during editing. Film edited in the camera will be very close to final form when filming is completed.
6. Page 211.

8-millimeter films (page 216)

1. Page 212.
2. —
3. Page 214.
4. Page 215.
5. Page 215.

CHAPTER 24. TELEVISION AND DISPLAY MATERIALS

1. Format and proportions; detail and size; and contrast and colors
2. Page 220.
3. Does the instructor need to handle them? In what form may they be most available?
4. Page 220.
5. The ability to make materials adhere to the surface is more certain with hook-and-loop. Heavier materials can be displayed on hook-and-loop boards.
6. The chalkboard surface permits writing as well as displaying materials.
7. Page 223.

Appendix C.

Books, Films, Pamphlets, and Periodicals

AUDIOVISUAL COMMUNICATIONS

Audiovisual materials in instruction

A-V Instruction: Materials and Methods. Second edition. James W. Brown, Richard B. Lewis, and Fred F. Harcleroad. McGraw-Hill Book Co., New York, 1964.

Audio-Visual Communication. United Business Publications, Inc. 200 Madison Ave., New York. (annual periodical)

Audiovisual Instruction. Department of Audio-Visual Instruction, National Education Association, Washington, D.C. (monthly periodical)

AudioVisual Communication Review. Department of Audio-Visual Instruction, National Education Association, Washington, D.C. (quarterly periodical)

"Automation and Education I: General Aspects." James D. Finn. *AudioVisual Communication Review,* vol. 5, no. 1, Winter 1957, pp. 343-360.

"Automation and Education II: Automating the Classroom—Background of the Effort." James D. Finn. *AudioVisual Communication Review,* vol. 5, no. 2, Spring 1957, pp. 451-467.

"Automation and Education III: Technology and the Instructional Process." James D. Finn. *AudioVisual Communication Review,* vol. 8, no. 1, Winter 1960, pp. 5-26.

Educational Implications of Technological Change. Appendix Volume IV in *Technology and the American Economy.* National Commission on Technology, Automation, and Economic Progress. Superintendent of Documents, Washington, D.C., February 1966.

"From Research to Mock-up in Three Years: Rensselaer's Experimental Classroom." *Audiovisual Instruction,* April 1963, pp. 206-207.

The Information Explosion. 16mm motion picture, sound, black-and-white with color segments, 34 minutes. Department of Photography, Ohio State University, Columbus, 1966. (includes 6 subfilms)

Instructional Media and Creativity. C. W. Taylor and Frank E. Williams, editors. John Wiley and Sons, New York, 1966.

Media and Educational Innovation. Wesley C. Meierhenry, editor. University of Nebraska Press, Lincoln, 1966.

"Multimedia Instructional Laboratory." Gerald F. McVey. *Audiovisual Instruction,* February 1966, pp. 80-85.

"Multiscreen Presentations: Promise for Instructional Improvement." Alvin B. Roberts and Don L. Crawford. *Audiovisual Instruction,* October 1966, pp. 528-530.

"The Schools, Industry, and New Knowledge." Ronald L. Hunt. *Audiovisual Instruction,* March 1964, pp. 162-165.

Studies in the Growth of Instructional Technology: Audio-Visual Instrumentation for Instruction in the Public Schools, 1930-1960: A Basis for Take-off. James D. Finn, Donald G. Perrin, and Lee E. Campion. National Education Association, Washington, D.C., 1962.

The Teacher and Technology. 16mm motion picture, sound, black-and-white, 49 minutes. Department of Photography, Ohio State University, Columbus, 1966. (includes 11 subfilms)

Technology in Education: Hearings Before the Subcommittee on Economic Progress of the Joint Economic Committee, Congress of the United States, June 1966. Superintendent of Documents, Washington, D.C., 1966.

Technology in Learning. Ontario Curriculum Institute, 344 Bloor Street West, Toronto, Canada, May 1965.

Training in Business and Industry. Gellert-Wolfman Publishing Co., 33 W. 60th Street, New York. (monthly periodical)

Visual Communications Instructor. Syndicate Magazines, Inc. 25 W. 45th Street, New York. (monthly periodical)

The instructional system

The Design of Instructional Systems. Robert G. Smith, Jr. Human Resources Research Office, The George Washington University, Alexandria, Virginia, November 1966.

"Educational Escalation through Systems Design." Alexander Schure. *Technology–Education,* Syracuse University Press, Syracuse, 1966, pp. 55-80.

"Essentials of a Training System." David H. Curl. *Training in Business and Industry,* March 1967, pp. 37-41.

Instructional Media: A Procedure for the Design of Multi-media Instruction. Leslie J. Briggs and others. American Institute for Research, 135 North Bellefield Avenue, Pittsburgh, Pennsylvania, 1967.

"An Instructional Systems Approach to Course Development." Michael R. Eraut. *AudioVisual Communication Review,* vol. 15, no. 1, Spring 1967, pp. 92-101.

An Integrated Approach to Learning, with Emphasis on Independent Study. S. N. Postlethwait, J. Novak, and H. Murray. Burgess Publishing Co., Minneapolis, 1964.

"A Point of Transition." Wesley C. Meierhenry. *Trends in Programmed Instruction.* National Education Association, Washington, D.C. 1966, pp. 272-277.

A Procedural and Cost Analysis Study of Media in Instructional Systems Development: Part A. John Barson. Michigan State University, East Lansing, September 1965 (for the U.S. Office of Education, Grant No. OE-3-16-030).

A Procedural and Cost Analysis Study of Media in Instructional Systems Development: Part B—Instructional Cost Analysis. Gardner M. Jones. Michigan State University, East Lansing, September 1965 (for the U.S. Office of Education, Grant No. OE-3-16-030).

Proceedings of the Engineering Systems for Education and Training Conference, June 14-15, 1966. National Security Industrial Association, Washington, D.C., 1966.

"Programmed Instruction as a Systems Approach to Education." Robert E. Corrigan. *Trends in Programmed Instruction.* National Education Association, Washington, D.C., 1966, pp. 36-45.

"Psychological Bases for Instructional Design." Robert Glaser. *AV Communication Review,* vol. 14, no. 4, Winter 1966, pp. 433-449.

Psychological Principles in System Development. Robert M. Gagné, editor. Holt, Rinehart and Winston, New York, 1962.

Studies in the Systems Engineering of Education I: The Evolution of Systems Thinking in Education. Leonard C. Silvern. Instructional Technology and Media Project, School of Education, University of Southern California, Los Angeles, 1965.

"Systems Approach Gets Results." William R. Tracey. *Training in Business and Industry,* June 1967, pages 17-21, 32-38.

"A Systems Approach to Botany." S. N. Postlethwait. *Audiovisual Instruction,* April 1963, pp. 246-252.

The Systems Engineering of Education II: Applications of Systems Thinking to Instruction. Robert Heinich. Instructional Technology and Media Project, School of Education, University of Southern California, Los Angeles, 1965.

"Toward a Behavioral Science Base for Instructional Design." Robert Glaser. *Teaching Machines and Programed Learning II: Data and Directions.* National Education Association, Washington, D.C., 1965, pp. 771-809.

Perception, communications, and learning theory

A Communications Primer. 16mm film, 20 minutes, sound, color. Classroom Films Distributors, Los Angeles, 1952.

The Conditions of Learning. Robert M. Gagné. Holt, Rinehart and Winston, New York, 1965.

Cybernetic Principles of Learning and Educational Design. Karl U. Smith and Margaret F. Smith. Holt, Rinehart and Winston, New York, 1966.

"Instruction and the Conditions of Learning." Robert M. Gagné. *Instruction: Some Contemporary Viewpoints.* Laurence Siegel, editor. Chandler Publishing Company, San Francisco, 1967, pp. 291-316.

"Instructional Communications and Technology." David K. Berlo. *Technology–Education.* Syracuse University Press, Syracuse, 1966, pp. 7-20.

Learning about Learning. Jerome Bruner, editor. U.S. Office of Education Monograph 15-OE12019. Superintendent of Documents, Washington, D.C., 1966. (catalog no. FS5.212:12019)

"Learning and Education." B. R. Bugelski. *The Psychology of Learning.* Henry Holt and Co., New York, 1956, pp. 449-479.

Learning Theory and AV Utilization. Wesley Meierhenry, editor. *AV Communication Review,* vol. 9, no. 5, September–October 1961.

The Mathematical Theory of Communication. C. E. Shannon and W. Weaver. The University of Illinois Press, Urbana, 1949.

"New Dimensions in Curriculum Development." Ralph W. Tyler. *Phi Delta Kappan,* September 1966, pp. 25–28.

Perception and Communication. 16mm motion picture, sound, black-and-white with color segments, 32 minutes. Department of Photography, Ohio State University, Columbus, 1966. (includes 6 subfilms).

Perception Theory and AV Education. Kenneth Norberg, editor. *AudioVisual Communication Review,* vol. 10, no. 5, September–October 1962.

"Principles of Learning." Edgar Dale. *The News Letter,* vol. 29, no. 4, January 1964. Bureau of Educational Research and Service, Ohio State University, Columbus.

The Process of Communication. 16mm motion picture, sound, black-and-white with color segments, 45 minutes. Department of Photography, Ohio State University, Columbus, 1966. (includes 8 subfilms).

The Process of Education. Jerome Bruner. Harvard University Press, Cambridge, Mass., 1960.

"Psychological Concepts and Audio-Visual Instruction." C. R. Carpenter. *AudioVisual Communication Review,* vol. 5, no. 1, Winter 1957, pp. 361-369.

Research, Principles, and Practices in Visual Communication. John Ball and Francis C. Byrnes. National Education Association, Washington, D.C., 1960.

Theories of Learning. Third edition. Ernest R. Hilgard and Gordon H. Bower. Appleton-Century-Crofts, New York, 1966.

A Theory of Instruction. Jerome Bruner. Harvard University Press, Cambridge, Mass., 1966.

Understanding Media: The Extension of Man. Marshall McLuhan. McGraw-Hill Book Co., New York, 1964.

"What Do We Know About Learning?" Goodwin Watson. *NEA Journal,* March 1963, pp. 20-22.

Research in design of audiovisual materials

"Controlled Variations of Specific Factors in Design and Use of Instructional Media." A. A. Lumsdaine. *Instruments and Media of Instruction* of *Handbook of Research on Teaching.* N. L. Gage, editor. Rand McNally and Co., Chicago, 1963.

Enhancements and Simplifications of Motivational and Stimulus Variables in Audiovisual Instructional Materials. Mark A. May. U.S. Office of Education Contract No. Œ-5-16-006, July 10, 1965. (a working paper)

Instructional Film Research 1918-1950. Charles F. Hoban, Jr., and Edward B. van Ormer. Technical Report No. SDC 269-7-19. Special Devices Center, U.S. Navy, Port Washington, New York, 1950.

Learning from Films. Mark A. May and A. A. Lumsdaine. Yale University Press, New Haven, Conn., 1958.

"Learning from Visuals: Some Behavioral Considerations." George L. Gropper. *AudioVisual Communication Review,* vol. 14, no. 1, Spring 1966, pp. 37-70.

Research and Theory Related to Audiovisual Information Transmission. Robert M. W. Travers. Campus Bookstore, Western Michigan University, Kalamazoo, 1967.

A Review of the Literature Pertinent to the Design and Use of Effective Graphic Training Aids. Ezra V. Saul and others. Technical Report SPECDEVCEN 494-08-1, U.S. Naval Training Devices Center, Port Washington, New York, 1954.

The Role of Student Response in Learning from the New Educational Media. Mark A. May. U.S. Office of Education Contract No. Œ-5-16-006, August 1966.

"Single and Multiple Channel Communication: A Review of Research and a Proposed Model." Frank R. Hartman. *AudioVisual Communications* Review, vol. 9, no. 6, November–December 1961, pp. 235-262.

Word-Picture Relationships in Audio-Visual Presentations. Mark A. May. U.S. Office of Education Contract No. Œ-5-16-006, July 20, 1965.

PLANNING AUDIOVISUAL MATERIALS

Objectives

"The Analysis of Instructional Objectives for the Design of Instruction." Robert M. Gagné. *Teaching Machines and Programed Learning II,* National Education Association, Washington, D.C., 1965, pages 21-65.

Controlling the Quality of Training. Robert G. Smith, Jr. Human Resources Research Office, The George Washington University, Alexandria, Virginia, June 1965.

Developing Vocational Instruction. Robert F. Mager and Kenneth M. Beach, Jr. Fearon Publishers, Palo Alto, California, 1967.

The Development of Training Objectives. Robert G, Smith, Jr. Human Resources Research Office, The George Washington University, Alexandria, Virginia, June 1964.

The Derivation, Analysis, and Classification of Instructional Objectives. Harry L. Ammerman and others. Human Resources Research Office, The George Washington University, Alexandria, Virginia, May 1966.

Educational Objectives. 35-millimeter sound filmstrip. Vimcet Associates, P.O. Box 24714, Los Angeles, California.

Preparing Instructional Objectives. Robert F. Mager. Fearon Publishers, San Francisco, 1961.

Taxonomy of Educational Objectives, Handbook I: Cognitive Domain. Benjamin S. Bloom, editor. David McKay Company, Inc., New York, 1956.

Taxonomy of Educational Objectives, Handbook II: Affective Domain. David R. Krathwohl and others. David McKay Company, Inc., New York, 1964.

Storyboards and scripting

Audiovisual Planning Equipment. Eastman Kodak Company, publication S-11, November 1966. (free)

How to Make an Effective Visual Presentation. 35-millimeter filmstrip and script. VariTyper Corporation, Newark, New Jersey, 1966.

Planning a Photo Essay. Eastman Kodak Company, publication AT-39, September 1966. (free)

Planning and Producing Visual Aids. Eastman Kodak Company, publication S-13, April 1966. (free)

Selecting media

The Conditions of Learning. Robert M. Gagné. Holt, Rinehart, and Winston, New York, 1965.

Instructional Media: A Procedure for the Design of Multi-media Instruction. Leslie J. Briggs and others. American Institutes for Research, 135 Bellefield Avenue, Pittsburgh, Pennsylvania, 1967.

"Media Stimulus and Types of Learning." William H. Allen. *Audiovisual Instruction,* January 1967, pages 27-31.

"Multiple Images," *Educational Screen and Audiovisual Guide,* February 1963, pages 84-85, 88.

"Selecting an Instructional Medium." Vernon S. Gerlach. *Media Competencies for Teachers.* Wesley Meierhenry, editor. University of Nebraska Press, Lincoln, 1966, pages 70-100.

"Two Screens—What For?" Eastman Kodak Company, *Audiovisual Notes from Kodak,* publication 63-1, 1962.

Wide-Screen/Multiple-Screen Showmanship. Eastman Kodak Company, publication S-28, April 1966. (free)

Using media

Audiovisual Projection. Eastman Kodak Company, publication S-3, May 1966. (free)

GENERAL PHOTOGRAPHY

Picture taking

Applied Color Photography Indoors. Eastman Kodak Company, publication E-76, March 1966.

Color as Seen and Photographed. Eastman Kodak Company, publication E-174, September 1966.

Color Photography Outdoors. Eastman Kodak Company, publication E-75, September 1965.

Composition. Eastman Kodak Company, publication AC-11, January 1966. (free)

Exposure. 16mm motion picture, sound, color, 12 minutes. Indiana University, Bloomington, 1959.

Exposure Meter—Theory and Use. 16mm motion picture, sound, color, 10 minutes. Indiana University, Bloomington, 1959.

How to Set Your Adjustable Camera. Eastman Kodak Company, publication AC-27, July 1965. (free)

Photography of Television Images. Eastman Kodak Company, publication AC-10, September 1966. (free)

Pictures Outdoors at Night. Eastman Kodak Company, publication AC-21, July 1965. (free)

Films

Data: Kodak Black-and-White Roll Films. Eastman Kodak Company, publication AF-16, October 1966. (free)

Filter Data for Kodak Color Films. Eastman Kodak Company, publication E-23, May 1966. (free)

Kodak Color Films for Still Cameras. Eastman Kodak Company, publication AE-41, November 1966. (free)

Lighting

Controlled Photographic Lighting. 16mm motion picture, sound, color, 9 minutes. Indiana University, Bloomington, 1959.

Flash Pictures. Eastman Kodak Company, publication AC-2, November 1965.

Studio Lighting for Product Photography. Eastman Kodak Company, publication O-16, July 1965.

Close-up and copying

Basic Copying. Eastman Kodak Company, publication AM-2, August 1966. (free)

Basic Titling and Animation. Eastman Kodak Company, publication S-21, May 1965.

Copying. Eastman Kodak Company, publication M-1, June 1965. (free)

A Simple Wooden Copy Stand for Making Title Slides and Filmstrips. Eastman Kodak Company, publication T-43, January 1964. (free)

Film processing and printing

Basic Developing, Printing and Enlarging. Eastman Kodak Company, publication AJ-2, May 1966.

Enlarging in Black-and-White and Color. Eastman Kodak Company, publication AG-16, October 1965.

"The Modern Monobath." Grant Haist. *Photographic Applications in Science and Technology,* summer 1967, pages 28-34, 47.

Photographic Darkroom Procedures. 35mm black-and-white filmstrips, 6 filmstrips in set 1 (developing and printing), 6 filmstrips in set 2 (advanced techniques). McGraw-Hill Book Company, New York, 1950.

Photolab Design. Eastman Kodak Company, publication K-13, March 1967.

Stabilization—What, Why, How. Eastman Kodak Company, publication J-24, January 1966. (free)

Handbooks and journals

The Focal Encyclopedia of Photography. Macmillan Co., New York, 1960.

Industrial Photography. 10 E. 40th St., New York. (monthly journal).

Photo-Lab Index. John S. Carroll. Morgan and Morgan, New York. (quarterly supplements).

Photo Methods for Industry. 33 W. 60th St., New York. (monthly journal)

Photographic Applications in Science and Technology. 257 Park Avenue South, New York. (monthly journal)

Photography: Its Materials and Processes. C. B. Neblette. D. Van Nostrand Co., New York, 1958.

GRAPHIC ARTS

Mounting

Better Mounting by the Dry Mount Method. Seal, Inc., Shelton, Conn., 1961.

Dry Mounting Instructional Materials. A series of 16mm motion pictures, sound, color, each 5 minutes in length, University of Iowa, Iowa City. (Basic Techniques, Cloth Backing, Display and Use, Laminating and Lifting, Special Techniques)

Lettering

Lettering Instructional Materials. 16mm motion picture, sound, color, 20 minutes. Indiana University, Bloomington, 1955.

Lettering Techniques. Martha F. Meeks. Visual Instruction Bureau, University of Texas, Austin, 1960.

Standards

Art-work Size Standards for Projected Visuals, pamphlet S-12. Eastman Kodak Company. (free)

Legibility Standards for Projected Materials, pamphlet S-4. Eastman Kodak Company. (free)

Space for Audio-Visual Large Group Instruction. University Facilities Research Center, University of Wisconsin, Madison, 1964.

Illustrating

Creating Cartoons. 16mm motion picture, sound, black-and-white, 10 minutes. Baily Films, Hollywood, California, 1955.

How to Do Cartoons. 16mm motion picture, sound, black-and-white, 20 minutes. Samuel Lawrence Schulman Productions, 23 Livingston St., Trenton, N.J., 1957.

Kodak Compass—Instant Artwork. Eastman Kodak Company, publication P-1-63-1. (free)

Paste-up procedures

Kodak Compass—Paste-up Drafting. Eastman Kodak Company, publication P-1-64-1. (free)

Modern Graphic Arts Paste-up. Gerald A. Silver. American Technical Society, 848 East 58th Street, Chicago, Illinois.

Graphs and statistics

Charting Statistics. Mary Spear. McGraw-Hill Book Company, New York, 1952.

Graphic Presentation. Frances J. McHugh. Tecnifax Corp., Holyoke, Mass., 1956.

Handbook of Graphic Presentation. Calvin F. Schmid. Ronald Press, New York, 1954.

Making the Most of Charts. K. W. Haemer. Tecnifax Corp., Holyoke, Mass., 1960.

Pictographs and Graphs. Rudolf Modley and Dyno Lowenstein. Harper and Bros., New York, 1952.

Technical Presentations. John Bateson. Tecnifax Corp., Holyoke, Mass., 1957.

Handbooks and journals

Display for Learning. Marjorie East. Dryden Press (Holt, Rinehart, and Winston), New York, 1952.

Graphics Handbook. Ken Garland. Reinhold Publishing Corporation, New York, 1966.

Graphic Science. Graphic Science, 9 Maiden Lane, New York.

Reproduction Methods for Business and Industry. NPD Corp., 33 W. 60th St., New York. (monthly journal)

Simplified Techniques for Preparing Visual Instructional Materials. Ed Minor. McGraw-Hill Book Company, New York, 1962.

SOUND RECORDING

Creative Teaching With Tape. Revere-Mincom Division, 3M Company, St. Paul, Minnesota.

The How to Do It Booklet of Tape Recording. 3M Company, St. Paul, Minnesota.

How to Use a Tape Recorder. Dick Hodgson and H. J. Bullen. Hastings House, New York, 1957.

Magnetic Sound Recording for Motion Pictures. Eastman Kodak Company, publication P-26.

The Tape Recorder. Robert Sloan, Jr. Visual Instruction Bureau, University of Texas, Austin.

Radio and Television Sound Effects. Robert B. Turnbull. Rinehart & Co., New York, 1951.

Tape Recording for Instruction. 16mm motion picture, sound, black-and-white, 15 minutes. Indiana University, Bloomington, 1956.

Tape Tips from Capital Audio Engineers. Capital Recordings, Los Angeles, California.

The Technique of the Sound Studio. Alec Nisbett. Hastings House, New York, 1962.

PHOTOGRAPHIC PRINT SERIES

Planning and preparing

Creative News Photography. Rod Fox and Robert Kerns. Iowa State University, Ames, 1961.

Graphic Graflex Photography. Willard Morgan. Morgan and Morgan, New York, 1958.

Making Service Pictures for Industry. Eastman Kodak Company, publication P-4.

Photo Journalism Manual: How to Plan Shoot Edit Sell. David P. Bergin. Morgan & Morgan, Inc., Publishers, Hastings-on-Hudson, N.Y. 10706, 1967.

Planning a Photo Essay. Eastman Kodak Company, pamphlet T-39. (free)

Displaying

Better Bulletin Board Displays. J. Preston Lockridge. Visual Instruction Bureau, University of Texas, Austin.

Bulletin Boards and Displays. Reino Randall and Edward C. Haines. Davis Publications, Worcester, Massachusetts, 1961.

Educational Displays and Exhibits. J. Preston Lockridge. Visual Instruction Bureau, University of Texas, Austin, 1960.

Preparation of Inexpensive Teaching Materials. John E. Morlan. Chandler Publishing Company, San Francisco, 1963.

SLIDE SERIES AND FILMSTRIPS

Adventures in Indoor Color Slides. Eastman Kodak Company, publication E-7.

Adventures in Outdoor Color Slides. Eastman Kodak Company, publication E-9.

Black and White Transparencies with Kodak Panatomic-X, 35mm. Eastman Kodak Company, pamphlet F-19. (free)

Effective Lecture Slides. Eastman Kodak Company, publication S-22, March 1966. (free)

Facts You Should Know about Filmstrips. Frank Holmes Laboratories, Inc., 1947 First Street, San Fernando, California, 1965.

Handbook for Production of Filmstrips and Records. John Lord and Robert Larson. DuKane Corporation, St. Charles, Illinois, 1962.

How to Make Better Pictures with Anscochrome and Super Anscochrome Film. Ansco, Binghamton, N.Y., 1961. (sold through photo dealers)

Photographic Slides for Instruction. 16mm motion picture, sound, color, 11 minutes. Indiana University, Bloomington, 1956.

Producing Slides and Filmstrips. Eastman Kodak Company, publication S-8, April 1966.

Production of 2"×2" Slides for School Use. Joe Coltharp. Visual Instruction Bureau, University of Texas, Austin, 1958.

Simple Ways to Make Title Slides and Filmstrips. Eastman Kodak Company, pamphlet T-44. (free)

TRANSPARENCIES FOR OVERHEAD PROJECTION

Diazochrome Slides for Visual Communications. Tecnifax Corp., Holyoke, Massachusetts.

A Guide to Overhead Projection and the Practical Preparation of Transparencies. Gaylen B. Kelley and Phillip J. Sleeman. Chart-Pak, Inc., Leeds, Mass., 1967.

High Contrast Photography for Instruction. 16mm motion picture, sound, color, 14 minutes. Indiana University, Bloomington, 1956.

How to Use the Overhead Projector in Mathematics Education. Stephen Krulik and Irwin Kaufman. National Council of Teachers of Mathematics, 1201 Sixteenth Street, N.W., Washington, D.C., 1966.

Making Black and White Transparencies for Overhead Projection. Eastman Kodak Company, pamphlet S-7. (free)

Overhead Projection. Horace Hartsell and Wilfred Veenendaal. American Optical Co., Buffalo, N.Y., 1960.

The Overhead System: Production, Implementation and Utilization. Richard E. Smith. Visual Instruction Bureau, University of Texas, Austin.

Projecting Ideas on the Overhead Projector. A series of 16mm motion pictures, sound, color. University of Iowa, Iowa City.
    (I—General, 17 minutes. II—Diazo Transparency Production, 11 minutes. III—Direct Transparency Production, 5 minutes.)

"Readable Letter Size and Visibility for Overhead Projection Transparencies." Sarah Adams and others. *AudioVisual Communication Review,* vol. 13, no. 4, winter 1965, pages 412-417.

Simplified Techniques for Preparing Visual Instructional Materials. Ed Minor. McGraw-Hill Book Company, New York, 1962.

They See What You Mean: Visual Communications with the Overhead Projector. Ozalid Audio-Visual Department, Johnson City, N.Y., 1959.

Vu-Graphics: A Manual on Vu-graph Projection. Charles Beseler Co., East Orange, N.J., 1952.

MOTION PICTURES

Techniques

Eastman Kodak Motion Picture Films for Professional Use. Eastman Kodak Company, publication H-1, September 1966. (free)

Film and the Director. Don Livingston. Macmillan Co., New York, 1958.

Film and Its Techniques. Raymond Spottiswood. University of California Press, Berkeley, 1957.

Film Making from Script to Screen. Andrew Buchanan. Macmillan Co., New York, 1951.

Film Problems. 16mm motion picture, sound, black-and-white, 8 minutes. Indiana University, Bloomington.

Filming Athletic Events with 16mm Camera. Joe Coltharp. Visual Instruction Bureau, University of Texas, Austin.

The Five C's of Cinematography. Joseph V. Mascelli. Cine/Grafic Publications, P.O. Box 430, Hollywood, California, 1965.

Handbook of Basic Motion Picture Techniques. Emil E. Brodbeck. McGraw-Hill Book Company, New York, 1950.

How to Shoot a Movie Story. Arthur Gaskill and David Englander. Duell, Sloane and Pearce, New York, 1960.

Industrial Motion Pictures, publication P-18. Eastman Kodak Co.

Kodak 16mm Movie Films: Data and Selection. Eastman Kodak Company, pamphlet D-22. (free)

Motion Picture Production for Industry. Jay E. Gordon. Macmillan Co., New York, 1961.

16mm Sound Motion Pictures: A Manual for the Professional and Amateur. William H. Offenhauser, Jr. Interscience Publishers, New York, 1958.

So You Wanna Shoot Newsfilm. Leo Willette. Leo Willette, 120 Rampart Street, New Orleans, Louisiana, 1960.

The Technique of Documentary Film Production. W. Hugh Baddeley. Morgan and Morgan, Inc., 25 Main Street, Hastings-on-Hudson, New York.

The Techniques of Special Effects Cinematography. Raymond Fielding. Film & TV Book Club, 250 W. 57th St., New York 10019.

Editing

Colburn Comments on Editing. George W. Colburn Laboratory, 164 N. Wacker Drive, Chicago, Illinois.

Editing Synchronous Sound. 16mm motion picture, sound, color, 10 minutes. Indiana University, Bloomington, 1957.

Film Editing: Interpretation and Values. 16mm motion picture, sound, black-and-white, 25 minutes. American Cinema Editors, 6775 Hollywood Blvd., Hollywood, California, 1958.

A Method of Editing Your Movies. Eastman Kodak Company, pamphlet D-26.

The Technique of Film Editing. Karl Reis. Farrar, Straus, and Young, New York, 1959.

Sound

Colburn Comments on 8mm Magnetic Sound. George W. Colburn Laboratory, 164 N. Wacker Drive, Chicago, Illinois.

Kodak Sonatrack-Coating Service. Eastman Kodak Company, pamphlet D-27. (free)

Magnetic Sound Recording for 16mm Motion Pictures. Eastman Kodak Company, publication P-26.

Sound Recording for Motion Pictures. 16mm motion picture, sound, color, 10 minutes. Indiana University, Bloomington.

Special applications

Animation Art in the Commercial Film. Eli L. Levitan. Reinhold Publishing Co., New York, 1960.

Animation: Its History, Techniques, and Applications. Associated Educational Services, 630 Fifth Avenue, New York, 1967.

Animation Techniques. 16mm motion picture, sound, color, 30 minutes. Animation Equipment Corp., 38 Hudson St., New Rochelle, N.Y., 1956.

Animation Techniques and Commercial Film Production. Eli L. Levitan. Reinhold Co., New York, 1962.

Basic Titling and Animation. Eastman Kodak Company, publication S-21.

My Ivory Cellar (Time-Lapse Photography). John Ott. Twentieth Century Press, 40 S. Clinton St., Chicago, Illinois, 1958.

The Technique of Film Animation. John Halas and Roger Manvell. Hastings House, New York, 1959.

Time Lapse Photography. 16mm motion picture, sound, color, 10 minutes. International Film Bureau, Chicago, Illinois, 1961.

8-millimeter

"8mm Motion Pictures in Education: Incipient Innovation." Louis Forsdale. *Innovation in Education.* Matthew B. Miles, ed. Teachers College, Columbia University, New York, 1964, pages 203-229.

Newsletter of 8mm Film in Education. Project in Educational Communications of the Horace Mann-Lincoln Institute of School Experimentation, Teachers College, Columbia University, New York. (occasional publication)

Handbooks and journals

American Cinematographer. A.S.C. Agency, Inc., 1782 North Orange Drive, Hollywood, California. (monthly journal)

American Cinematographer Manual. Joseph V. Mascelli. American Society of Cinematographers, North Orange Drive, Hollywood, California, 1960.

The Aperture. Calvin Productions, 1105 Truman Road, Kansas City, Missouri. (free monthly publication)

Journal of the University Film Producers Association. Ohio State University, Department of Photography, Motion Picture Division, 1885 Neil Avenue, Columbus.

Rewind. General Film Laboratories, 1828 Walnut Street, Kansas City. Missouri, and 1546 N. Argyle Avenue, Hollywood, California. (free monthly publication)

TELEVISION MATERIALS

Creating Visuals for TV. John Spear. National Education Association, Washington 6, D.C., 1962.

Movies for TV. John H. Battison. Macmillan Co., New York, 1956.

The Technique of Television Production. Gerald Millerson. Morgan and Morgan, New York, 1961.

Television Production Handbook. Herbert Zettl. Wadsworth Publishing Co., San Francisco, 1961.

Television Programming and Production, 3rd edition. S. Hubbell. Holt, Rinehart, and Winston, New York, 1960.

TV and Film Production Data Book. Ernest M. Pittaro. Morgan and Morgan, New York, 1959.

Sources for Equipment and Materials

Many of the common items needed for the preparation of your audiovisual materials can be purchased from local art, stationery, photography, and engineering-supply stores. Other equipment and specialized materials are listed here. Although the headquarters or main-office address is given, you will find local offices or local dealers distributing most products. If you do not, write to the address given for further information.

The following sources are organized under headings that approximate the order by which topics are presented in this book.

GENERAL ART SUPPLIES

Dick Blick, P.O. Box 1267, Galesburg, Illinois.
Arthur Brown and Bros., Inc., 2 W. 46th St., New York.
Flax's Artist Materials, 250 Sutter St., San Francisco, Calif.

ILLUSTRATIONS

Clip art and books

American Mail Advertising, 61 Newbury St., Boston, Mass.
A. A. Archibold Publisher, 419 S. Main St., Burbank, Calif.
Multi-Ad Services, 118 Walnut St., Peoria, Ill.
ModulArt, Artype Inc., Barrington, Illinois
Tecnifax Corporation, 195 Appleton St., Holyoke, Mass. (translucent art)
Harry Volk, Art Studio, Pleasantville, N.J.

Photo modifiers

Arthur Brown and Bros., Inc. 2 W. 46th St., New York. (Lacey-Luci and Cromwell Art Aid)
Tecnifax Corporation, 195 Appleton St., Holyoke, Mass. (Visucom)

COLORING AND SHADING MATERIALS

Bourges Color Corp., 80 Fifth Ave., New York. (Cutocolor)
Cello-tak Lettering Corp., 131 W. 45th St., New York.
Chart-Pak, 1 River Road, Leeds, Mass. (Contak)
Craftint Manufacturing Co., 1615 Collmar Ave., Cleveland, Ohio. (Craf-tone)
Mico/Tape, 6551 Sunset Blvd., Los Angeles, Calif.
Para-tone, 512 W. Burlingame Ave., La Grange, Ill. (Zip-a-tone)
Peerless Color Laboratories, 11-13 Diamond Place, Rochester, N.Y. (transparent water colors)
Thayer & Chandler, 331 S. Peoria St., Chicago 7, Ill. (transparent water colors and airbrush)

LETTERING EQUIPMENT AND MATERIALS

Boldface typewriters

Local dealers for I.B.M., Royal, Smith-Corona.

Paper cut-outs

Mutual Aids, 1946 Hillhurst Ave., Los Angeles 27, Calif.
Stik-a-Letter Co., Route 2, Box 286, Escondido, Calif.

Dry-transfer letters

Arthur Brown and Bros., Inc., 2 W. 46th St., New York. (Instant Lettering)
Chart-Pak, Inc., Leeds, Mass. (Deca-dry)
Graphic Products Corp., P.O. Box 94, Arlington Heights, Ill. (Formatt)
Instantype Inc., Los Angeles, Calif. (Instantype)
Prestype Corp., 136 W. 21 St., New York. (Prestype)

Gummed-back paper cut-outs

The Ticket and Tablet Co., 1021 E. Adams St., Chicago, Ill.
Stik-a-Letter Co., Route 2, Box 286, Escondido, Calif.
The Holes-Webway Co., St. Cloud, Minn.

3-dimensional cut-outs

Gaylord Brothers, 155 Gifford St., Syracuse, N.Y.
Grace Letter Co., 77 Fifth Ave., New York.
Hernard Manufacturing Co., 21 Saw Mill River Road, Yonkers, N.Y.
Mitten's Display Letters, 2 W. 46th St., New York.
Redikut Letter Co., 185 N. Prairie Ave., Hawthorne, Calif.

Stencil guides

Wood-Regan Instrument Co., Nutley, N.J. (Wrico)

Template lettering guides

Keuffel & Esser Co., 300 Adams St., Hoboken, N.J. (Leroy)
Letterguide Co., Box 99, Lincoln, Neb.
Varigraph Co., 841 W. Lakeside St., Madison, Wisc.

Photocomposing units

ProType Division, Electrographic Corp., 323 E. 38th St., New York. (ProType)
Strip-Printer, P.O. Box 18-895, Oklahoma City, Okla.
VariTyper Corp., 720 Frelinghuysen Ave., Newark, N.J. (Headliner)

Hot presses

Olsenmark Corp., 124-132 White St., New York. (Kensol)

SOS Camera Supply Corp., 602 W. 52nd St., New York. (Tel-Anima)

MOUNTING EQUIPMENT AND MATERIALS

Rubber cement

Craftint Manufacturing Co., 1615 Collmar Ave., Cleveland, Ohio. (Kleen-Stik)

Union Rubber and Asbestos Co., Trenton, N.J. (Best Test)

Dry mount

Eastman Kodak Company, Rochester, N.Y. (dry-mount tissue)

Seal, Roosevelt Drive, Derby, Conn. (dry-mount press, dry-mount tissue, Chartex cloth, Sealamin laminating film)

Brandywine Photo Chemical Co., Avondale, Penn. (Spray-Mount photo adhesive)

Ditto Inc., 6800 McCormick Rd., Chicago, Ill. (Masterfax)

Laminators

General Binding Corp., 1101 Skokie Blvd., Northbrook, Ill.

Nationwide Adhesive Products, Inc., 19600 St. Clair Ave., Cleveland, Ohio. (Transeal)

Wax coaters

Addressograph-Multigraph Corp., 1200 Babbitt Road, Cleveland, Ohio. (striped adhesive wax coater)

Daige Speedcote Co., 160 Denton Ave., New Hyde Park, N.Y. (Daige Speedcote)

M.P. Goodkin Co., 112 Arlington St., Newark, N.J. (Goodkin)

Letro-Stik Co., 4545 North Clark St., Chicago, Ill. (Letro-Stik)

Photo-stabilization equipment

Eastman Kodak Company, Rochester, N.Y.

Federal Manufacturing and Engineering Corp., 1055 Stewart Ave., Garden City, N.Y.

BINDING AND DISPLAYING MATERIALS

Cloth tape

Demco Library Supplies, Madison 1, Wisc. (Fastape)

Mystic Adhesive Products, 2635 N. Kildare Ave., Chicago, Ill.

Plastic rings

General Binding Corp., 1101 Skokie Highway, Northbrook, Ill.

Tauber Plastics, 200 Hudson St., New York.

Display adhesive

Chemex Industries, Inc., Tampa, Fla. (Base-Tape)

Delkote, Berkeley, Calif. (Delkote Tak)

Brooks Manufacturing Co., P.O. Box 156, Cincinnati, Ohio. (Plasti-tak)

PROJECTORS

See *The Audio-Visual Equipment Directory,* National Audio-Visual Association, Fairfax, Virginia (annual publication) for manufacturers and sources of the following:

    2″×2″ slide projectors

    Tape recorders

    2″×2″ slide projector and tape recorder combination units

    35mm filmstrip projector and record player combination units

    Individual slide and filmstrip viewers

    Individual slide or filmstrip viewers—synchronized tape recorders

    8mm and 16mm motion-picture projectors

Tape-slide programming units

Bausch & Lomb Optical Co., 83760 Lomb Park, Rochester, N.Y. (Balsync)

Eastman Kodak Company, Rochester, N.Y. (Programmer)

Michael DeAngelo, 146-29 Laburnam Ave., Flushing, N.Y. (Synchro-Sound Slide Sync)

V-M Corp., 375 W. Main St., Benton Harbor, Mich. (V-M Synchronizer)

Meridian Enterprises, Inc., 1645 S. La Cienega Blvd., Los Angeles, Calif. (Cue Slide)

Minnesota Audio Visual, 1012 Marquette Avenue, Minneapolis, Minn. (Arion)

SLIDE MOUNTS

Karl Heitz, 979 Third Avenue, New York. (Linda)

Eastman Kodak Company, Rochester, N.Y. (Readymount cardboard frames)

Mr. E Enterprises, P.O. Box 45586, Los Angeles, Calif. (plastic mounts)

PLASTIC SHEET SLIDE HOLDERS

Plastic Sealing Corp., 1507 N. Gardner St., Los Angeles, Calif. (Vis File Folios)

Plastican Corp., P.O. Box 157, Butler, N.J. (Slide Frame)

Joshua Meier Co., Inc., 601 W. 26th St., New York (Slide-Sho)

35MM FILMSTRIP AIDS

Filmstrip cans

Film Kare Products Co., 446 W. 43rd St., New York, N.Y.

Richard Manufacturing Co., P.O. Box 2041, 5914 Noble Ave., Van Nuys, Calif.

Printer and slide copier

Heiland Division, Minneapolis-Honeywell Regulator Co., 5200 E. Evans Ave., Denver, Colo. (Repronar)

Bogen Photo Corp., 232 S. Van Brunt Street, Englewood, N.J. (Bowens Illumitran)

OVERHEAD TRANSPARENCY PROJECTION MATERIALS

Transparency supplies

Audio Visual Communications, Inc., 159 Verdi Street, Farmingdale, N.Y.

Charles Beseler Co., 219 So. 18th St., East Orange, N.J.

Metro Supply Co., 1420 47th Street, Sacramento, Calif.

Technifax Corp., 195 Appleton St., Holyoke, Mass.

Clear acetate

The Holson Co., Belden Ave., Norwalk, Conn.

Newstat Plastics, 8501 Agusta St., Philadelphia, Pa.

Valiant Industries, 172 Walker Lane, Englewood, N.J.

Frosted (matte) acetate

Arthur Brown & Bro., 2 W. 46th St., New York.

Keuffel & Esser Co., 300 Adams St., Hoboken, N.J.

Ozalid Division, General Aniline and Film Corp., Johnson City, N.Y.

Mounts

The Holson Co., Belden Ave., Norwalk, Conn. (cardboard)
Sherburn Graphic Products, Inc., P.O. Box 7503, Ft. Worth, Texas (plastic)

Polarizing materials

Technical Animations, 11 Sintsink Drive, East Port Washington, N.Y.
Tecnifax Corp., Holyoke, Mass.

Tapes

Applied Graphics Corp., Glenwood Landing, N.Y.
ACS Tapes, 217 California St., Newton, Mass.
Chart-Pak, 1 River Road, Leeds, Mass.
Craftint Manufacturing Co., 1615 Collmar Ave., Cleveland, Ohio
Labelon Tape Co., Rochester, N.Y.
Mico/Tape, 6551 Sunset Blvd., Los Angeles, Calif.
Para-Tone, 512 W. Burlingame Ave., La Grange, Ill.

Diazo equipment and materials

Keuffel & Esser Co., 300 Adams St., Hoboken, N.J. (Saturn)
Ozalid Division, General Aniline and Film Corp., 140 W. 51st St., New York.
Tecnifax Corp., 195 Appleton St., Holyoke, Mass.
VariTyper Corp., 720 Frelinghuysen St., Newark, N.J.

Heat-process equipment and materials

A. B. Dick Co., 5700 W. Touhy Ave., Chicago, Ill.
Ditto, Inc., 6800 McCormick Road, Chicago, Ill. (Masterfax)
Printing Arts Research Laboratories, Inc., La Arcada Building, Santa Barbara, Calif. (Parlab)
3M Company, 900 Bush Ave., St. Paul, Minn. (Thermo-fax)

Xerography film

Arkwright, Main Street, Fiskeville, R.I.
Sepsco Plastics, Atlanta, Georgia (Zelar)

Diffusion-transfer (photocopy) equipment and materials

Ampto, Hix Ave., Newton, N.J.
Cormac Photocopy Corp., 80 Fifth Ave., New York.
A. B. Dick Co., 5700 W. Touhy Ave., Chicago, Ill.
Electrocopy Corp., 10401 Decatur Road, Philadelphia, Pennsylvania (Copease)
Eastman Kodak Company, Rochester, N.Y. (Verifax)

Picture-transfer film and equipment

National Adhesive Products, Inc., 19600 St. Clair Ave., Cleveland, Ohio
Seal, Shelton, Conn. (Transpara-film)

High-contrast film

Ansco, Binghamton, N.Y. (Reprolith)
E. I. du Pont de Nemours and Co., Wilmington 98, Del. (Cronar)
Eastman Kodak Company, Rochester, N.Y. (Kodalith)
Ilford, 37 W. 65th St., New York. (Formalith)

MOTION-PICTURE EQUIPMENT

General

Camera Equipment Co., 315 W. 43rd St., New York.

SOS Camera Supply Corp., 6331 Hollywood Blvd., Hollywood, Calif., and 602 W. 52nd St., New York.

Lighting

Mole-Richardson Co., 937 N. Sycamore Ave., Hollywood, Calif.
Natural Lighting Corp., 612 W. Elk Ave., Glendale, Calif. (Colortran)
Smith-Victor Corp., Griffith, Ind.

Background and light supports

Polecats, Old Lyme, Conn.

TELEVISION DISPLAY SUPPLIES

Easels and display boards

Advance Furnace Co., 2310 E. Douglas, Wichita, Kan.
Arlington Aluminum Co., 19011 W. Davison Ave., Detroit, Mich.
Chart-Pak, 1 River Road, Leeds, Mass.
Oravisual Co., Box 11150, St. Petersburg, Fla.
Reynolds Metals Co., Louisville, Ky.

Flannel boards and materials

Educational Supply and Specialty Co., 2833 Gage Ave., Huntington Park, Calif.
Jacronda Manufacturing Co., 5449 Hunter St., Philadelphia, Penn.
The Judy Co., 310 N. Second St., Minneapolis, Minn.
The Ohio Flock-Cote Co., 5713 Euclid Ave., Cleveland, Ohio.
Visual Specialties Co., 5701 W. Vernor, Detroit, Mich.
L. A. Whitney Associates, 331 Madison Ave., New York, N.Y.

Hook-and-loop boards and materials

Maharam Fabric Co., 130 W. 46th St., New York; 1113 S. Los Angeles St., Los Angeles, Calif.
Charles Mayer Studios, 776 Commins St., Akron, Ohio.
The Ohio Flock-Cote, Inc., 13229 Shaw Ave., East Cleveland, Ohio.

Magnetic boards

Bangor Cork Co., Pen Argyl, Pa.
Madison A-V Co., 62 Grand St., New York, N.Y.
Magna Visual Inc., 1200 N. Rock Hill Road, St. Louis, Mo.

Magnetic boards

Brunswick-Balke-Collender Co., Chicago, Ill.
Weber Costello Co., 1212 McKinley, Chicago Heights, Ill.

Magnets

Hollywood House of Magnets, 6912 Hollywood Blvd., Hollywood, Calif.
Maggie Magnet Co., 39 W. 32nd St., New York.
Miami Magnet Co., 3240 N.W. 27th Ave., Miami, Fla.
Ronald Eyrich, 1091 N. 48th St., Milwaukee, Wisc.

Rear-screen material

Commercial Picture Equipment Co., 5137 N. Broadway Ave., Chicago, Ill.
Polacoat, 9750 Conklin Road, Blue Ash, Ohio.
Trans-lux Corp., 625 Madison Ave., New York, N.Y.

Appendix E.

Services

Various services are available to assist you in the preparation of your audiovisual materials. For a complete listing of laboratories and services see the annual directory issue of *Photo Methods for Industry,* PMI Directory, 33 W. 60th St., New York. Samplings of laboratories from various sections of the country are listed. Those selected offer a wide range of services under each of the following categories.

COLOR PRINT, SLIDE, AND FILMSTRIP SERVICES

Includes processing color films; making color prints; producing slides from art work and color negatives; duplicating slides; and complete filmstrip preparation.

Northeast

Admaster Prints, 425 Park Ave., New York.
Bebell and Bebell Color Laboratories, 108 W. 24th St., New York.
Color Corp. of America, 43 W. 61st St., New York.
K & L Color Services, 10 E. 46th St., New York.
Slides, Inc., P.O. Box 2, Orchard Park. N.Y.
World-in-Color Productions, P.O. Box 392, Elmira, N.Y.

Midwest

George W. Colburn Laboratories, 164 N. Wacker Drive, Chicago, Ill.
Colind Photography, P.O. Box 165, Peoria, Ill.
Visual Education Consultants, 2066 Helena St., Madison, Wisc.

Southwest

Brooks Photo Service, 401 Edith Blvd., N.E., Albuquerque, N.M.
Roland Jeanneret, 4526 Main St., Kansas City, Missouri

West

Marvin Becker Films, 915 Howard St., San Francisco, Calif.
Colorage, 116 S. Hollywood Way, Burbank, Calif.
Frank Holmes Laboratories, 1947 First St., San Fernando, Calif.

TRANSFER VIDEOTAPE TO FILM SERVICES

West

Acme Film Laboratories, Inc., 1161 N. Highland Ave., Hollywood, Calif.
Technicolor Corporation, 6311 Romaine Street, Hollywood, Calif.
Teleview Recording Services, 6325 Santa Monica Blvd., Hollywood, Calif.

MUSIC LIBRARIES AND RECORDING SERVICES

Includes recorded title and background music; sound effects; transfer of tape recordings to disk; and multiple duplication services.

East

Audio Master Corp., 17 E. 45th St., New York.
Boosey & Hawkes, 30 W. 57th St., New York.
Corelli-Jacobs Film Music, 723 Seventh Ave., New York.
Charles Michelson, 45 W. 45th St., New York.
Recorded Publications Laboratories, 1558-1570 Pierce Ave., Camden, N.J.
Thomas J. Valentino, 150 W. 46th St., New York.

Midwest

Speed-Q Sound Effects, P.O. Box 141, Richmond, Ind.
Standard Record Transcription Services, 360 N. Michigan Ave., Chicago, Ill.

West

Capital HQ Library Services, Hollywood and Vine, Hollywood, Calif.
MP-TV Services, 7000 Santa Monica Blvd., Hollywood, Calif.

MOTION PICTURE SERVICES—16MM

Includes film-planning services; processing black-and-white and color films; preparing workprints; printing and special effects; and sound services.

Northeast

All Service Film Labs Inc., 35 W. 45th St., New York.
Capital Film Laboratories, 1905 Fairview Avenue, N.E. Washington, D.C.
Color Service Co., Inc., 115 W. 45th St., New York.
DeLuxe Laboratories, Inc., 850 Tenth Ave., New York.
Movielab Film Laboratories, 619 W. 54th St., New York.

Southeast

Motion Picture Labs, 781 S. Main Street, Memphis, Tenn.
Reela Films, Inc., 17 N.W. 3rd St., Miami, Fla.
Southeastern Film Processing Co., 1305 Geiger Ave., Columbus, S.C.

Midwest

George W. Colburn Laboratories, 164 N. Wacker Drive, Chicago, Ill.

Film Associates, 4600 S. Dixie Highway, Dayton, Ohio.

Film Services, 113-119 W. Hubbard St., Chicago, Ill.

Fischer Photographic Laboratory, 6555 W. North Ave., Oak Park, Ill.

Southwest

Calvin Productions, 1005 Truman Road, Kansas City, Mo.

Jamieson Film Co., 3825 Bryan St., Dallas, Texas.

West

Consolidated Film Industries, 959 Seward St., Hollywood, Calif.

Hollywood Valley Film Laboratories, 2704 W. Olive, Burbank, Calif.

W. A. Palmer Films, 611 Howard St., San Francisco, Calif.

Technicolor Corporation, 6311 Romaine St., Hollywood, Calif.

Western Ciné Services, 312 S. Pearl Street, Denver, Colo.

MOTION-PICTURE SERVICES—8MM

The following laboratories are noted for their services relative to 8 millimeter film work:

Calvin Productions, Inc., 1105 Truman Road, Kansas City, Mo.

George Colburn Laboratory, Inc., 164 No. Wacker Drive, Chicago, Ill.

Hollywood Valley Film Laboratories, 2704 W. Olive, Burbank, Calif.

W. A. Palmer Films, Inc., 611 Howard St., San Francisco, Calif.

Technicolor Corporation, Motion Picture Division, 6311 Romaine St., Hollywood, Calif.

Technicolor Corporation, Cartridge Branch, 3402 West Osborn Road, Phoenix, Ariz. (cartridge loading service)

Glossary

accent light a spotlight which accentuates and highlights a person or an object in a scene.

acetate (clear) a plastic sheet permitting a high degree of light transmission, resulting in a transparent appearance.

acetate (coated or treated) a clear-appearing plastic sheet to each side of which a special coating has been applied; the coating will accept ordinary drawing inks.

acetate (matte or frosted) a plastic sheet with one side etched or roughed so as to take regular inks and colored pencil markings easily.

animation a filming technique that brings to apparent life and movement inanimate objects or drawings.

answer print the first duplicate copy of an audiovisual material (slides, filmstrip or motion picture) made from the original, with exposure corrections and special effects included.

background light the illumination thrown on the background to lighten it, giving the scene depth and separating the subject from the background.

captions the printed explanations to accompany the visuals of an audiovisual material.

clearance form (see *release form*)

clip books printed booklets containing a variety of commercially prepared black-and-white line drawings on various subjects.

close-up a concentration of the camera on the subject, or on a part of it, excluding everything else from view.

colored adhesive a translucent or transparent color printed on a thin acetate sheet having adhesive backing for adherence to cardboard, paper, acetate, or film.

communications specialist a person having broad knowledge of audiovisual media and capable of organizing the content of audiovisual materials to be produced so that the stated purposes will best be served.

conforming the process of matching original motion-picture footage to the edited workprint.

contact print a photographic print the same size as the negative, prepared by exposing to light the negative and positive films (or paper), placed together.

continuity the logical relationship of one scene leading to the next one and the smooth flow of action and narration within the total audiovisual material.

continuous-tone subjects illustrations consisting of shades of gray, varying from black to white.

copy stand a vertical or horizontal stand for accurately positioning a camera when photographing flat subjects very close to the lens.

credit title a listing of those who participated in or cooperated with the audiovisual project.

cut-away shot a motion-picture scene of a subject or action taking place at the same time as the main action, but separate from it, and placed between two related scenes which have a discontinuity of action.

cut-in shot a close-up feature of a subject being filmed as a motion picture and usually placed between two scenes having a discontinuity of action.

depth of field the distance within a scene from the point closest to the camera in focus to the farthest in focus.

developer a solution in which the chemicals set the image by acting upon silver salts on exposed film that have been affected by light during picture-taking.

diazo process a method for preparing overhead transparencies requiring film containing one of a possible number of dye colors, which is exposed, in contact with a translucent original, to ultraviolet light, and then developed in ammonia vapor.

diffusion-transfer process a method for preparing overhead transparencies requiring the exposure to light of negative paper placed against the original material, then development of the negative in contact with a sheet of positive film in a photographic solution.

dissolve an optical effect in motion pictures involving two superimposed scenes in which the second one gradually appears as the first one gradually disappears.

documentary approach a method of taking pictures without preplanning or detailed script preparation.

double-frame filmstrip a series of pictures aligned lengthwise along 35mm film, each double frame being 24×36mm.

dubbing the transfer of recorded sound from one unit to another; commonly record-to-tape, tape-to-tape, tape-to-film.

edge number a series of matching numbers printed at 1-foot intervals along the edge of original motion-picture footage and also along the workprint edge so that after the editing the workprint and original can be easily matched together.

editing the selection and organization of visuals after filming and the refinement of narration or captions.

electronic mixer a control mechanism through which a number of sound-producing units can be fed in order to combine voice, music, or sound effects at desired recording levels onto a single tape or film sound track.

electrostatic duplication use of coated, electrically charged, light-sensitive paper or film to reproduce original and printed pages.

establishing shot   a medium or long shot that establishes the whereabouts of a scene and serves as orientation to action photographed at close range.

exposure index   a number assigned to a film by the manufacturer which indicates the relative emulsion speed of the film for determining camera settings (*f*/ number and shutter speed).

exposure meter   (see *photographic light meter*)

exposure-value system   (*EV*)   a series of numbers for setting exposures by a single number which represents combinations of *f*/ number and shutter speed, and which will vary depending on the exposure index of each film.

***f*/ number (*f*/ stop)**   the lens setting selected from a series of numbers consisting partially of . . . 2, 2.8, 4, 5.6, 8, 11, 16, 32, . . .

fade-in   an optical effect in motion pictures in which a scene gradually appears out of blackness.

fade-out   an optical effect in motion pictures in which a scene gradually disappears into blackness.

fill light   the secondary light source illuminating a scene which brightens dark shadow portions created by the key light.

film chain   the part of a television system which includes the slide and motion-picture projectors connected optically to a television camera.

film clip   a brief, filmed sequence used generally on television without having titles or special effects.

filmograph   a sequence of still pictures on a motion-picture film.

fine cut   the final step in editing a motion picture, on completion of which the scenes are of proper length and action between adjacent scenes is matched.

fixer   a solution in which the chemicals harden the developed film image and change all undeveloped silver salts so they can be removed by washing.

flannel (felt) board   a presentation board consisting of a flannel or felt surface to which objects backed with flannel, felt, or sandpaper will adhere.

focal frame   a camera attachment that overcomes the parallax problem and permits accurate framing and focusing of objects very close to the lens.

focal length   a classification of lenses, being the distance from the center of a lens to the film plane within the camera when the lens is focused at infinity.

frame   an individual picture in a filmstrip or motion picture.

guide number or exposure guide number   a number assigned to a film for the purpose of calculating exposure when flashbulbs or electronic flash units are used; it is based upon the film speed, the type of flash bulb or electronic unit, and the shutter speed.

halftone subjects   printed illustrations consisting of uniformly spaced dots of varying size, which blend together and convey shades of gray.

high-angle shot   a scene photographed with the camera placed high, looking down at the subject.

high-contrast subject   an illustration consisting solely of black lines or marks on white paper.

hook-and-loop board   a presentation board consisting of a cloth surface textured with minute nylon loops to which display materials backed with strips of tape having minute nylon hooks will intermesh and hold firmly.

incident-light method   the measurement of light falling on a scene by the use of an incident-light meter held in the scene and aimed at the camera.

instruction guide   suggestions for good utilization of an audiovisual material; it normally includes a description of content and preparatory, participating, and follow-up questions and activities.

instructional system   a coordination of all aspects of a problem toward answering a specific objective and following a logical series of steps to reach a solution.

jump action   a discontinuity in the smooth action within a motion-picture scene, caused by momentary stopping and then starting the camera motor or by incorrectly removing a section of film within a scene during editing.

jumper cord   (see *patch cord*)

key light   the brightest light source on a scene, forming a large portion of the total illumination.

lens diaphragm   the opening through which light enters a camera; its size is controlled by an adjustable diaphragm.

lighting ratio   the relationship between the intensity of the key light and the intensity of the fill light as measured with a light meter.

lip synchronization (lip sync)   a recording of the speech of a person appearing in a motion picture so that the sound is heard at the same time his corresponding lip movements are observed.

log sheet   a written record of all pictures taken, including scene numbers, takes, camera settings, and special remarks.

long shot   a general view of a subject and its setting.

low-angle shot   a scene photographed with the camera placed low, looking up at the subject.

magnetic chalkboard   a presentation board consisting of a metal sheet, covered with chalkboard paint, to which magnetic-backed objects will adhere and on which chalk marks may be made.

magnetic-striped film   8mm or 16mm motion-picture film to which a narrow stripe of magnetizable material is added which will accept sound impulses in the form of magnetic variations.

main title   the name of the production, shown at the start of an audiovisual material.

matched action   the smooth continuation of action between two adjacent, related motion-picture scenes.

medium shot   a view of a subject which eliminates unnecessary background and other details.

monobath   a combination developer-fixer solution for one-step black-and-white film processing.

montage   a series of short scenes in a motion picture used to condense time or distance or to show a series of related activities or places.

multicamera filming   recordings of the same action with two or more cameras operated at the same time and located at different position in relation to the subject.

multimedia (multiple image)   use of two or more audiovisual materials at same or closely related times.

narration   the verbal comments made to accompany the visuals.

negative opaque   a water-soluble carbon material brushed on high-contrast negatives to eliminate marks, spots, and areas.

objective scene   a scene recorded with the camera aimed toward the subject, from a theater-audience point of view.

opaque projector   a projector that can enlarge information from paper, pages from a book, or other nontranslucent or nontransparent materials.

optical sound track   a narrow band of light and dark areas or lines along one side of motion-picture film which through the action of light is converted into the film's sound.

overhead projector   a projector which accepts transparent and translucent film or other plastic and projects the information prepared on them onto a screen.

overlay   one or more additional transparent sheets with lettering or other matter that may be placed over a base transparency or an opaque background.

overprint   the superimposition of one scene over another; generally titles, captions or labels over a background scene or a specially prepared background.

out-takes usable motion picture footage that has been removed during the editing process.

pan (panorama) the movement of a motion-picture camera, while filming, in a horizontal plane (sideways).

pantograph a linked-lever device for enlarging or reducing diagrams by tracing the original under one point and duplicating it at the other point in suitable proportion.

paste-up the combination of illustrations and lettering, each unit of which is rubber-cemented in position on paper or cardboard by a temporary method.

patch cord an electrical wire used to connect together two pieces of sound equipment (as tape recorders and record players) so that electrical impulses can be transferred between the units in order to make a recording.

parallax the difference between the vertical position of an object in a filmed scene as viewed through a viewfinder and that recorded on film through the camera lens.

permanent mounting the application of rubber cement to the back of a flat material to be mounted and also to the mount surface, then permitting the two surfaces to dry before adhering them together; or the use of dry-mount tissue placed between the material and the mount surface, with heat and pressure being applied to seal the layers together.

photocopy process (see *diffusion-transfer process*)

photographic light meter a device for measuring light levels, either incident upon or reflected from a scene.

photo modifier a large-size camera used to enlarge or reduce art work.

photo stabilization a two-step rapid processing method for photographic paper.

picture transfer the transfer of printing ink from a magazine picture to a special acetate sheet after the two are sealed together with heat and/or pressure and then submerged in water to remove the paper.

pinboard (see *register board*)

planning board a 3′×4½′ board with strips of acetate channels, designed at Eastman Kodak Company, for holding storyboard cards.

progressive disclosure exposing a series of items on a transparency or slide by moving an opaque mask during use or preparation.

pumping in (pumping out) the change of camera position from one motion-picture scene to the next without change of camera angle with relation to the same subject.

rangefinder the camera attachment which upon proper setting indicates the distance from camera to subject or sets the lens in focus at that range.

rear-screen projection projecting on the back side of a translucent screen, the projector being behind the screen or off to one side projecting on a mirror.

reflected-light method the measurement of light reflected from a scene by the use of a reflected light meter held near the camera and aimed at the subject.

register board a surface with two or more small vertical posts for holding paper, cardboard, or film materials all correctly aligned when more than one layer must be assembled for filming.

release form the form used to obtain written permission for use of pictures taken of persons or of their copyrighted materials.

release print a duplicate print of an original audiovisual material prepared for general use.

reversal film film which, after exposure, is processed to produce a positive image on the same film.

rough cut the second step in editing a motion picture, on completion of which the length of scenes has been shortened somewhat but not necessarily to final length, and action between adjacent scenes is not yet exactly matched.

scene (shot) the basic element that makes up the visuals of an audiovisual material; each separate picture or amount of motion-picture footage exposed when the release button is pushed and then released.

script the specific directions for picture taking or art work in the form of a listing of scenes with accompanying narration or captions.

sequence a section of an audiovisual material, more or less complete in itself, and made up of a series of related scenes.

shading film textures and patterns printed on acetate sheets having adhesive backing for adhering to cardboard, paper, acetate, or film.

shot (see *scene*)

shutter speed the interval between opening and closing of the shutter of a camera, measured in fractions of a second.

single concept a discrete skill or limited aspect of a topic.

single-frame filmstrip a series of pictures oriented horizontally across the width of 35mm film and of such a size that two adjacent pictures (or frames) combined are 18×24mm.

single-framing exposing one frame at a time on motion-picture film, as opposed to continuous exposure (8 frames per second or faster).

single-lens reflex camera a compact camera employing a mirror or prism for accurate viewing directly through the camera lens.

slating putting on film a few frames of printed information prior to the regular filming of a motion-picture scene in order to identify the scene and take number.

sound striping (see *magnetic-striped film*)

specifications the framework and limits within which audiovisual materials are produced; may include such factors as length, materials, special techniques, assistance required, completion date, and budget.

squaring method the method for enlarging or reducing a diagram by placing a grid over the original and copying relative positions of lines on a grid of another size (smaller or larger scale, or proportioned).

stop bath a solution in which the chemicals stop the action of developer on exposed film.

storyboard a series of sketches or pictures which visualize each topic or sequence in an audiovisual material to be produced; generally prepared after the treatment and before the script.

string out the first step in editing a motion picture, on completion of which all scenes are of original camera length and have been spliced together in proper sequence.

subject specialist a person having broad knowledge of the subject content for an audiovisual material to be produced.

subjective scene a scene recorded with the camera placed in the subject's position and aimed at action he is performing.

subtitles words, phrases, or sentences that appear over a visual to explain, emphasize, or clarify a point.

take (of a scene) one exposure among two or more for the same scene; successive takes of the same scene are numbered from one upward.

telephoto lens a camera lens which permits a closer view of a subject than would be obtained by a normal lens from the same position.

technical staff a person or persons responsible for the photography, graphic-art work, and sound-recording in producing audiovisual materials.

temporary mounting the application of rubber cement to the back of an illustration or lettering and immediate placement on a mount surface while the cement is still wet.

thumbspot a visible mark placed in the lower left corner of a slide which indicates the proper position for correctly viewing the slide.

tilt   the movement of a motion-picture camera in a vertical plane.

time-lapse photography   the exposing of individual motion-picture frames at a much slower rate than normal, for projection at normal speed; the method accelerates action that normally takes place too slowly for motion to be perceived.

toner   a black powder used in the electrostatic duplicating process to deposit on the charged paper or film and provide the visible, opaque image.

transitional devices   the use of such techniques as fade-out-fade-in and dissolves to bridge space and time in motion pictures.

treatment   a descriptive synopsis of how the content of an audio-visual material may be organized and presented.

wide-angle lens   a camera lens which permits a wider view of a subject and its surroundings than would be obtained by a normal lens from the same position.

wipe   an optical effect in motion pictures in which a new scene seems to push the previous scene off the screen.

workprint   an inexpensive copy of original motion-picture footage used during editing, and to which the original film is matched before duplicate copies are made.

zoom lens   a camera lens of variable magnification which permits a smooth change of subject coverage between distance and close-up without changing the camera position.

Index

MASK FOR OVERHEAD TRANSPARENCIES

7½″

9½″

The area enclosed in the black line gives the outline of a mask opening for a transparency to be used with an overhead projector.